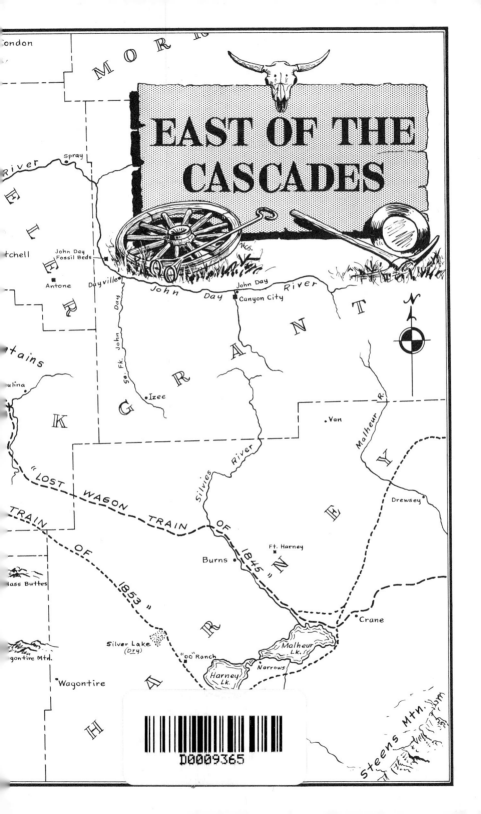

EAST OF THE CASCADES

EAST

of the

CASCADES

EAST

Portland · Oregon · 1965

OF THE
CASCADES

by Phil F. Brogan

edited by L. K. Phillips

BINFORDS & MORT, *Publishers*

PREFACE

Many persons have helped with this book. Some of them assisted unknowingly, around desert campfires. Others added important bits during hikes over mountain trails, or in isolated range cabins, revealing their early-day experiences in this lonely land of tilted mountains, plateau vistas, and juniper-fringed rims. Often they spoke of the range saga of the rimrock lands east of the white and beautiful Three Sisters of the Oregon Cascades. Many of these old-timers have long since headed out over trails of no return, and with them disappeared a rich part of pioneer history.

It was my good fortune to have lived a part of the frontier life of the Central Oregon range country and to have viewed, as a boy, passing events from a homestead high on a grassy upland facing the hills of the John Day basin. Still in memory, I hear the thunder of the hoofs of wild horses rushing to corrals in spring roundups. I feel the tremor of blasts in the Deschutes Gorge when two railroad giants raced to Bend. I recall many nights when my blankets were spread under summer stars.

Events, dates, names, and places have all been carefully checked. In this task, Deschutes County librarians were especially helpful, as was Martin Schmitt of the University of Oregon Library. As historian of the Lost Wagon Train of 1853, Leah Collins Menefee of Eugene made considerable contribution. Sincere thanks go to Major General William Dunckel, who searched Pentagon records in Washington, D.C., to verify his own vivid memories of the High Desert "war" in which more than a hundred thousand men took part. Special thanks go to the Oregon Historical Society for assistance in searching records, diaries, and old newspapers which hold intriguing history of this range country.

27/09

The story of mid-Oregon, and of towns that grew up where stock once grazed, remained in the planning stage for years. It would still be unwritten if Robert W. Chandler, editor and publisher of the Bend *Bulletin*, had not insisted that I take time out from routine work on the staff to get the material into shape. To Bob Chandler, my deep thanks.

To scores of individuals, especially earth-scientists with whom I worked in the Central Oregon field for some forty years, I wish to express my gratitude. The dust of caves was never too thick to becloud morsels of information that anthropologists and spelunkers dropped. I am grateful to the kindly, yet insistent, urgings of my wife Louise, who kept me at this task—writing the story of a region largely bypassed by historians.

Once started, the book virtually flowed into shape, possibly because for more than thirty-five years I enjoyed the advice, the wisdom, and the stories of this region's top historian, the late Robert W. Sawyer. At work we shared the same roof for more than thirty years. We climbed the same lofty peaks. We hiked the same lonely trails, and together we studied their creatures and their history. Those were the days when I rehearsed the story of this fascinating land east of the Cascades.

To all who helped, this book is dedicated.

Phil F. Brogan

CONTENTS

Part One

PREHISTORIC TIMES

CHAPTER 1

Geologic Story

MILLIONS OF YEARS AGO the story of Central Oregon was the story of the Pacific Northwest, even of North America. Only in fairly recent times has this region east of the Cascades become unique.

There were no Cascade Mountains when the inland country started its fossil record in the ooze of ancient oceans. Far off to the west, a thousand-mile chain of volcanic islands was in violent eruption, spreading its dust and lavas eastward. Except for foundation islands, most of Oregon and California lay under shallow seas whose waves lapped against uplifts ancestral to the Blue Mountains. Then, some sixty million years ago, all the western part of the continent was slowly transformed.

When the floor of the last ocean to sweep over Oregon rose, the inland region became a plain, its elevation only slightly above that of the receding waters. This folding, rising interior revealed records of the old seas, back to the Age of Fishes, some 225 million years ago. These time-markers are marine fossils found in brown limestone on Beaver and Grindstone creeks, east of Crooked River. They set the date for the oldest known formation in Oregon.

The Age of Reptiles, ending more than sixty million years ago, added its own interesting chapter to the prehistoric past. This includes the story of a spectacular mountain range, the

1

Mesozoic Alps of Oregon, so-called by Dr. E. L. Packard, an early Oregon paleontologist. Roots of the old mountains in the Suplee country of Eastern Crook County and in Western Grant County indicate these mountains were three miles high. Reaching from the northwest to the southeast, they ruled the mid-Oregon landscape for millions of years.

As the last of the seas rolled away from the inland region to spill into the Pacific basin, there appeared the Chico and Horsetown embayments, named for Northern California formations holding similar marine fossils. The Age of Mammals came to inland Oregon in the wake of the receding waters.

Clarno Period

In the John Day River region, geologists have given a local name to the first epoch of the Age of Mammals. They call it the Clarno, after a community rich in fossils, located twelve miles east of Antelope. The Clarno yielded the first record of land mammal life in Oregon, a record consisting of Dawn Age creatures whose bones, eons ago, turned to rock. Fossil hunters unearthed them from the tan hills shouldering up to lava-capped Iron Mountain, a short distance northeast of the community of Clarno.

Giant "thunderbeasts" ruled the lush land in Clarno times. Rhinoceroses wallowed in swamps. Tiny horses, still with four toes, grazed along streams. Crocodiles swam in rivers and lakes, along whose edges grew semitropical plants and trees. Covering much of the region was dense vegetation. Fossils, formed from plants entombed in gray cliffs, tell part of the story of that ancient land of rhinos and sheep-like ponies, giant dogs and flesh-tearing cats.

Even while animals grazed or sought their prey in the verdant lowlands of Clarno times, many volcanoes were erupting to the south. These built up Sugarloaf, Coyote Mountain, Burnt Butte, and other peaks. They spilled lavas into deep valleys, forming lava traps that held in the earth a wealth of that silvery metal known as mercury.

John Day Fossil Beds

The time lapse between the Clarno and the John Day periods was possibly ten million or more years. That mammal life continued to flourish in this later period is proved by the fossil record of the John Day Valley, adjacent areas along Crooked River, and even in the Deschutes Canyon.

More than a hundred different species of fossil mammals are represented in the John Day fossil beds, including numerous flesh-eaters—horses and camels, fierce pigs, and peccaries. However, all these species differ greatly from those out of the Clarno clays; and none of them much resemble animals now living. Rhinoceroses, which first appeared on the local scene in Clarno times, continued into the John Day epoch, but were considerably changed; and the four-toed horses of the Clarno had evolved into the three-toed horses that grazed on the John Day horizons.

Columbia Lavas

When the Columbia lavas spread over the Pacific Northwest millions of years ago, they covered much of inland Oregon. Only the highlands remained—ancient "islands" in a black sea of rock. All regional life must have perished, or moved out. The massive, many-layered lavas were sometimes folded and warped, sometimes tilted. Drainage basins were blocked; rivers and streams were dammed. With this choked drainage, huge lakes took shape on the prehistoric landscape.

After the lavas had cooled and new land had formed, life returned to the John Day country. Once more, a new species of horse appeared, but now only one of the three toes was functional. Deer included a species with club-like horns, and among flesh-eaters was a dog resembling a bear. Rhinos also roamed the new lands above the Columbia lavas, but they too differed from those of both the Clarno and John Day periods.

Paleontologists have a strange name for this period sandwiched between the John Day and the Ice Age lands—they call it the Rattlesnake. Curiously, it was named for a creek, not a reptile. Only a scant record of this epoch is found in the region, as bones of animals and leaves of plants were rarely being entombed in the swamps or in the mud of streams. However, on this horizon of "Rattlesnake rims" and thin lava flows, mastodons left a fine record of their sojourn in Oregon. Over to the west, the Cascades were now rising, and a rain shadow was spreading throughout the once-verdant land.

The Age of Ice

After the Age of Mammals came the Ice Age. This refrigerated era left its icy thumbprint many places in the interior country. The original crest of the present Cascades, composed of "first generation" volcanoes, was deeply notched by glaciers, while some of the older peaks, such as Broken Top, Thielsen, and Mt. Washington, lost much of their mass to the moving fields of ice. Oregon's glaciers were not part of the northern continental sheet of the Ice Age; its glaciers were mountain-born. Mountain ice cut the Cascade peaks, scoured deep U-shaped valleys on the Steens, and transformed the topography of higher mountains.

The Ice Age was indirectly responsible for the huge lakes of South-Central Oregon. Great ice sheets to the north changed the pattern of weather, bringing south the storms that dropped heavy moisture. This moisture was trapped in areas of lava-choked drainage and in basins adjacent to fault-block mountains, such as the Steens and Warner, and in the Abert Rim country. Countless animals and birds lived in this old lake region, and their bones are well represented in the fossil record. Their fossils have appeared in the silt and sands of the lake beds, especially in the Fossil, Thorn, Christmas, and Silver Lake basins. Though the Ice Age lasted for the better part of a million years, there is evidence of periods of mild and even arid weather in this over-all epoch of refrigeration.

Trails into the Past

A pastor with Bible in pocket and pick in hand was the first person to read from the rocks the ancient story of the lands east of the Cascades. This was Thomas Condon, Oregon's first geologist. For a time, Condon was stationed at Fort Dalles on the Columbia River, the jump-off point for the virtually unknown inland country. To the southeast, cavalrymen still rode trails well beaten by Paiute ponies. Captain John M. Drake, a cavalryman stationed at Camp Maury on upper Crooked River, was the first to tell Condon that the hills of the area he scouted held many fossils. On July 19, 1864, Captain Drake wrote to the pastor:

Last week during my absence from our camp on Beaver Creek, a tributary of Crooked River, in pursuit of a party of Snake Indians, some soldiers made a discovery that I take to be of interest geologically.

While wandering over the colored hills, Drake's men found mammal fossils and also some marine shells. Drake sent Condon a number of fossils from the Beaver Creek hills, including several fine specimens of sea shells. This was the first evidence that, long ago, a salty embayment swept over the inland country, which was later warped and elevated into highlands. The specimens, Condon learned, included shells from the last of the oceans of the Age of Reptiles, whose waves had pounded the Pacific headlands of an emerging continent, and had eddied into quiet water to build coral reefs.

These fossils were the first Condon received from the country southeast of The Dalles. Most of his marine shells had come from high, eastern tributaries of Crooked River, a location that in later years was to get much attention. Eager to explore the new field, Condon obtained permission to make a trip into Central Oregon with a company of cavalry that was serving as an escort to an Army caravan moving supplies to Harney Valley.

The trip was made in 1865 or 1866, according to his daughter, Ellen Condon McCornack.

On the return journey, by way of Camp Watson, Condon first glimpsed a field in which he was destined to make scientific discoveries of world-wide interest—the John Day Basin. The road was through the Bridge Creek country, past gaudily colored hills. In those hills with their tilted tufa tops, Condon, on later trips, found bones of rhinoceroses, oreodons, huge dogs, big cats, and a strange creature scientists named Moropus, a "clawed horse."

The kindly pastor from Fort Dalles, who was to head the first geology department at the University of Oregon and become Oregon's first state geologist, made many other trips into the region. Slowly he pieced together the geologic story of the land that emerged from ancient seas to buckle into the high interior plateau. During some of his earlier trips, he apparently collected specimens under trying conditions. In a letter to Dr. John Strong Newberry of Columbia University, dated February 28, 1869, he noted:

On my last visit to the place of the outcrops (leaf impressions) I found some new things, new leaves, new fruit, and several insect impressions. As the region in which they occur was, when I was there, infested by hostile Indians, whose fresh tracks were on the trail I traveled, I could examine but little of the surroundings.

Also in 1869, Condon wrote Dr. Newberry that he had to postpone a planned trip into the newly discovered fossil field "for there is some reason to apprehend the breaking loose of some of the Snake Indians again. . . . The fossils are in their country near a road where Indians once loved to infest." Referring to the fossil locality east of the Cascades, he said: "I am hungry for a sight of that hill again, when no fear of prowling Indians shall compel me to hold a rifle in one hand and my pick in the other."

By the following year Condon could report: "I have not been able to go into Crooked River, but hope to do so: only a few small bands of Indians remain to be gathered on the reservation, and then one may go there without an escort."

The Three-Toed Horse

Condon's discoveries in the John Day, Bridge Creek, and Crooked River areas soon attracted world-famous scientists—or their representatives—to Eastern Oregon. O. C. Marsh of Yale and Professor E. C. Cope of Philadelphia, were among the first. Condon's prestige grew fast, especially after his field work led to the discovery of a Tertiary horse that was new to science. This was the three-toed creature called Miohippus, nine species of which were found. One, *Miohippus condoni,* honors the pastor-paleontologist.

In 1876, Condon enlarged his fossil-hunting field. A former Oregon governor, John Whiteaker, while on a camping trip, had discovered sand-blasted, black bones on the dusty beds of old lakes, in Lake County. This he reported to Condon. The following summer, with Whiteaker's son Charles as his guide, Condon crossed the Southern Cascades and made his way into the Silver Lake area. On the morning of August 4, he started on horseback for the fossil beds. Detouring sand dunes and riding around big sage, early in the day the pair reached the area where winds were whipping away sand from an old lake bottom and exposing fossils. Condon wrote in his diary of the trip:

We staked our horses and went to work. We found the remains of elephants, camels and horses and other mammals; a good many bird bones, and some specimens of fossil fish. After a search of six or seven hours we packed our specimens and returned to Button's (ranch) and on Monday we started home.

Fossil Lake Discoveries

That trip by Condon into the old lake country opened for science a new geologic horizon of the Ice Age. The abundance of horse bones led to a new name, one that was to become widely known—the Equus (horse) Beds of Oregon. When the land was green and water was plentiful, several types of horses ranged the inland basin. Elephants plodded the shores of the pluvial lakes, and camels grazed on the lush foliage—as did many ground sloths. A large species of beaver lived in the waters of this green land.

Among the mineralized, well-preserved mammal and bird fossils were many arrowheads. This caused Condon to ponder:

If the sands, the fossils, the arrow points, and the fresh-water shells were all of the same period, and the fossil bones were early Glacial Age, then the arrow points were fashioned before the Ice Age, and the mixture of these artifacts may be due entirely to the simple law of gravity, for both the arrow points and the recent shells may have settled down among the fossils as the dust and sand upon which they rested was gradually blown away.

Condon's discoveries at Fossil Lake immediately attracted other paleontologists to the area. First to arrive, and within three weeks, was C. H. Sternberg, who collected for Professor Cope and also picked up some background for his own book of later years, *Life of a Fossil Hunter*. In 1879, Cope himself came to Oregon to confer with Condon and to collect at Fossil Lake. He also hunted fossils in the Crooked River country and along the John Day.

Condon's Famous Theory

Earth scientists have continued to retrace Dr. Condon's famous trails and theories. Condon was the first boldly to conceive that the region had its start in two islands. One he called Siskiyou. This, he said, was in the southwestern part of Oregon and northern California, a land that has yielded its share of mineral riches. The other island he called Shoshone. This he placed in the uplifted northeastern corner of Oregon.

Through the years, Dr. Condon's "two-island" theory has been modified by geologists who have probed into old formations unknown to the pastor of pioneer days. To some it may appear that a 1960 discovery refutes the Condon theory—the 350-million-year-old outcroppings near the head of Crooked River. That is not so. These primordial rocks merely extended the Shoshone cornerstone.

CHAPTER 2

The Landscape Changes

FROM THE BEGINNING of the Age of Mammals to the end of the Ice Age—a period of more than sixty million years—profound changes took place in the mid-Oregon landscape.

The interior region remained near sea level long after the last great marine bays disappeared westward, to lap for a time the seaward shores of the old Cascades in the Eugene-Salem area. Rocks of the first lands to take shape in Central Oregon hold a record of swampy conditions, and of lazy streams depositing silt, mud, sand, and fossils. The streams, many of them apparently well fed by Pacific moisture, brushed the roots of a nest of volcanoes in the Clarno country, then reached across the John Day basin to flow directly west past the humps of new mountains that were to become the original Cascades.

The Western Cascades were formed by a chain of small but highly active volcanoes. Ash from these fire mountains drifted inland, filling valleys and blanketing swamps. Other volcanoes thundered and blazed east of the Cascades, sending broad aprons of lava into damp valleys and over swampy terrain.

The string of volcanic mountains, close to the edge of the receding ocean that covered the Eugene country and spread north toward Portland, apparently never attained great height: the mountains sank into the plastic earth under their own weight. Possibly their average height was only a few hundred feet above sea level, with occasional volcanic peaks reaching several thousand feet into the sky. Yet this was sufficient to screen some of the flow of moist air from the ocean, increasing aridity to the east, in the land of the Clarno volcanoes. Here grew tropical trees, broad ferns, and giant plants of the horsetail family.

10

As a mountain barrier formed in the west and climatic conditions changed, the interior country gradually became cooler. Subtropical vegetation retreated southward. Redwoods, however, continued to grow on higher slopes. These slopes were dampened with possibly forty inches of moisture annually, compared with a present annual average of around ten inches.

The High Cascades

The High Cascades, forming along a north-south zone of weakness just to the east of the old Western Cascades, slowly took impressive shape. This vast barrier, dominated by bulky shield volcanoes, shut off inland Oregon from ocean moisture and left the country immediately to the east of the Cascades in a rain shadow. Even the redwoods finally disappeared, but their fossils are still abundant in many places. Stony wood of the big trees is scattered over the High Desert northeast of Hampton Butte, about halfway between Bend and Burns.

Two generations of volcanoes grew along the High Cascade summit. First were the massive cones of the epoch that directly preceded the Ice Age. These included today's pinnacled peaks, such as Three Fingered Jack and Broken Top. Radiating from the ice-sheathed domes were many glaciers, some thousands of feet thick. These choked western valleys on the high flanks of the Cascades and spread east from foothills that tapered to the Deschutes River.

The older volcanoes of the High Cascades were followed by the grand mountains of the present—Hood, Jefferson, and the South Sister, the highest of the trio of peaks called the Three Sisters. The North Sister was at least partly a product of the epoch that chilled into the Ice Age. Glaciers gnawed deeply into its sides during the earth's long, cold winter when one fourth of its bulk was worn away.

Throughout the Age of Mammals, lava intermittently spilled over inland Oregon, reaching its peak in the period of fire that followed John Day times. These great lava floods altered the entire face of the land, which was even further changed by the elevation of the interior plateau, the warping of the Ochocos, the cracking of the earth, and the rising of the Steens, Warner, and other fault-block mountains. High Abert and Warner rims show the role played by the faulting of the old lava plain in carving the inland Oregon terrain. Faulting is believed to have occurred when great stresses forced layered lavas of the region beyond their elastic limit.

Mt. Mazama

Southwest of the Deschutes country towered Mazama, Oregon's Crater Lake mountain. It was a huge mountain, entirely the product of volcanic action, but possibly with marine beds as its deep foundation. Mazama began to form prior to the Ice Age, when the first chill of the approaching earth winter came to the region. Geologists estimate that when Mazama was covered with ice, in its mature years, it reached a height of around twelve thousand feet.

Mazama erupted violently in fairly recent times. As the volcanic blasts shook the earth, the mountain engulfed its own broad dome. Billowing clouds of ash drifted east before the prevailing winds, then shifted to the northeast as the currents changed. Valleys on the high slope of the beheaded mountain filled with ash, some of which rushed in flowing avalanches over the low country. Lava dust drifted north seventy-four miles to deposit a veneer of pumice on the slopes of another huge volcano, Mt. Newberry. No less than five thousand square miles of the inland country was covered with Mazama ash. This explosion occurred around 6,600 years ago, according to radiocarbon dating. That Indians were in the lands east of the Cascades at the time is proved by arrowheads, scrapers, and other artifacts discovered under Mazama ash in the Wickiup Reservoir area of the upper Deschutes basin. Now Mazama's rims enclose the blue waters of Crater Lake.

Newberry Crater

About the time Mazama was growing on the crest of the southern Cascades, a shield volcano thirty miles in diameter started near the southern edge of the Deschutes plateau. This was Mt. Newberry, highest point of a small volcanic range known as the Paulinas. This range is immediately east of the headwaters of the Deschutes River.

Newberry did not reach the imposing height of its volcanic twin, Mt. Mazama, but it apparently was a grand mountain before it lost its dome. Newberry engulfed its top on reaching an estimated elevation of ten thousand feet above sea level. Today lovely Paulina and East lakes nestle in the Newberry caldera.

Collapse of the Newberry summit, though, did not chill the earth fires deep in the stump of the big volcano. Besides caldera craters, a rash of small fire cones broke out around the base of the sprawling mountain. Lava spilled from craters and cracks; and big cinder cones, such as Mokst Butte, were formed. It is estimated that there are at least two hundred and fifty parasitic cones on the Newberry slopes.

Rivers of lava spread over the surrounding area, some of the liquid rock flowing into pine forests to leave molds of trees in its wake. These tree molds are found in the Lava Cast Forest, high on the northern Newberry slope; also in flows near Sugar Pine Butte and Lava Butte. They can be reached over mountain roads branching from U. S. Highway 97, south of Bend.

Newberry's banked fires remained active until about a thousand years ago, providing the final topographic touches for the Central Oregon scene in the lands just east of the Sisters.

CHAPTER 3

The Strange Deschutes

EAST OF THE CASCADES is a stream often described as one of America's strangest rivers. It is a river of remarkably even flow because normal high water is trapped in a great lava sponge. It is a stream that has held its right-of-way against flooding lava, which at times entirely erased the original channel. It is a river fed by a thousand springs.

This river is the Deschutes. Its source is close to Elk Lake, not far from the South Sister. Here the river spills through lava, gathers force as a small, cold stream, then suddenly loses its vigor and its identity in a man-dammed basin—Crane Prairie Reservoir. During the long winter months in the high country, it burrows through deep snow. When the snow melts, the stream meanders in old channels across meadows where deer feed.

Downstream a short distance, the Deschutes is trapped in another big reservoir, the Wickiup. In the Pringle Falls and Benham Falls areas, the fast-flowing river is churned into white water as it tumbles over lava ledges. There it stores most of its flood in shattered rock. Finally gathering new strength, the river races past Lava Island, winds its way to Bend, lingers in a scenic mirror pond, then, freed of man's impediments, plunges into a rocky canyon. In the Cove country west of Culver, the river picks up the flow of two other strong streams, the Metolius and Crooked rivers. It then twists past two high dams, serpentines through deep gorges walled with lava, and eventually—after a 240-mile journey—spills into the west-flowing Columbia.

Old Shortcuts Traced

From mile-high lakes east of the Three Sisters, the Deschutes

14

races wildly along the eastern Cascades, then drops to a point only 150 feet above sea level, as it reaches the Columbia. Upstream from Bend, the river has many sharp curves, and many abandoned channels. Through the ages, the virile Deschutes has taken a number of shortcuts on the first sixty miles of its course. Some of the shortcuts left old beds in the lodgepole pines that reach to meadow edges.

Often the Deschutes changed its course, not from choice but from necessity. This occurred when streams of lava spilled into the canyon. Despite these frequent interruptions of flow from Bend to the Cove, the Deschutes cut a deep and awesome gorge in the Central Oregon plateau that crowds west to the Cascade foothills.

The source of the Deschutes River is Lava Lake, which takes its name from rocky flows near Elk Lake. Ordinarily, Lava Lake has no surface outlet, but in periods of high water, it sends a small stream through an open channel to its nearby twin, Little Lava Lake. Feeding the Deschutes near its source are many large streams. One of these is Fall River, a Deschutes tributary less than a mile long. Spring River is another of the spring-fed tributaries; and Little River, an important feeder, comes in from the southeast.

The Deschutes has been likened to a tree having nearly all its branches on the same side. With the exception of Crooked River, all feeder streams originate in the Cascades, where winter storms drop heavy snow. To the east of the Deschutes is the semiarid Central Oregon plateau, devoid of streams except for Trout Creek and streams from the timbered Ochoco, that flow through the Crooked River Valley.

The geologic story of the Deschutes apparently goes back to epochs when most streams east of the embryonic Cascades flowed westward to empty into a gulf flanked far out at sea by a long line of volcanic islands. Fed by much heavier moisture than at present, the westward-flowing streams battled for right-of-way around volcanic mounds—the humps of the slowly grow-

ing Western Cascades. The low Cascade barrier, later increased
in height by today's mountains, turned the Deschutes north to
join the Columbia, a mighty river that had been able to hold its
course over the rising mountains.

Lava Flows Blocked Channel

Troubles of the Deschutes continued even after it changed its
course into the north. In various places, some of this lava spilled
from Cascade cones. Other flows came from fissures and vents
on the ruptured slopes of Mt. Newberry. The Deschutes had
scoured a channel 137 feet below the present Benham Falls,
when lava poured in from the east to fill the valley. Eventually,
the river, dammed for centuries, detoured around the rocky
barrier to cut a new channel. Before the lava dam was breached,
the impounded river filled its upstream basin with silt. On that
silt and fine soil, great meadows evolved, and on those meadows,
ranches took shape when the white men came.

Streams of syrup-like, porous rock, flowing from a vent on the
south wall of Lava Butte, ten miles south of the Bend site, served
as a natural sponge when the area below Benham Falls was
settled. This impounded the surplus flow of the river in seasons
of heavy runoff. The level of the Deschutes at Bend remains
virtually the same the year around. Since not all the water
absorbed by the "lava sponge" in the Benham Falls area of the
Deschutes finds its way back into the channel, the loss of water
to irrigationists is heavy. Construction of a bypass has been considered for the diversion of the water from the lava-strewn
channel, during the irrigation season.

Between Bend and the Cove, the Deschutes plunges in white
spray over a number of spectacular falls. These were cataracts
that thundered during the years preceding the era of upstream
storage and irrigation diversion. Below Cline Falls, the river
gains some water from canyon springs to replenish part of the
upstream loss from irrigation. Farther north, the Deschutes is
fed by Crooked River, which pours in from the Ochocos, follow-

ing a temporary halt at the Prineville Dam. Another big mid-Deschutes feeder is the Metolius, which drains a section of the eastern Cascades. Other streams come in from the west at Tygh Valley, and in the Warm Springs areas.

Crooked River's Ancient Course

Crooked River is by far the most important of the few tributaries that feed the Deschutes from the east. Born in the high country where weak streams reach to the desert edge and the John Day Divide, Crooked River bears a name that tells its physical story. It is a stream that slashes through some of the oldest lands in the Pacific Northwest. Its direction of flow is possibly the same as in remote ages when all inland rivers headed west. It loses its identity when it reaches Lake Billy Chinook at the Cove. Here a high peninsula towers over the dual, converging Crooked River-Deschutes canyons.

Crooked River originates in large springs about seventy miles southeast of its junction with the Deschutes. It flows through a range country long known to Indians, where juniper and sage vie with grass for the scant soil moisture. Its appropriate name dates back to fur-trading days. John Arrowsmith's map of North America, bearing an 1824 date—with pen corrections in the early 1830s—shows Crooked River by name, and in fairly good detail.

Cove Island

The westward flow of Crooked River was not always peaceful. Lava flowed into its channel in various places, Columbia basalts filling many of the basins and valleys of the region. Later, lava from the Newberry eruptions to the south spilled into the old canyon in the Smith Rock locality. There the lava completely filled the gorge, then flowed downstream and choked the confluence of the Deschutes and Crooked rivers with a "plug" about eight hundred feet high. This is the spectacular "Cove Island," the landmark known to pioneers as the "Plains of Abraham." It is grandly visible from the rim viewpoints of the Cove Palisades State Park.

But the sluggishly moving lava did not stop at the Cove. It continued downstream, filling the gorge to a depth of nearly a thousand feet. Undaunted by this impressive lava challenge, the twin rivers went to work cutting their present spectacular gorges through the blockading rock. Lava flows that choked the two rivers at their confluence, as well as some distance downstream, created a type of scenery unique in the West. This gorge has been called "The Grand Canyon of Oregon."

Ice Age Fossils

When Newberry lava spilled into Crooked River near Smith Rock, it created a dam which backed water to a point upstream from Prineville. That natural reservoir left full evidence of its story and its antiquity. In gravel bars near the shore of the old lake east of Terrebonne, fossils have been discovered of a giant species of Ice Age beaver. Browsing camels also lived there, as did elephants and Glacial Age ponies. Fossils of rhinos have been sifted from the gravels, but apparently they were washed in from old formations in the Crooked River country.

This big lake remained in the mid-Crooked River valley until the untiring stream cut a new and deep channel across the lava barricade. In carving this channel, Crooked River created unique "box canyons." These are the perpendicularly walled, deep inner canyons within older lava-filled valleys that pose problems for reservoir builders because of the danger of leakage between the older lavas, or sedimentary beds, and the recent flows.

River of Many Uses

The Deschutes long has been recognized as an ideal power-producing stream, primarily because of its uniform flow. It is also regarded as one of the nation's best fishing and recreation streams. Impoundments in the upper reaches of the Deschutes and Crooked rivers supply summer irrigation water to Central Oregon farmlands.

In 1964, Portland General Electric Company completed construction of its Pelton-Round Butte hydroelectric project on the main stem of the Deschutes River in North Central Oregon, ten miles west of Madras. The two principal dams are capable of producing a total of 424,000 kilowatts of electric power.

The two reservoirs formed by the dams provide 4,200 acres of lake ideal for recreation. Lake Simtustus, behind Pelton Dam —completed in 1958—reaches southward seven and a half miles to Round Butte, behind which was formed Lake Billy Chinook. Round Butte is the largest hydroelectric dam wholly within the State of Oregon.

CHAPTER 4

Fort Rock Cave Men

A SHALLOW, ROCK-STREWN CAVE, in the remnant of a wave-cut volcanic cone of the Fort Rock basin, is the oldest known habitation of man in the Oregon country.

Sagebrush sandals unearthed from the dust of Fort Rock Cave have a radio-carbon date of around nine thousand years. The sandals—some of them scorched by hot pumice from a nearby volcano—were discovered deep in the debris of the cavern. Fort Rock Cave, once the home of hunters who tipped their spears and arrows with obsidian, is now part of the Reuben Long ranch in northern Lake County.

Those ancient Oregonians wove sagebrush bark into durable sandals and wore them along the muddy shores of a lake never seen by white men. Some of the sandals, when found, still bore mud from the rim of the lake that spread over the broad Fort Rock Valley thousands of years ago. The discovery, in 1938, of these prehistoric sandals attracted the attention of anthropologists throughout America. It modified the pre-history of Oregon and earned national recognition for Dr. L. S. Cressman, the University of Oregon anthropologist who supervised the exploration of the cavern.

Protected by masks from the choking dust, students working under Dr. Cressman in earlier research in caverns of the region had found matting and basketry, bones of animals that lived in the old lake country, and implements shaped from volcanic glass. Lying deep in cave litter and under rocks which had fallen from the ceiling, were scrapers, knives, arrowheads, stone awls, and even sinkers used in weighing nets. Those stone-anchored nets once saw service in a lake-filled basin, across which dust devils now whirl on warm summer days.

The Fort Rock Cave differs little from other caverns of the old lake country that is rimmed by tilted mountains. Apparently cut by wind-whipped lake waves, the cave slopes from a high, wide entrance back to a point where rock meets dust. The cave mouth looks down on the big Fort Rock amphitheater, about two miles southeast. Across the basin are the brush-covered Connley Hills. Miles to the south are the pine-covered hills of the Fremont National Forest.

The "Lost Oregonians"

Just who these Fort Rock hunters were remains a mystery. Anthropologists who have traced their dim trails through the northern Great Basin can only hazard a guess. Like the "lost men" in the Southwest during Folsom times and the ancient people of the Yuma camps and Sandia caves, the Fort Rock hunters left only their artifacts to record their long stay in this land of vanished lakes. However, it is possible to piece together much about their way of life.

In the Ice Age, or early-recent times, the long fault-block valleys of South-Central Oregon impounded the runoff from a wide region of mountains and basins. This runoff, heavy in pluvial days, formed great land-locked lakes. These lakes, virtually inland seas, reached flood stage and marked their high shore lines through the lashing action of wind-chopped waves. At the same time other big lakes spread over other broad basins of the west. One of these was Lake Bonneville, in the mountain-rimmed Salt Lake Valley to the east. Another was sprawling Lahontan. Arms and bays of ragged-shore Lahontan covered parts of Nevada and sent a broad inlet into southeastern Oregon, up the Quinn River Valley.

In that same damp, warm era between ice encroachments, both prehistoric Winter Lake and Lake Chewaucan flooded the basin south from Picture Rock Pass to the high rims of the Abert country. Separated from now-vanished Lake Chewaucan by Picture Rock Pass, huge Silver Lake gradually formed to the north. This lake flooded Thorn and Christmas Lake basins and the Fort Rock Valley. Some of its water came from Alkali Lake, to the east. Many small but active volcanoes fringed old Silver Lake, whose waves splashed against the southern slope of Fort Rock Cave. The lashing waters slowly gnawed into the volcanic rocks, creating similar but smaller caves at the bases of various volcanic humps.

As the level of the lake lowered, hunters entered the basin, possibly lured by game that lived close to the shore, where vegetation was dense and prey was plentiful. They likely came from the Great Plains, members of tribes that had crossed the Rockies and moved through the Snake River gateway to the Oregon country. They could, though, have been members of Asian tribes following a well-blazed trail to North America. They might even have been descendants of the Folsom and Sandia men of the Southwest, who had wandered around the shores of Lake Lahontan, trailing bison herds and other game.

Prehistoric Wildlife of Fort Rock

In the damp days following the last ice age, Fort Rock Basin must have been a lush land. Feeding on its verdant meadows were bison, deer, and antelope. Somewhat earlier, Fossil Lake, across the basin to the southeast, was the range of two types of camels. Elephants lived along the shores; their fossils marked their trails. Across the ancient basin, dunes slowly moved, massing into a great white barrier at the edge of a "lost forest" of pines in the northeast.

Waterfowl were abundant; there were many Canada geese and many swans. There were ducks, grebes, shore birds, herons, and even flamingos. Their bones, now turned to stone, have been found near small arrowheads, of the type used by early-day Indians in hunting birds. Nevertheless, Thomas Condon's century-old question remains unanswered: Were those stone-tipped arrows shot at Ice Age birds? It is hard to say. Bones and "points" of different ages might have sifted to a common level by the erosive action of wind whipping over the now-dry lake basins.

Conditions under which Fork Rock hunters lived must have been harsh. Winds would have blasted into exposed Fort Rock Cave and lashed across the cold, stony floor. Overhanging rocks would have provided little shelter. The cave opens to the southwest, from which direction biting winds still sweep during Great Basin storms. However, the cave did serve as a protection from northern blasts. In winter, cattle and horses still seek that protection, but today there are few traces of the extensive excavation; and stock wintering there have given the cave a barnyard appearance.

Hunters Fade into Oblivion

What was the physical appearance of Oregon's Fort Rock hunters? No one knows. They did not leave a single skeleton in cavern dust to give a clue. In Cougar Mountain Cave, nearby, the skeleton of a young person was discovered in 1958, but its age was not determined. Evidence of human habitation has also been found in other caves of Oregon's Great Basin.

Interior Oregon's first people possibly saw volcanoes in eruption, and tongues of lava reaching out of the eastern Cascades. Their arrowheads and scrapers are present under glacial debris near Odell Lake. Descendants of Glacial Age tribes faced a prolonged dry period in which the great lakes dwindled, and occasionally disappeared. As a wet cycle followed dry years, basins again partly filled with water. Old shore lines prove this.

Descendants of "Lost Oregonians"

If these prehistoric Oregonians moved out of the brushy basins in arid years, their descendants must have returned, because there is plenty of evidence of later cultures in this lonely land. Proof exists not only in the dust and debris of caves, but at old, widely scattered camp sites. These are on ancient lake shores in the rim country of southeastern Oregon and even on the High Desert, where small lakes once existed. Obsidian chips and occasional artifacts mark these camps.

Artisans who chipped "points," knives, scrapers, awls, and other tools from volcanic glass had several fine sources. The largest was in Newberry Crater, where black glass spilled from a high vent to create one of the most spectacular flows of its kind on the continent. This is the Great Obsidian Flow, between Paulina and East Lakes. The U. S. Forest Service road connecting the twin lakes skirts the north edge of the big flow.

Just over Newberry Rim to the south, was the home of the Fort Rock hunters. To the east were the camps of the tribes whose water supply was ice found the year around in caves such as Arnold, Edison, East, and South Ice caves. Directly over the Newberry Rim to the north, on the slope of the old volcano facing Bend, is mysterious Charcoal Cave. There partly burned wood was found bearing the imprint of stone axes.

Glass Buttes on the High Desert, seventy miles east of Bend, was another rich source for spear points and arrow tips. Strewn over the grassy slopes is considerable obsidian, including the rare iridescent variety.

Some evidence exists that horses still ranged over the interior of Oregon when the Fort Rock hunters and their kin arrived. Horse bones, broken "points" and chipped obsidian have appeared in the same gravels and dust. Horses, though, were extinct on the continent before the arrival of the first white men. There were horses in the inland region of Oregon when the first explorers came, but these ponies were descendent from European horses, not from the animals that ranged over western America for millions of years.

Whites Followed Indian Trails

The first trappers and explorers saw many Indians in the

semiarid lands east of the Cascades. They often followed trails long used by Indians, and later by the cavalrymen. These well-worn trails indicated a heavy seasonal movement of Indians from the Klamath Basin and the interior plateau to Columbia River fishing sites.

Few parts of western America have yielded more artifacts representative of ancient stone industries than the lake region of South-Central Oregon. Some early arrowhead hunters collected up to ten thousand specimens, mostly from along lake shores, above which loom high fault-block mountains or "rims." Many artifacts have occurred around range springs, or where springs existed in damper times. By now, though, the old camp sites have been fairly well gleaned.

Construction work in Central Oregon accidentally revealed a number of arrowheads and spear points. Years ago when a street in Bend was being widened close to the Deschutes River and mill area, a worker blasting rocks discovered a bushel of beautifully formed spear points. Apparently they had been hidden in a rocky crevice after having been shaped from volcanic glass. Another cache came to light north of Bend, when a road was being built across a small cove to a new trailer plant.

Many small but scattered bands of plateau Indians made plenty of trouble for explorers, trappers, miners, and ranchers. They stole the white man's horses, occasionally returning them for a fee. They attacked smaller parties and raided prospectors' camps; they waylaid soldiers and burned ranch homes.

Roaming bands of Indians eventually became so troublesome that, in the early 1860s, soldiers were sent to establish camps and outposts. These were in the range country, adjacent to mining-camp trails. However, raids continued to grow in intensity following the discovery of gold at Canyon City in 1861, when many prospectors followed Indian trails into the John Day River country. The rich booty of miners and packers became an irresistible lure to the nomadic Indians who lived on the land.

Part Two

INDIANS AND THE FIRST WHITE MEN

CHAPTER 5

Early Explorers

A MOTLEY BRIGADE, tired after a long ride, camped near the mouth of a southern tributary of the Columbia River on the evening of December 1, 1825. Heading that party of trappers was one of the most colorful "mountain men" of the West. Peter Skene Ogden of the Hudson's Bay Company was surveying the fur possibilities of the little-known land east of the Three Sisters and Mt. Jefferson. That land was Central Oregon.

The swift stream by which Ogden halted was the River of the Falls—the Deschutes of the Oregon country. If Ogden realized on that wintry evening of 1825 that he was destined to make the first recorded exploration of the inland Oregon region, his diary does not show it.

Camp was made on the east bank of the Deschutes, where the stream, rushing over giant boulders, pours into the westward-flowing Columbia. Indians from several tribes, including even the Iroquois, were in the group, as well as a considerable number of French Canadians. Historians believe that women and children were also in the brigade, members of the families of the Canadian trappers. This was customary. Entire families even accompanied fur-hunting expeditions into the dangerous Snake country.

When Ogden's trappers moved into the area, they found about a hundred Indians gathered there to offer horses for sale, but "they were too extravagant in their demands."* However, the day before, his trappers—looking forward to a hard journey into the unknown land—had obtained two horses by trade.

Now, while they slept within sound of the Deschutes pouring through its rocky gorge, Indians stole several of their horses. Despite this loss, the trappers made an early start next morning. They had some difficulty in crossing the Deschutes, near its wide, swift mouth. The river was high, its banks flooded, "no doubt owing to the mild weather and the late rains."

Once across the swollen river, the party struck inland. They slowly gained elevation by following zigzag trails up the "elephant-back" hills facing the Columbia from the south. The southerly route was through Wasco County of the present, southeast of The Dalles site. Ahead of the men lay dangerous adventure that was a daily part of their lives. The prize they sought was not new lands, but furs. Many times the party faced death from starvation, and on one of these occasions, Ogden notes that "Prayers were made."

Who Was Peter Skene Ogden?

It has been said that of all the mountain men who penetrated the Far West in the early decades of the nineteenth century, none trapped more beaver, played wilder practical jokes, fought harder, or left his name on more places, from Utah to the Pacific, than did Peter Skene Ogden. Born in Quebec, in 1794, of Loyalist parents who had left New Jersey at the outbreak of the Revolutionary War, he was educated in London, where he studied law. On returning to Canada from England, he went into the wilderness, accepting employment with the North West Company.

Ogden first entered the Oregon country at the age of twenty-

---

*Unless otherwise noted, all quoted material in this account of the Peter Skene Ogden party is from Ogden's *Journals*, published by the Hudson's Bay Record Society.

four, when he headed a trapping party with headquarters at Fort George, now Astoria. He continued with the Hudson's Bay Company after its merger with the North West Company in 1821. Four years later, when Ogden was in the upper Columbia River area, John McLoughlin, chief factor at Fort Vancouver, ordered him to go into the central part of the region that was to become the State of Oregon. It was to be a trapping mission.

Ogden's diary reports little about the country through which he passed. He sought beaver for furs and game for food. He was apparently unimpressed by landmarks such as the deep gorge of the Deschutes, the spectacular Smith Rock formation above Crooked River, or the elevation later known as Powell Buttes. However, there were exceptions. On December 5, 1825, as the brigade was slowly moving up from the Columbia into the highlands, Ogden wrote:

Started this morning about 8 o'clock. Our guide informed us there were some small deer to be seen in this quarter. I dispatched my three hunters off: at 12 o'clock came to the end of the hills. Here certainly was a grand sight: Mt. Hood bearing due west and Mt. St. Helen and Mt. Nesqually (Mt. Adams) northwest covered with I may say eternal snow, and in the S.W. direction a number of other lofty mountains in form and shape of sugar loaves.

This view was from the top of Tygh Grade, a few miles east of the present highway leading from Central Oregon, through Maupin and Tygh Valley, to The Dalles. The close-up view of Mt. Hood probably inspired Ogden to make this unusual entry. To the south was majestic Mt. Jefferson. In the distance loomed Three Fingered Jack and Washington. Still farther away, astride the Cascade crest, rose the Three Sisters, to be known for a while as Faith, Hope, and Charity.

Rendezvous on the Deschutes

At the same time that he dispatched Ogden from Fort Nez Perce (Walla Walla), McLoughlin ordered another of his aides,

Scotland-born Finan McDonald, to cross the Cascades from the west and rendezvous with Ogden at an inland point on the River of the Falls. This was the *Riviere des Chutes* of the French Canadians, now the Deschutes. To keep the rendezvous with McDonald, Ogden and his trappers bore into the southeast, crossing Wasco County of the present into the Warm Springs region.

First to reach the rendezvous point on the Deschutes River was McDonald, accompanied by the faithful Thomas McKay from Fort Vancouver. On the evening of December 9, 1825, the Ogden party joined him. The meeting place likely was at the mouth of Shitike Creek, or a short distance downstream at the mouth of Dry Creek. It is easy to picture that wilderness reunion by the Deschutes—a river still unharnessed by giant dams and irrigation reservoirs, a river still carrying its mountain flood north to the Columbia.

There was plenty of forage for the horses, plenty of trout in the stream, game in the hills, as well as brushy tributary creeks for the beaver hunters. It was a natural meeting place. But how was it selected, and how did Ogden's big party so unerringly pilot its course to the evening campfire of Finan McDonald? Ogden apparently had guides, whereas McDonald had none. Yet McDonald crossed the Cascades, ahead of schedule, set up his camp, and awaited the arrival of the Ogden party.

Perhaps Finan McDonald had been in Central Oregon before. Some historians believe he had. He was in the Northwest as early as 1809-10, with David Thompson, after leaving Glengarry in Ontario, Canada. One of the classic stories of far western literature is McDonald's fight with a wounded buffalo. Although he apparently was the first white man to penetrate Central Oregon, no landmark in the sprawling inland country east of the Cascades bears his name.

The trappers faced an immediate problem, that of crossing the Deschutes to get into the inland plateau and its streams with their expected beaver colonies. Following heavy rains, the river undoubtedly was a big, swift stream, gaining strength for its plunge past rocky ramparts, then on north through Mutton Mountain gorges. Finally a place for the crossing was selected. Four horses were lost in the attempt to get over the swollen river, in the first recorded crossing of the Deschutes by white men in this, the geographic center of Oregon. From the river, the trappers rode over the Agency Plains, past the site of the present Madras. Many abandoned Indian lodges marked this trail leading through the Lamonta area of later years.

Crooked River Country

The party made its first camp on Crooked River, on the night of December 17, setting out one hundred traps. Deer and antelope were bagged and a raccoon "nearly as large as an Indian dog" was caught. The party next moved on up Crooked River, where the trappers came on grass seven feet high. (In pioneer days, high ryegrass covered the Crooked River bottom, spreading over the present site of Prineville.)

Christmas day was spent in camp. Bitterly cold weather had settled over the valley, under the high rims to the west and the sloping hills to the east, and the party had less than forty pounds of food "of any kind." As the river froze over, they took their traps from the water. Rough days lay ahead. Slowly they worked their way toward the highlands of upper Crooked River, which they found "nearly fast with ice." They used ice chisels to free the traps but caught few beaver. On the morning of December 30, Ogden's guide refused to proceed farther, saying there were no animals of any kind in the wintry highlands ahead. Horses, he warned, would die for want of grass. To emphasize the reason for quitting, the guide said it would be impossible to get over the mountains in winter. However, on being promised a gun, he changed his mind, consenting to continue his efforts to get the party over the high country in the "Dey" (John Day) River region.

The beaver seekers were still in the Crooked River area at year's end. Because of the intensity of the cold, the families, the trappers, and the horses all suffered greatly. In addition, the food supply was practically exhausted: "One beaver gave the men half rations for tomorrow, but which no doubt will be devoured tonight as three-fourths of the party has been two days without food."

On New Year's day, Ogden wrote: "We remained in camp. Gave all hands a dram and I have only to observe there was more fasting than feasting."

Despite the great cold and suffering, Ogden ordered his men to scout the area. On an upper tributary of Crooked River, they found many beaver houses, causing Ogden to vow that he would steer his way through this area on his way home. A horse was butchered for food on January 3. Later, two more horses were killed and eaten. On January 10, two men who had been missing for three days returned to camp, starving.

Not until January 11, 1826, did the party—the first ever to pass through Central Oregon and leave a record—"bid adieu to the waters of the River of the Falls." By dusk the following day, the trappers reached the sources of the John Day River, the stream mentioned as "Dey's River," to move out of the Deschutes country. The combined parties of Ogden and McDonald apparently numbered about "50 gentlemen and servants." This entire group had to live off the country through which it passed during this bitterly cold season.

Keeping his earlier vow, Ogden returned across Central Oregon, from east to west, in the summer of 1826, going over a Cascade Pass, possibly the Santiam, and down the Willamette.

Ogden's Second Trip

Ogden made still another trip through Central Oregon, south from the Columbia, in 1826-27, with thirty-five men. Tom McKay was along with additional men. Gervais and Payette, other members of the group, each boasted five or six men. On this second trip to the interior, Ogden left his old tracks of the year before, going from the present Dufur area directly to White River, a western tributary of the Deschutes, past the falls. From that point, the party moved downstream to the Deschutes, where they made a crossing at Sherars Falls.

There, Ogden found an Indian camp of twenty families, and the trappers also discovered "a bridge made of slender wood." When the crossing was attempted, five horses broke through the Indian-made span, falling into the white water of the Deschutes, where it churns its way through lava channels. Mention of an Indian-built bridge over the Deschutes at the Sherar site has attracted considerable comment from old-timers and historians, for it was not the practice of tribes of this region to engage in such engineering activity. The family of John Y. Todd, which lived at Sherars Bridge in the 1860s, said Indians told them the span was not a bridge but a fishing platform, built out from each side of the channel and joined in the center.

At the camp on Crooked River, Ogden noted harassment by the Indians. On October 4, 1826, he wrote:

We certainly had a most providential escape. Last night the Indians crossed the river and set fire to grass within 10 yards of our camp. The watch perceived it and gave the alarm. Had there not been a bunch of willows to arrest it, everything would have been lost: a gale blowing at the time. This morning every Indian had decamped. If ever Indians deserved to be punished, these do.

From the upper Crooked River country, Ogden made his way to a "Country of rivers and lakes," the Malheur-Harney region. It was a land explored the previous year by Antoine Sylvaille, who headed a group of Ogden's trappers. The Silvies River was named for him.

East, Paulina Lakes Discovered

It was on Ogden's return trip from that second expedition

After getting a fast start high in the Cascade Range, Central Oregon's Deschutes River flows through blooming sage northwest of Redmond as it journeys north to join the Columbia.

Majestically ruling over the Central Oregon scene are the Three Sisters and Broken Top, pictured here in a wintry setting across Dutchman Flat. Jagged Broken Top looms to the right.

Looking south toward the Three Sisters and Broken Top (far left), part of the High Cascades of Oregon. This is a land of great forests, lakes, and rivers as well as volcanic mountain peaks.

that he apparently discovered, on November 16, 1826, East and Paulina lakes, in Newberry Crater. He noted: "We ascended a divide, descended and had the pleasure of finding two lakes. . . . It was a consolation to see our poor horses quench their thirst."

Presumably he had gone over the eastern rim of the crater, stopping at East Lake. From the upper Klamath country, he and his party continued south to the Klamath basin, then on to California to discover and name beautiful Mt. Sastise (Shasta).

First visitors to the Harney basin were greatly impressed by the number of Indians in the region. On his trip into this country in 1826, Ogden observed: "It is incredible the number of Indians in this quarter. We cannot go 10 yards without finding them. No Indian nation so numerous as these in all North America." Apparently Ogden came across the tribes when they were concentrated in their winter quarters. In the open seasons, the Indians were widely scattered. Early explorers of the Great Basin province, the old Oregon lake country, and the high plateau, generally described the Indians in these areas as living under starving conditions and occasionally being cannibalistic.

Ogden found the Indians of the Klamath country well provided with bows and arrows. On December 6, the trappers reached an Indian village of five huts in this area: "Huts large size made of earth, flat on top, the top a defense against arrows but not balls. Some 200 Indians gathered around the camp and traded for four days. The two chiefs delivered traps lost by Mr. McDonald last year with eight beaver. This is much in favor of their honesty." In the *Snake River Journals* of the Hudson's Bay Company, Ogden estimated that the "Clammitte" nation was composed of about 250 men. The Indians served as guides for Ogden's trappers in penetrating unknown areas.

Ogden described and named many geographic features of the Snake region east of the Cascades, yet attained his greatest recognition in American history, not as an explorer and trapper, but as the rescuer of the Whitman massacre survivors in December of 1847. Seven years later, on September 27, he was laid to rest in Oregon City, beside a river he knew well—the Willamette —and was buried in the Mountain View Cemetery there. An Oregon State park, facing the deep, spectacular gorge of Crooked River on U. S. Highway 97, honors this early explorer of Central Oregon.

A dozen or so years after his travels there, trails of Peter Skene Ogden through interior Oregon had reverted to Indian paths, and all traces of his camps on the River of the Falls and Crooked River had disappeared.

John Work, Trader

The trails of John Work, chief trader for the Hudson's Bay Company, possibly crossed those of Peter Skene Ogden in the early 1830s. In command of the Snake River Expedition of 1830-31, Work followed north along the Snake River to the Raft River, a southern tributary of the Snake, then crossed the northwest corner of Utah, and visited the Nevada country, where he trapped the tributaries of the Owyhee and the Humboldt. Swinging northwest across the dry bed of Tum Tum Lake, he reached the southern end of Steens Mountain, a landmark visible from the high country east of the Deschutes.

From there he moved north along Harney Lake, which he described as "high, brackish and very bad," and went up the Silvies River, where he spent six weeks trapping and fishing. His "take" was thirty-six beaver, six antelope, two elk, and five deer. Some of the hunters possibly covered the country tributary to Crooked River. The entire party returned east by way of the John Day, crossing spurs of the Blue Mountains.

In the season of 1831-32, Work was again in command of a Snake River Expedition in quest of furs. On the return journey he sent eight men, under command of Charles Plante, into the Malheur region and across the headwaters of the Silvies River. Plante's instructions were to proceed to Fort Vancouver by way of the Deschutes and the Columbia. There is no record of

Plante's route across Central Oregon, but it is assumed that, being in quest of beaver, he followed the river courses.

Wyeth, Trader and Patriot

A heavy storm was brewing over the Cascades, and the highlands of the upper Deschutes basin were white with pre-Christmas snow when a new trail blazer came out of the north. He was Nathaniel J. Wyeth, trader and patriot. Some historians say he was on a trapping expedition as was his predecessor, Peter Skene Ogden; but there is a chance that he was seeking Sandwich (Hawaiian) Islanders who had left one of the Wyeth construction camps on the Columbia River. Wyeth failed to find his Kanakas, but he left an interesting account of the journey that appears to be the first recorded visit of white men to the present site of Bend.

Behind Wyeth—a native of Cambridge, Massachusetts—is an interesting story. Historian George Bancroft said of him: "He it was who, more directly than anyone else, marked the way for the ox teams which were shortly to bring the Americanized civilization of Europe across a roadless continent." In his early thirties, Wyeth's interest turned westward. Having learned of the Astor enterprise, he conceived the idea of doing something similar. He started for the Columbia with a land party and a sea party. When the parties met, they established a post near the mouth of the Willamette River. On Sauvie Island, in 1834, he established Fort William.

Regardless of the motive for the trip, Wyeth and his party picked a poor time of the year to visit the upper Deschutes River country. On December 22, 1834, as they passed upstream on the west bank of the Deschutes, a winter storm was increasing in severity. Soon they encountered deep snow, and Wyeth was forced to send some of his men back to the lower country with horses, where feed would be available. He and three of his men remained to build canoes for use in exploring upper reaches of the River of the Falls. Their camp was about twelve miles south of the Bend site.

When the canoes were launched, Wyeth and his companions had progressed only about five miles when they came to the rapids of Benham Falls and were unable to ascend farther. One canoe broke away, and the men had to run several miles before they could retrieve it. They made a portage at the falls, then continued their upstream exploration to Pringle Falls, where they camped overnight. Despite bad weather and deep snow, Wyeth obviously explored the upper Deschutes more extensively than he noted in his diary—in notes written with chilled fingers. He made side trips up Deschutes tributaries when four feet of snow covered most of the region.

On the return trip, Wyeth abandoned the boats a short distance south of the Bend location. "Killed one deer just in time," he wrote. At the time the kill was made, there was nothing in the larder but a bit of swan meat. In all, twenty deer were killed. Wyeth met the main party at the head of Squaw Creek, with "men and horses well fed." Ending the two-months' exploration, or Kanaka-hunting trip, the party returned to the Columbia on February 8, 1835.

Wyeth's winter trip, the first on record into the upper Deschutes region south of Crooked River, has been strangely neglected by historians. His name is not attached to a single geographic feature in the area, and not until one hundred years afterwards did his visit to inland Oregon receive any recognition. In all Oregon, only one place, Wyeth on the Columbia, bears the name of this man who "marked the way for ox teams that brought civilization from the east."

Fremont Given Western Assignment

Eight years passed before Central Oregon was again visited by an explorer. This person was John C. Fremont, then a thirty-year-old lieutenant in the Topographic Engineers of the U. S. Army. Guides for this trip in 1843 were Kit Carson, of frontier fame; and Billy Chinook, a Warm Springs Indian. The trip took Fremont through the Deschutes country and southeast to the Klamath Marsh, the point from which he headed east into the Rim Country.

That year, Fremont's superiors decided he should explore the West. There had been much jealousy among his fellow officers, possibly because of articles he had written on his explorations and his sudden rise to leadership. Whatever the reason, an effort was made to stop him. A few years before this journey west, Fremont had eloped with Jessie Benton, daughter of Senator Thomas Benton—for whom Benton County, Oregon, was named. After Benton finally forgave his daughter and took Fremont into the family, the senator proved helpful in many ways. For one thing, he assisted Fremont in getting the important assignment of exploring the West.

When the party was about ready to begin the journey, some-one learned that Fremont was taking along a howitzer. This news was relayed to Washington, with the idea of stopping him. The charge was made that his could not be a peaceful expe-dition if he were toting a cannon. A runner was immediately sent after him. Somehow his wife Jessie heard of the plot against her husband. She sent him a note, advising that he start at once and keep going. Fremont had faith in his wife, and the runner never caught up with him.

Early in November 1843, he reached The Dalles, where he outfitted his men for the journey south through inland Oregon. On the 25th, they started up the Deschutes, following an old trail from The Dalles to Tygh Valley. After crossing White River, they moved inland across the Warm Springs country, eventually reaching the upper meadows of Tumalo Creek. They journeyed south past Benham Falls to Klamath Marsh, where they found Indians in established villages. There for the first time, Fremont discharged the cannon. The Indians did not attack, but Fremont feared trouble was brewing. The frightened Indians sent a brave and his squaw to the camp, offering gifts.

From the marsh, the explorers turned directly east. Moving into the highlands through a snowstorm, they suddenly emerged from the pine forest to walk out on a high, vertical ledge. Far below was a beautiful lake, its shores bordered with green grass. As the sun broke through the clouds, the men on the ledge—still enveloped by heavy snowfall—saw a magnificent view spread out before them. Fremont named the high rim Winter Ridge. The great body of water below he called Summer Lake.

He now headed toward Warner Valley, reaching Abert Lake on December 20. This lake was named for his chief, Colonel J. J. Abert of the U. S. Topographic Engineers. However, Fremont was not the first to see Abert Lake. John Work had called it Salt Lake when he and his brigade were there on October 16, 1832, and his diary implies that other trappers even preceded him.

From southeastern Oregon, Fremont went into California, crossing the Sierra Nevada during a bad winter storm and through deep snow. Not until 1855 did another party of explorers cross Central Oregon, when agitation for a railroad culminated in the Pacific Railroad Survey under Robert S. Williamson.

CHAPTER 6

Wandering Wagons

FIERCE HARDSHIP, even death, faced the first immigrants to cross the almost waterless expanse of the Central Oregon high country. Across a sage-covered land of buttes and rims, they rode into a strange, forbidding country. Over a period of eight years, three different groups made the crossing.

Other smaller parties followed the paths of these first iron-rimmed wagon wheels through the sage desert, but their stories have largely been merged with those of the larger trains—the Blue Bucket Mine party, the Clark Massacre survivors, and the Elliott Cutoff group.

Aside from explorers, soldiers, and prospectors, members of these earliest wagon trains were the first to view the broad land that is now Central Oregon. None of the seekers of new homes in the West lingered to build cabins beside the old roads of the pioneers; but in later years, some returned to settle on lands along Crooked River and in the Upper Deschutes. Such was the primary role of these first people to help open interior Oregon for settlement.

The Blue Bucket Mine People

First to cross the interior country in a wagon train were members of the Blue Bucket Mine party in 1845. That party was organized on April 28, at the Oregon Encampment on the Missouri River bottom. Men stood up to be counted, and stern rules governing the train were approved. Anyone guilty of willful murder was to be punished by death. A person guilty of manslaughter would be delivered to the authorities in Oregon. Anyone guilty of open adultery would receive forty-nine lashes on the bare back. Every dog found running about camp could be shot at the discretion of the captain. The rules were harsh, but so was the long road ahead—the Oregon Trail. Yet it should have been a routine crossing, for the trail had already been traversed by many parties.

This Blue Bucket train was destined to become one of the most famous to make the western trek because it got lost in the High Desert of Central Oregon and somewhere there—or in the Malheur River area to the east—discovered a mine that is now legendary, the Blue Bucket.

There were some eight hundred men, women, and children in the train. With them were numerous oxen and more than two thousand head of loose cattle. The trip from the Missouri was largely uneventful until Oregon was reached. Here leaders decided to leave the wheel-cut, dusty Columbia River route to The Dalles, and instead cut across virtually unknown Central Oregon. Undertaking the task of guiding the immigrants over the unknown land was Stephen Meek. Leaving the Oregon Trail west of Fort Boise, they wandered over the barren lands, moving from waterhole to mountain spring and making many dry camps. Some historians report that twenty-four persons died between Boise and Prineville. The location of several of the graves remains unknown.

Nuggets of Gold

Legend says that, sometime during the agonizing trip over Central Oregon from the Malheur country, the party discovered nuggets of gold. One widely accepted version holds that during a night camp several youngsters were sent to a nearby stream to get water in a blue bucket. Yellow metal was later noticed in the bottom of the bucket but was not identified until the train had moved on and a golden nugget was pounded into a disc on the wheel of a wagon.

The story of "gold in the blue bucket" expanded and changed through the years. Members of the party retraced the route of the wandering wagon train in an attempt to locate the creek with the reputed gold. Veteran miners also followed the trail. Attempts to find the mine continued in earnest more than a century after the reported discovery; occasionally even today one hears of new searchers. Some historians believe that a segment of the Meek party strayed into the gullies leading into the Canyon City country, where nuggets were found in 1861.

It was east of the John Day River that Meek, the only member of the train who knew interior Oregon, lost his direction and led the immigrants into the High Desert. Thirsty and near starvation, they all drank heavily of the alkali water from playa lakes. Soon a fever epidemic struck. Children fell ill and some died. Eventually the lost immigrants reached Crooked River, after Meek and the Reverend Elijah White had hurried north to The Dalles to report the plight of the lost train.

Some segments of the train moved downstream in the bed of Crooked River, where high, rocky walls crowd to the stream edge. On the night of September 22, the immigrants stopped in the ryegrass bottoms, where Prineville was later to take shape. There the group was met by a rescue party from The Dalles. It is possible that one unit of the train did not go into Crooked River, but, before backtracking, moved west through the present Alfalfa community to the Bend site.

Rejoined by splinter groups and guided by men from The Dalles not too sure of their direction, the party made camp one night on the high Deschutes rim northwest of the Madras location, another night at Sagebrush Springs (Gateway), and still another on Hay Creek. The immigrants doubled teams to get up to the brushy Shaniko flats. From the plateau, the weary group went down Buck Hollow, ferried over the Deschutes in wagon beds, then moved through Butler and Immigrant canyons, and on into The Dalles.

In the Meek cutoff party were Solomon Tetherow, wagon master, and his wife and their son, Andrew Jackson Tetherow. Like many another immigrant to Western Oregon, years later the son became a resident of Central Oregon, moving there from the Willamette Valley in 1873. From his home on the Deschutes, at a location long known as Tetherow Crossing, he could watch a backwash of immigrants roll by over the Santiam Pass to the Ochoco meadows—to settle in a land they had bypassed years before.

Clark Massacre Party

The second immigrant train to cross Central Oregon was a comparatively small party, more of a family group than a train. In it were the survivors of an Indian attack on Raft River, near its confluence with the Snake, in the fall of 1851. The story of this ill-fated party dates to the time Thomas Clark left the Sacramento gold fields for the East, to buy blooded and purebred stock. In Illinois, home of the Clark family, the small train was formed for the trip to Oregon. The westward start was uneventful, with wagons moving slowly for the grazing of stock.

Clark, who had been in the Oregon country, was making the journey west accompanied by several members of his family—his mother; his nineteen-year-old sister, Grace; and his brother, seventeen-year-old Hodgson. In St. Louis, Missouri, Clark had purchased a hack, in which his mother and sister traveled. Other members of the slow-traveling party were mainly engaged in moving the many horses and cattle.

Autumn had already set in, and there was a chill in the air when the group reached the Snake River, the land of the Snake Indians. Clark had charted his course to reach the Snake at Hell's Gate. Boys rode ahead of the wagons, slowly following the grazing cattle and horses. Also ahead of the main party were Thomas Clark, Mrs. Clark, Grace, and Hodgson.

The little group was making camp when suddenly some thirty Indians—with the horses and the cattle as their targets—swooped out of the dusty sage. Eight headed for the spot where Mrs. Clark and Grace were setting up camp. Both Hodgson Clark and his mother were killed in the attack. Grace was shot and partly scalped. Hearing the shooting, men quickly arrived from the main group to drive off the attackers. After spending the night on the river and secretly burying their dead, the Clark party continued sadly westward. Clark had made his sister as comfortable as possible in one of the wagons.

West of the Snake River, Clark decided to branch from the Oregon Trail. In some places his route over Central Oregon approximated that of the Blue Bucket Mine party, but his was more direct. On an earlier trip, he had been advised to use three white mountains (the Sisters) as his westward guide. He was also told about a low volcanic cone, called Red Butte—directly in front of the Sisters as viewed from the mid-Oregon plateau— that would guide him to a good camping spot on the Deschutes River. This is now Pilot Butte, at the eastern city limits of Bend, and the central feature of a state park.

The Clark party stopped for several days on the Deschutes, apparently at the site of Bend's Pioneer Park. As Grace slowly gained strength, the group moved north from the Bend site to cross the new Barlow Pass, then turned south to Cottage Grove.

Passage of the Clark party through Central Oregon possibly played no major role in the opening of this little-known part of the region; but in the early 1890s, a Clark descendant, William P. Vandevert, son of Grace Clark Vandevert, returned to homestead on the upper Deschutes River. Claude Vandevert—grandson of the girl wounded by the Indians in the Snake River attack —now operates the old homestead, a landmark in the Deschutes country south of Bend.

A monument in Pioneer Park, on the east bank of the Deschutes River in Bend, commemorates the camp made there by the Clark party. As far as is known, that camp was the first ever made on the site of the present city.

The Elliott Cutoff Party

In the fall of 1853, the largest of all trains to cross Central Oregon became lost after leaders mistook the Three Sisters for

Diamond Peak, the landmark that was to guide them to a new Cascade crossing. This was the Elliott Cutoff Party. It included 250 wagons, 1,027 persons, and considerable stock. It was a loosely-associated train, traveling in sections days apart, and frequently over different routes. It is a train virtually lost to Oregon history, principally because its story of suffering and death merged with that of the Blue Bucket Mine group.

The story of the Elliott Cutoff Party had its beginnings in March 1852, when a group of men met at the Mahlon Harlow home in Lane County to discuss the possibility of opening a new road over the Oregon Cascades, through the Middle Fork region of the Willamette. Out of that meeting came authorization for a road-viewing expedition. Seven men were commissioned to go up the Middle Fork from the west, to determine whether a feasible route for wagons could be found. In the party were John Diamond, W. M. Macy, Joseph Meadows, Alexander A. King, W. T. Walter, J. Clarke, and William Tandy. The viewers found a pass just south of a large mountain on the Cascade summit. Diamond climbed the mountain and named it for himself. The men continued east over the Cascades to the head-waters of the Deschutes, then followed the river north to the Bend area, before swinging into the east.

Well to the east of the Bend site, the party was attacked by Indians. Diamond, Clarke, and Macy were wounded as the men fought a retreating battle to the Vale area. The wounded were placed on wagons and returned to western Oregon over the Barlow Pass. A report on the new route was later submitted to the Oregon Territorial legislature, but strangely, the men did not mention the Indian attack. In their report, the road viewers said that the new route—up the Middle Fork of the Willamette and east past Diamond Peak—could be used by wagons and estimated that the road could be built at a cost of about $3,000. A contract for construction was afterwards let for $12 a mile. Work started immediately.

In 1853, stout-hearted Elijah Elliott of Lane County decided to go east to meet his family. After joining them at Fort Boise, he agreed to head a contingent of wagons over the new cutoff—a route that was to bear his name. Assured that the new Willamette Pass road would be ready by fall, Elliott was confident that three weeks could be saved by heading west across Central Oregon from the Vale area, up the Malheur River, and across the High Desert. At the start of the trip, the Elliott wagons apparently used the Meek party route. Later parties noticed the new tracks of wagon wheels leading into the west and swinging away from the Oregon Trail.

In the Harney Lake country, members of the Elliott train seem to have differed as to the route that should be followed. Some moved south along the lake fringe, close to the Steens foothills, then headed back into the Central Oregon highlands after passing the southern lake marshes. Others, shifting to the north of the lake, attempted to follow the erratic tracks of the Meek train.

Realizing their leaders were lost, young men from different wagons volunteered to ride ahead of the slow-moving party to get bearings on the unknown land beyond—or cross the Cascades for help. This occurred when the immigrants realized they were on a waterless, rough, canyon-furrowed plateau. Horses were becoming weak. Some were dying. Cattle were wandering away, seeking water. Many wagon owners were forced to lighten their loads. Furniture, chests, bedding, and heirlooms from a dozen eastern states were hidden in desert caches, to which their owners never returned. Some wagons were abandoned, and stock wandered through the sage.

This was the plight of various segments of the train as the young riders headed west for help. In one group were seven men; in another, five. An additional group of three elected to ride north to The Dalles for help, as had leaders of the Blue Bucket Mine train eight years earlier.

In one of the advance parties that crossed the mountains west of the Bend site were V. F. Owen of Missouri, Robert

Tandy of Oregon, Joab Denning of Indiana, and Calvin I. Nolan of Missouri. Another member, Andrew S. McClure, kept a diary that told of the men's suffering. In the high country west of the Bend site, the small party abandoned their horses, believing they were now in the Diamond Peak country, not the Sisters. Later they sighted Diamond Peak far to the south. McClure recorded in his diary, October 2:

Our guides have come to the conclusion that we did not pass around the foot of Diamond's Peak, as was intended, but being mistaken in the mountain, passed between two of the Sisters and north of the intended pass 40 to 50 miles. Surely no part of the mountains can be more rugged than we passed over.

At least one of the advance parties crossed the Cascades over the Chambers Lake Pass between two of the Sisters whose peaks reach skyward more than ten thousand feet.

Wagon masters of the various units slowly moving over the High Desert behind the advance scouts expected to find a road when they came to the "foot of the mountains"—those great white peaks visible from the high country well to the east. But on reaching the Bend area they found no road, nothing but occasional blazes on scattered trees. It was late October and already storm clouds were capping the Cascades. Finally they found blazes cut into trees by the road viewers of the previous year; these led into the south from the Bend site.

After a number of crossings of the Deschutes and its upper tributaries, the wagons reached the Middle Fork Pass, south of Diamond Peak. There an indifferent road had been slashed through the timber, but by now trees had fallen in cleared areas. In some places they were forced to construct "bridges" over firs and move wagons across the log spans by hand, but they made little headway. More immigrants arrived daily, frightened by mountain storms. All knew the sad story of the Donner party in the blizzard-swept Sierra summit in 1846-47.

When no word came from the young men who had gone for help, the immigrants—starving on the Cascade Divide south of Diamond Peak—sent a young schoolmaster, Martin Blanding, ahead down the Middle Fork. Blanding bravely borrowed a mule and started over the mountains and into the wilderness. His progress was slow and he was near starvation when one night he made camp near Butte Disappointment, not far from the present Lowell community of Lane County. When morning came, he started a fire and was preparing a meal from a newborn colt when he was discovered by a youth from the settlement, who had sighted the smoke of the fire.

Soon riders were hurrying down the valley to spread word that immigrants were stranded on the high pass. A rescue party hurried up to the divide. There they built campfires and cooked huge stacks of pancakes for the starving families. Wagons laden with food followed up the dim trail from the west, in an epochal relief operation. The story of that rescue—and of the sufferings of the young scouts, who eventually made their way into the valley—is part of the heroic and tragic history of Lane County.

The contribution of the Elliott Party to Central Oregon history was the opening of a new route over the Cascades—the Willamette Pass.

CHAPTER 7

Central Oregon Indians

RENEGADE CHIEF PAULINA of the Walapi tribe of the Snake Indians, who had outwitted soldiers in many skirmishes, died under the gunfire of a rancher on April 25, 1867. His time at last ran out in a grassy cove bordered on three sides by rocky cliffs which face the narrow gorge of Trout Creek, where it starts its race to join the Deschutes, just west of the village of Ashwood.

The chief—a title possibly bestowed by his white enemies rather than his own warriors—died as he had lived, a cattle rustler. A bullet from a Henry rifle downed him while he and his men were feasting on a beef killed from a herd of cattle they had stolen from a John Day River ranch. The rancher credited with firing the shot that killed Paulina was Howard Maupin, a veteran of the Mexican War, who had served under Zachary Taylor.

Chief Paulina's Raiders

On a night ride into the John Day River country near the present Clarno community, Paulina and his followers raided the ranch of Andrew Clarno and stole a herd of cattle. From the ranch, Paulina headed south into the high country, then southwest, possibly down Little Trout Creek. He crossed the route of the Canyon City road east of Antelope, where he was sighted by a stage driver, James N. Clark, who took the word to Maupin at the Antelope stage station. The Indians and the trail tramped by the stolen cattle were followed into Trout Creek.

With Maupin were Jim Clark, the stage driver, who left his rig at the Antelope station to join in the chase; William Ragan, and, some accounts indicate, John Atterbury.

Trout Creek was a lonely land on that late spring day in

1867, when the small group of ranchers rode out of the north in the dawn hours to trap the chief and his men. The big ranches of later years had not yet been established. Unfenced, rolling lands, here and there broken by lava rims and aged Clarno volcanoes, reached southeast to the timbered Ochocos. There was not a hamlet or a town in the still-wild land of Central Oregon. At the time, Howard Maupin was the lone resident of Antelope Valley, crossed near its head by the wagon road to Canyon City gold fields. Paulina was killed about halfway between the Antelope Valley stage station and the Ochoco settlement at the edge of the Blue Mountain timber.

Occasional prospectors undoubtedly visited the Trout Creek country to probe into the colored hills which much later were to yield the sulphide ores of the "Oregon King" and other diggings. As early as 1862, Felix and Marion Scott wintered in the general area, well to the northeast of Trout Creek, in the Trout Creek country. The map of Oregon still showed the interior range country as an unknown land.

But Paulina, the "Attila of the sagelands," was well known to the few settlers of the region and also to the soldiers sent into Central Oregon to protect the scattered ranches of stockmen and the trails traveled by miners.

Warlike Indians Blocked the Way

In 1864, Colonel C. S. Drew of the U. S. Army was ordered by the Department of the Pacific to make a reconnaissance trip into eastern Oregon to size up the Indian situation and determine the conditions of the various posts established to protect immigrants, miners, stagecoach drivers, freighters, and isolated ranchers. With his company, Drew rode east from the Klamath country and ran into a group of warlike Indians believed to be headed by Paulina. Fortunately he had a howitzer along. This weapon is believed to have caused the wily Paulina—well acquainted with the white man's military machine—to wait for another day before attacking. Some of the frontiersmen believe Paulina was bullet proof, as did the Warm Springs Indians, who hoped to avenge the death of Chief Queapama, who was slain by Paulina.

Klamath Peace Meeting

In 1864, the whites attempted to make peace with the Oregon Indians. A large group of Indians, including a small tribe of Snakes, attended a peace meeting at Fort Klamath, but Paulina did not show up, even though he was invited. He had other appointments in Central Oregon, where trails into the John Day gold fields were well traveled and hunting was good. J. W. P. Huntington, superintendent of Indian affairs for Oregon, was present at the Klamath meeting; and en route back to The Dalles, he and his party discovered Paulina's camp. It was in the upper Deschutes country near the Crescent location. At the camp they found three men, three women, and two children. In their attempt to seize the white men's guns, the three tribesmen were killed, and the women and children were taken to Fort Vancouver as hostages. One of the three women proved to be Paulina's wife.

Possibly because his wife was a hostage, Paulina showed up at Fort Klamath, after word had been sent to him that he would not be molested if he came there. While at the fort, he promised to return the next summer to make peace with the whites, but scarcely had the pact been signed before Paulina struck again, in a move to massacre the Fort Klamath garrison. The chief lost fourteen men. His attack was believed to have been in resentment over the white soldiers' practice of using Warm Springs scouts to watch the Snakes and the Shastas to the south.

Paulina Out-Maneuvers Troopers

It is ironical that Paulina died in a one-sided fight with a small group of ranchers, after having on a number of occasions successfully out-maneuvered troopers. One of the occasions on which Paulina escaped the pincers of an entrapping army maneuver occurred on upper Crooked River, the night of May 17, 1864. It was in this fight that Lieutenant Stephen Watson of the 1st Volunteer Cavalry was killed while charging a natural rock fortress that the Paiutes used in making a stand against the soldiers and the Warm Springs scouts.

Captain John M. Drake of Fort Dalles commanded the expedition into the Crooked River country, where Paulina's raiders were causing considerable trouble. The captain took with him young Stephen Watson, who had enlisted in 1861, and had served as territorial representative from Jackson County prior to this.

The expedition headed into the sparsely-settled Crooked River region, cautiously moving into the highlands, where Paulina and his men had been seen. The soldiers made camp at the junction of the north and south forks of Crooked River, at a spot later to be known as Camp Maury, in honor of Colonel R. F. Maury, who commanded the First Oregon Volunteer Cavalry.

Operating out of this camp, Warm Springs scouts made first contact with the Snakes late on the evening of May 17. Starting at 9:30 p.m., they rode northeasterly for about twelve miles. Scouts detailed to watch the Indian camp reported that the braves had been taking part in a war dance, making a noise that could be heard for miles. This noise from the Indians later led to the belief that the dance was for the purpose of enticing the whites into battle at a site of Paulina's own choosing.

About 4 a.m., soldiers and scouts moved into battle from three sides. As the dawn attack was launched, the Indians immediately retreated to a rocky cliff where they were impregnable. From the rocks, the entrenched Snakes fired a volley that killed Lieutenant Watson and two privates of Company B. Five other whites were wounded. The soldiers fell back to a safe place and waited reinforcements. On receiving word from Lieutenant John McCall of the attackers' plight and the death of

Watson and the soldiers, Captain Drake and his men started at once toward the scene of the fight.

On arrival, the soldiers found that the Snakes had fled about an hour before, leaving the dead on the battlefield, horribly mutilated. Only three of Paulina's braves were killed in that fight under the cliffs.

The soldier dead and the Warm Springs scouts were buried on a low ridge in the Ochocos, in the marginal timber through which flows a small stream. This was the site of Camp Watson. However, the remains of the young lieutenant killed in the wild charge on that early May morning in 1864, were not buried with his fallen comrades. They were taken to Fort Vancouver.

The body of Lieutenant Watson was first moved to Fort Dalles, with horses the source of transportation. Word reached the soldiers at Fort Dalles in advance of the arrival of the mounted escort. In dress uniform, the soldiers saluted their fallen comrade, then escorted the body to the Columbia River, a short distance from the fort. There the body was placed on a boat for the final journey to Fort Vancouver.

"Bullet-proof" Paulina

Part of the Paulina story centers in the year 1865, when James N. Clark and his wife located on the new military road between The Dalles and Canyon City. The Clark place was near the John Day River, east of Cherry Creek, where colored hills are mantled with old rimrock lava. Clark, hoping to profit from the heavy traffic over the route to the gold diggings, opened a stage station about the same time that Howard Maupin went into business in Antelope Valley, well to the west. In 1866, Paulina raided Clark's station and burned the buildings. Thus originated the name Burnt Ranch, well known to Central Oregon pioneers who traveled today's Ashwood-Mitchell road. At the time of the attack, Clark's wife was in the Willamette Valley. Clark himself, with his nephew George Masterson, was busy cutting firewood. The raiders struck suddenly from the hills. Clark's first knowledge of the Indians' attack came when he looked toward his ranch home and saw it in flames. Clark and Masterson decided to outrun the Indians on horseback, but only Clark succeeded in getting away.

Young Masterson was under the fire of approaching Indians as he headed for his horse. He mounted, but as the gunfire continued, he slipped from his horse and hid in the water of a creek while the Paiutes hunted the banks. Before setting fire to the house, the raiders took everything of value, even ripping open mattresses.

Eight miles down the road, Clark met a group of packers led by William (Bud) Thompson and bound for Canyon City. The packers, some of whom were later to play a role in the death of Paulina on Trout Creek, joined a group of friendly Indians and started in pursuit of the pillaging Paiutes. In Crook County at the head of McKay Creek, the party overtook the Snakes and killed four. "Bullet-proof" Paulina again escaped. He was next located in a rocky hideout overlooking Malheur Lake. The scout Donald McKay and his men attempted to get Paulina out of his fortress cave but they failed, though not before killing three of the braves while fighting in snow some two thousand feet above the lake level. Paulina's brother, Wahweveh, was among those who died there, high on the Steens.

Snakes Molest Warm Springs

In their attempts to trap the Paulina renegades, soldiers frequently were assisted by scouts and volunteers from the Warm Springs reservation, which lies in the evening shadow of Mount Jefferson, west of the Deschutes River. The Warm Springs tribes had just reason to join the whites in the effort to check Paulina, whose horse-riding warriors frequently raided their reservation, taking captives, killing the peaceful tribesmen, and stealing horses. The result was an appeal by Agency officials for military assistance.

Tribesmen were kept within reservation boundaries, partly for their own protection and partly because of treaty requirements. However, on September 26, 1866, Agent John Smith reported to the head of Indian Affairs in Oregon that permission had been granted to Poust-am-i-nie—one of the reservation chiefs —and seven of his men to cross the Deschutes to the east on a hunting trip. Several days out and having heard reports that a stage had been attacked on the Canyon City Road by the Snakes, the hunters started back for the reservation. On Trout Creek, about fifteen miles east of the Agency, the small band of Warm Springs hunters was attacked in camp by fifteen to twenty Snakes. Under a flag of truce and laying down their arms, the Warm Springs party attempted to make peace with the Snakes. Suddenly a group of Snakes fired from a ravine, mortally wounding Poust-am-i-nie. The Snakes then disappeared, taking with them the horses of the Warm Springs hunters.

Angered by the attack, seventy of the reservation braves rode to The Dalles, to enlist for military service. Two companies of Warm Springs scouts later enrolled to serve under Lieutenant Colonel George Crook in the final campaigns against the Snakes.

Army Outposts Established

Despite the combined efforts of soldiers, Warm Springs volunteers, and ranchers, Paulina and his braves continued their attacks on miners and settlers. Finally a growing fear of Indians led the army to set up a number of outposts and camps, one of which was Camp Polk, established in 1865, about three miles northeast of the Sisters site on the bank of Squaw Creek, where that stream meanders through a pine-bordered meadow. Little there now shows that it was once the location of a short-lived military post on the Oregon frontier. Meadows stretch away into the distance, timber crowds to the edge of grassy bottoms where army horses once grazed, and on a knoll in marginal timber is a pioneer cemetery.

Camp Polk on Squaw Creek was never the scene of a battle,

nor did troopers from the camp ever move into the semi-desert interior where Paulina and his warriors rode and killed.

All efforts to corner and conquer the scattered bands of Indians had failed. Roads were unsafe. The few ranch homes were virtual stockades. This was the condition that existed when Colonel George B. Currey was assigned to the command of the Department of the Pacific, on August 8, 1865. Colonel Currey reasoned that in winter months the restless Indians would be forced to "hole up" at places where they could obtain feed for their horses and sustenance for themselves. He planned a broad winter campaign covering most of Eastern Oregon, including the breaking up of unruly bands and halting their depredations. Among nine sites selected for winter camps, one was on Sic-se-que (Squaw) Creek.

Captain Charles LaFollette, with forty men from Company A, 1st Oregon Volunteer Infantry, was ordered to establish this camp near the junction of the Eugene and Santiam roads. One of these roads, little more than a rocky trail, led over the McKenzie lava fields, the other over the Santiam and down rugged Seven-Mile Hill, close to the old Wiley Trail. The camp, it was reasoned, would have the advantages of protective friendly relations with the Indians on nearby Warm Springs Reservation.

LaFollette's company left Fort Yamhill on September 4, 1865, the first military group to cross the Cascades on the new Santiam Road—a winding, dusty wagon route up through the fir country, over the summit, and into the pinelands. En route east, the volunteers met the road construction party at a prairie near the summit and delayed their journey a week to help clear seven miles of road to Fish Lake.

Possibly there was another reason that the soldiers, eager to get on the trail of Paulina, stopped for a week at the mountain lake: fishing was good. In his later reminiscences, Sergeant J. M. Shelley said that the fish "congregated in such numbers that they fairly touched elbows, . . . a lot of the boys took off their trousers and, wading in, made the fish jump out on dry land."

At Camp Polk, named by Captain LaFollette after his own county, the volunteers laid out a fair-sized parade ground, trimmed the tallest tree near the center for a flagpole, and constructed eight cabins. Long afterwards, Sergeant Shelley recalled that the volunteers never had a roll call or a guard mount, spending most of their ammunition hunting mule deer. One soldier reported he had killed more than a hundred deer, "some weighing as much as 300 pounds gross."

Before the winter campaign could be undertaken, word was received from the Army Chief in Washington, D. C., to muster out the volunteers, that the program was to be given up, and the camps abandoned. The detachment at Camp Polk stayed in winter quarters there until the spring of 1866, when the soldiers left for their homes. Thus ended the military history of Camp Polk.

In 1870, the site of the camp was homesteaded by Samuel M. W. Hindman in the community now known as Sisters. He established a store at the old site and was the community's first postmaster. In 1888, the post office was moved three miles southwest to the new village of Sisters and given the name of its adopted town.

Indian Fight in Crook County

An Indian fight took place in Crook County soon after the Camp Polk soldiers marched back across the Santiam Cascades to their Polk County homes. That fight was on Dry Creek, about thirteen miles from Prineville.

Donald McKay, a scout of the days of the Indian unrest in the range realm of Paulina, was camped on a creek now bearing his name. It was the summer of 1866. With McKay was a group of the friendly Warm Springs Indians, along with Billy Chinook, who had served as a scout and guide for John C. Fremont and Kit Carson in 1843, in their Oregon expedition. McKay ordered Billy Chinook to take twenty-five men and reconnoiter for possible Indian bands in the area where the Ochoco timber fades west into the rugged country around the head of Willow Creek.

One day out of camp, the scouts spotted a band of Paiutes on Dry Creek. After counting wigwams and fires, the scouts decided they had a strength equal to that of the encamped Indians. Though the scouts had orders, if they located the enemy, to return, not attack—to Billy Chinook and his men, the opportunity looked too good to resist. The first fires in the morning were to be the signal for the attack. At the earliest sign of smoke over the small camp, the Warm Springs fighters struck. Though the surprised Paiutes put up a stiff defense, the entire band of about thirty-two was either killed or captured.

At the very time the legend of Paulina's invulnerability was most widespread, events were shaping that would lead to his death in the isolated cove of Central Oregon's Trout Creek. Time was running out for the raiding chief of the Paiutes that spring day of 1867, when his braves stole a big herd of cattle from Andrew Clarno, then headed southwest over the divide, past the Maupin station where the town of Antelope was to be founded later.

When Maupin, Clark, Ragan, and Atterbury located the cattle at dawn, the animals were contentedly grazing in a broad cove, whose westerly rocky walls were nearly perpendicular. The Indians were breakfasting on a steer they had killed. This was the scene when the ranchers—who had left their horses near Trout Creek and crawled to the cove rim—opened fire. The battle was on: a couple of whites against the invulnerable chief and his men. The Henry rifles of Clark and Maupin blazed. The Indians broke and ran. One of them fell, his hip shattered by a bullet. The wounded man was Paulina, now deserted by his braves.

While the other Indians scrambled up the steep walls of the rock-rimmed basin that bears Paulina's name, Maupin approached, gun cocked. Legend has it that the chief plunged his knife into the ground, then sprinkled his forehead and chest with dust of the cove. He died in the high-rimmed cove apparently at Maupin's hands—but there are some who dispute this and say it was Clark who fired the final shot. It was Clark's home on the John Day, at Burnt Ranch, that had earlier been razed by the Paulina raiders. Not even a cairn was erected to mark the spot where Paulina fell. For years the skeleton of the chief bleached in the sun that arches across the deep gorge of Trout Creek. There the saga of Paulina, the raider, ended.

Paulina's Name Given Landmarks

Despite his record as a killer and a raider, Paulina has been honored by having his name bestowed on more Central Oregon places than any other individual. An outlying mountain range on the skyline south of Bend, the Paulinas, bears his name, as do beautiful Paulina Lake and its crater rim, Paulina Creek and falls, high Paulina Peak, and Paulina Prairie—through which meanders Paulina Creek.

On Upper Crooked River, the community of Paulina is also namesake for the raider chief. A railroad siding of the Southern Pacific's Natron Cutoff, Paunina, is a variant of the usual spelling. Apparently some of these places had their own Paiute names. For instance, Paulina Prairie was known as Mil-ka-ke. Other variant place names, such as Panina, Pahihi, and Pahnaina, also seem to honor Paulina of the Paiutes. A mesa-like butte, overlooking the John Day Valley from the highlands northeast of Antelope, is the only geographic name that honors Howard Maupin. It was past Maupin Butte that Paulina moved his stolen cattle on that April night of long ago for his rendezvous with death near Trout Creek.

The Walapi tribe of Snakes extended its pillaging beyond Central Oregon, raids reaching into Eastern and Southern Oregon, east of the Cascades, and into parts of Nevada, and even Northern California. Indian trouble was general in parts of Idaho. Paulina could not have been considered chief of all the scattered bands of Walapi who had lived on these ancestral homelands. His leadership and activities evidently were confined to interior Oregon, where part of the time he set up his willow-framed wickiups in the upper Deschutes country. Those wickiups have given their name to a big reservoir on the upper Deschutes River. Despite his vicious attacks on settlements, miners, packstrings, and wagons, Paulina was a colorful and challenging character of the Oregon frontier. Both Colonel C. S. Drew of the United States Army and Hubert Howe Bancroft, Pacific Coast historian, confirm that Paulina was an excellent military tactician.

After tracking down Paulina and bringing to an end the era of Indian raids on Central Oregon, Howard Maupin went back to his stage station up near the head of green Antelope Valley, where he was to become the community's first postmaster in 1871. He also lived and operated in other parts of Central Oregon, one of his enterprises, with his son Perry, having been a ferry over the Deschutes near the mouth of Bakeoven Creek. The ferry subsequently was owned by W. E. Hunt. When the railroads were built up the Deschutes Canyon, W. H. Staats bought the site and named it Maupin's Ferry. In 1909, postal officials shortened this to Maupin, in memory of the pioneer.

Maupin later shifted his ranching operations to Trout Creek, where he erected a ranch home within sight of the cove in which Paulina had been killed. Paulina's scalp—taken by Maupin as a trophy—for years remained nailed over a door of the ranch home, but was lost when fire destroyed the building in 1902. The rifle with which Paulina was killed and the scalping knife used by Maupin are relics in the Oregon Historical Society, gifts of J. W. Robinson, early-day Ashwood merchant.

On a low ridge leading to the edge of Trout Creek, across the site of the old ranch home, is a graveyard that holds the tombs of many of the pioneers of that area. There in 1887, Howard Maupin was laid to rest with his wife. Later their sons, Perry and Garrett, were buried nearby.

CHAPTER 8

Early Trails and Roads

MOUNTAINS AND RIVERS, lava fields and sagelands dictated travel routes through Central Oregon in pioneer days. Military parties made "roads" that disappeared in dust and sage in short order. Wagon-wheel ruts of lost immigrants were too meandering to become permanent roads.

With the discovery of gold in the early 1860s in the John Day Basin, in Eastern Oregon, and in Idaho, several important trails and temporary roads took shape across the mid-Oregon plateau. Gold seekers from California and Southern Oregon attempted shortcuts, blazing their own packstring trails, some of which bisected the wheel marks of early-day immigrants on the High Desert.

Probably more than any other factor, watering places determined the courses of pioneer trails across Central Oregon. In most areas, these were far apart; it was not always possible to reach a spring or creek for each night's stop. Dry camps on the desert were common. It was said that watering holes "stand out in the great Oregon desert like beacon lights and guiding points to a mariner at sea."

Miners were in the area in the 1850s, prior to the discovery of gold in the Blue Mountains and along the John Day tributaries. On June 12, 1853, John W. Hillman, with a group of prospectors, was attempting a crossing of the southern Cascades into Central Oregon when he discovered Crater Lake, which was then christened Deep Blue Lake. The Newberry Crater and the Ochocos off to the east undoubtedly attracted many prospectors who left no record of their adventures.

Another stream of prospectors moved northeast through the Klamath and Lake county areas in 1862, headed for the gold-beaded creeks in the John Day country. One of the routes of the prospectors, the Yreka-Canyon City road, cut through the Silver Lake community, northeast past Thorn and Fossil lakes, and on to the high horizon that marked the drainage divide between the Great Basin and the Columbia River. This trail skirted Dead Indian Spring, not far from Picture Rock Pass. Through that area now swings the Fremont Highway—named for the "Pathfinder," Captain John C. Fremont.

Northeast of the Silver Lake-Christmas Lake communities, the old trails divided, one leading into the Crooked River area and across the Izee highlands to Canyon City, the other into the Burns country, with its fine creeks and lush springs. Wagontire Mountain was a famous pilot to trail travelers in search of water. A large spring bubbles from the earth in its foothills. Old-timers knew the landmark as Ram's Peak. Many travelers, likely including part of the lost wagon train of 1853, camped in those foothills. In later years, it was the site of a range war.

Fort Dalles to Salt Lake

Army men on the Oregon frontier early saw the need of a shorter and easier road from Fort Dalles to Salt Lake. Such a road would bypass the rugged route over the Blue Mountains from the Columbia. In April 1859, General William S. Harney, in command of the Military Department of the Columbia with headquarters at Fort Vancouver, named Captain Henry D. Wallen to command an expedition to determine whether a short-cut across Central Oregon to the east would be feasible. Major Enoch Steen believed that such a route might be established up the John Day River, over the headwaters of the Malheur, and down the Snake.

Two months later, Captain Wallen left Fort Dalles with nine officers and 184 enlisted men. It was an imposing contingent that moved upland along the Columbia on that June day. Wagon wheels cut their own road as the company passed through Tygh Valley and crossed the Deschutes on pontoon bridges near the Warm Springs River. In the company were 116 horses for the dragoons, 344 pack mules, 38 horses for the quartermaster, 131 oxen to draw 30 wagons, and 60 beef cattle. Certainly those grazing cattle were an appetizing site for the Paiutes watching from lava rims.

Pontoon floats were taken along for crossing streams. Likely the big company moved southeast close to the site of present Madras, where Willow Creek winds from timbered highlands to the east and slashes a deep canyon from "The Basin" at Madras to the Deschutes. The route of the road blazers must have led through the gap west of Grizzly and on to Crooked River.

Captain Wallen and his party continued up Crooked River to its forks, where Camp Division was established and the party divided. Lieutenant John S. Bonnycastle headed a group instructed to explore and work a road back to the Columbia from Crooked River. Captain Wallen explored the south fork of Crooked River, crossed the divide from Buck Creek, and reached the Harney country. Then he moved over the southern slope of the mountains to the Malheur. His topographic engineer, Lieutenant Joseph Dixon, who considered the country northeast of Lake Harney too mountainous, recommended that the road from Lake Harney east to Salt Lake be built by way of the Owyhee. The road was never built.

Harney Lake to Eugene City

In the following spring of 1860, a second expedition, this time under the command of Major Steen, left Fort Dalles for the purpose of "opening a wagon road from Harney Lake to Eugene City." The party headed inland along the east side of the Deschutes River and across Crooked River. They traveled 275 miles to reach Lake Harney. Steen's company apparently traveled inland from Fort Dalles through one of the canyon passes, possibly Cow Canyon or Antelope Creek. It was a region Bonnycastle must have scouted the previous year when he explored north and west from Camp Division on Crooked River, on his return to the Columbia River.

Major Steen followed the Walla Walla Road from Fort Dalles to the crossing of the Deschutes at its mouth. From that point he swung into the highlands to Trout Creek, in the Hay Creek area. "The plateau is covered with a fine luxuriant growth of bunchgrass, but it is nearly destitute of timber," Major Steen noted in his report, referring to the high country between the Deschutes and the John Day rivers and the plains that reach to Willow Creek.

On his way into the southeast, Steen is believed to have passed through the upper Deschutes country, just east of Pilot Butte.

Indian Attacks

In the meantime, parties of miners in ever-imposing numbers daily crossed the region. From their rocky lookouts, Indians watched the gold seekers in nearby canyons. Some miners who were encamped in a small tributary of the Malheur were attacked and killed by Indians on June 13, 1860. These Indian depredations also slowed road explorations in the isolated interior of Oregon. Two weeks after the assault on the miners, an army-surveying expedition, under the command of Andrew J. Smith, was attacked. On June 29, when Steen heard of this attack, he was some twenty-five miles east of the upper Deschutes River, engaged in the Eugene City road survey. Steen then abandoned his road project and united his troops with those of Smith to establish Camp Union on Silver Creek, thirty miles north of Harney Lake.

One of South-Central Oregon's most prominent landmarks bears the name of the man who commanded Camp Union in those restless days. This is Steens Mountain, which overlooks much of the old lake country of the region. In early times, this towering, fault-block rim was known as Snow Mountain. The change in name occurred after one of Major Steen's battles with the Snake Indians of the region. On this occasion he chased a group of Indians over the snow-capped mountain.

Although they were called roads, the early military routes over Central Oregon were really only trails. Most transportation was by pack animals. When gold was discovered on Canyon Creek in the John Day country in 1861, prospectors followed some of the routes blazed by Wallen and Steen.

The primary barriers to travel between western and Central Oregon were the Cascades. About six months of each year, these were blocked by snow. Even in summer they were difficult to pass because of steep slopes, dense timber, and lava fields.

Sherars Crossing

The Deschutes River was also a formidable barrier. Few good crossings occurred between the Cove, at the junction of the Deschutes and Crooked rivers, and the Columbia. One of the fords was at the Sherars site, in a rock-walled gorge whose rims towered about one thousand feet above the river. This crossing was to play an important role in shaping the pattern of travel to inland Oregon from The Dalles, metropolis of the area for many years.

Here in 1860, John Y. Todd built a successful toll bridge. Through this pioneer gateway moved packstrings, Pony Express riders, stages, and freight-laden wagons to the John Day gold fields and beyond. Military units, generally with packstrings, frequently used the bridge on sweeps into the inland country in search of unruly Indians. The narrow bridge served as a link between two of the Pacific Northwest's largest cities—Canyon City on the John Day and The Dalles on the Columbia. Millions of dollars in gold dust and nuggets were carried over it in the wild days of mining fever.

In all Oregon, few river crossings hold such historic interest as the Sherars site on the stream known to Ogden as the "River of the Falls," and to his French trappers as the *Riviere des Chutes*. Its story goes back to Indian days, continues through

Grandly exposed in various parts of Central Oregon are the colored strata known as the John Day Formation. Here is a fine outcropping near Mitchell, on Bridge Creek.

Formations in Painted Hills State Park were once part of ancient horizons in the Central Oregon country. It is a region sculptured into fantastic shapes and stained a hundred shades, from delicate purple to brilliant red.

Oregon State Highway Dept.

Exposed on Crooked River in Central Oregon, at Smith Rock State Park, is a bit of an ancient world—the Clarno horizons of the dawn age of mammal life. On the skyline to the right are the Three Sisters.

The late Lon Hancock holds one of his own fossil "finds" as he stands beside a memorial to Thomas Condon in the John Day Fossil Beds State Park. Condon was the first to read from the rocks and fossils the primordial story of these ancient lands.

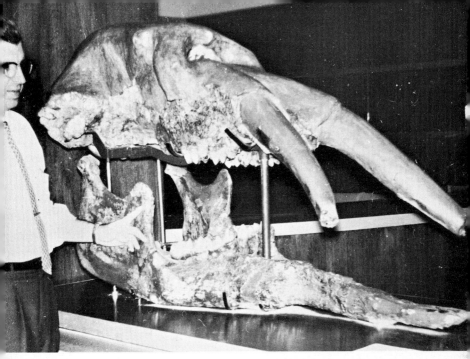

Even shovel-tusked elephants lived in the ancient Oregon country, as this picture illustrates. Dr. Arnold Shotwell is shown beside a huge head found in Eastern Oregon by Lon Hancock.

Persons studying the ancient Central Oregon story frequently must work under a burning sun. Shown here is a protective covering over a fossil quarry, devised by Lon Hancock (left foreground).

Ancient Oregonians who lived here in Roaring Springs Cave, of Catlow Valley, devised atlatls or "spear flings." The cavern was excavated by Dr. L. S. Cressman and his archeology students.

Barlow Cave, four miles east of Bend, was the seasonal home of early-day Indians for long ages. The cavern's overhanging lava rims provided much-needed shelter. Sandals were found here similar to those discovered at Fort Rock Cave.

the era of early exploration, gains importance with the discovery of gold in the eastern part of the state, and reaches its climax with the settlement of interior Oregon.

The bridge built over the Deschutes at a site that was to become historic as Sherars crossing was wide enough for wagons, but there were no approach roads in the deep canyon; wagons were still rare in Central Oregon. Possibly, though,Todd—homesteader and cattleman of the Tygh Valley area—hoped that eventually his bridge would be used as a military crossing. Even while packstrings were still the only users of the gorge route, on the long journey from The Dalles to Canyon City, Todd constructed approaches. One, from the west, was built down the White River, a route in later years to be approximately followed by State Highway 216. The approach from the east was through winding canyons and around rocky bluffs.

Road construction did not keep Cattleman Todd busy. He had other projects in the awakening wilderness east of the Cascades. With the discovery of gold in Idaho, he started operating a packtrain to the Orofino mines. Long afterwards, Todd's son, John C. Todd, reported:

The pack train undertaking proved successful. My father said that in a short time he made $10,000. A mule loaded with two kegs of whiskey was worth a lot of money to miners.

Shortly after building the bridge, Todd discovered a new source of revenue—toll for use of the span. Most of this toll, however, went into the improvement and upkeep of the approach roads. The Todd Bridge was carried away by the Deschutes flood of 1861, but was replaced in 1862.

While operating the toll road over the Deschutes, Todd took as his partners Robert Mays and Ezra L. Hemingway. Mays was a blacksmith at Tygh Valley. Hemingway lived at the bridge and collected tolls. When Todd moved his cattle south to Farewell Bend, he sold his interest in the Tygh Valley holdings and in the bridge. In 1871, the bridge was purchased by Joseph Sherar—for whom it was named.

A Pony Express making the run between The Dalles and the John Day gold fields used the Sherars span for about two years. The first run started at Canyon City and ended at The Dalles, on July 4, 1862, with N. F. Nelson as rider. He was associated with Tom Brent in that first operation of the Pony Express through Central Oregon. On the second run, riders were attacked by Indians, and John Espy was shot. Later, Tracy and Company operated a Pony Express over the route, making the 225-mile run in twenty-eight hours, in competition with a stage.

Brent and Nelson charged fifty cents each for letters carried. The charge for gold dust was three per cent of the weight of the metal.

Indians Attack Wheeler Stage

In 1864, the Sherars span was enlarged, and Henry H. Wheeler started operating a stage. For a brief time, the competition was keen between the Pony Express and the Wheeler stages. The first run of a Wheeler stage from The Dalles to Canyon City was in May 1864, with eleven passengers aboard. The coach was drawn by four horses. Not until the following spring did Wheeler carry the mail.

On September 7, 1866, Wheeler, driving his own stage, was about three miles east of the Mitchell location when he was attacked by some twenty Indians. A bullet fired by one of them passed through his cheeks. The attack came in a narrow, winding canyon, on the high west slope of the Mountain Creek-Bridge Creek Divide. In the area are some large sheltering rocks, ideal hiding places for the Indians.

The road was too rough and winding to attempt to outdistance them. While Wheeler's lone passenger, H. C. Page— riding gun that day—held off the Indians with gunfire, Wheeler unhitched his leaders, neither of which had been ridden. Page and the wounded Wheeler mounted these horses and raced to safety, leaving the stage and its cargo to the Indians. The cargo included $10,000 in currency, which the Indians scattered in the brush; but they tore the coach apart for its leather. The white men continued to The Dalles, where Wheeler received medical attention, and in a short time returned to his stage line. A monument beside U. S. Highway 26, just east of Mitchell, marks the place of the attack.

Wheeler improved his service by establishing stage stations at such places as Sherars, Bakeoven, Cross Hollows, Antelope, and Burnt Ranch.

Improvement of the Sherars Bridge in 1864 made it possible for many immigrants using the Oregon Trail to leave that dusty route and take a shortcut by way of Grass Valley and Sherars to the Wamic country and the new Barlow Pass over the Cascades. This provided a new and important business for the operators of the Sherars Stage Station.

Joe Sherar Colorful Figure

The man for whom the crossing of the Deschutes was named actually did not enter the picture until 1871, when he acquired the bridge and stage station for $7,041.

A native of Vermont, Sherar came west to the California mines in 1855, and in 1862 passed through Oregon with a pack train en route to the Powder River mines. On his return, he stopped in The Dalles, where he decided he could make money by packing supplies from that city to the John Day gold fields. Foreseeing that travel into Central Oregon was bound to increase and that the man who owned the toll bridge over the Deschutes at the established crossing would practically possess a gold mine, he bought the John Y. Todd bridge and filed on a homestead along the river edge.

Toll was collected, generally in a large bucket, at the bridge site. The charge apparently was $3.75 for each yoke of oxen or team and wagon, and one dollar extra for the driver. Joe Sherar put most of this money to good use in improving the bridge and access roads. For thirty miles on either side of the bridge, he improved the approaches.

Sherar soon faced competition in the river-crossing business. Howard Maupin of Antelope was operating his ferry over the Deschutes at a point about eight miles upstream, near the mouth of Bakeoven Creek, and some of the inland travel was using this new crossing. Despite upstream competition, as travel continued to increase, Sherar enlarged his stage station. He built a large barn, with one wall on the edge of the river gorge—and some years later, a three-story building. This was a comfortable tavern of thirty-three rooms, on the west bank of the river," where travelers might dream to the roar of the waters of the Deschutes." The tavern became famous as a stopping place for inland travel.

The road over Sherars Bridge for years continued to be the main route not only to the gold country, but to towns developing in the range lands and ranches taking shape in lush valleys. At its new location near the Maupin stage station, Antelope was an important branching point for two roads serving the region. From Antelope, The Dalles Road—which came out of the Deschutes Canyon at Sherars—continued east to Canyon City and on to Fort Harney. The other road branched down Antelope Creek to cross Crooked River upstream from Smith Rock and then swing west to Camp Polk.

The Dalles-Ochoco Road

A petition asking for the establishment of "The Dalles-Ochoco Road" was received by the Wasco County Court in The Dalles, on May 8, 1872. This road was to reach from Bakeoven—where it branched from the Canyon City Road—to the Prineville country, known at the time as "The Ochoco." Road viewers were William Douthit, James Combs, and E. Barnes. This route approximated the Cow Canyon section authorized in 1869 as a toll road.

Toll was collected by Charles Haight at a station about halfway down Cow Canyon, now a million-dollar section of U. S.

Highway 97. At the foot of Cow Canyon were the green meadows of Trout and Hay creeks, where early-day ranchers, one of them the John Bolter family, provided meals and overnight accommodations for travelers.

From the foot of Cow Canyon (now Willowdale), the new inland route veered to the south, crossed Willow Creek, moved over the Ochoco summit, and headed down McKay Creek. It bypassed the hamlet of Prineville and ended at the Ochoco Creek bottoms. There, in the higher Ochoco area, the City of Prineville might have been founded if Barney Prine had not set up shop near the confluence of Crooked River and Ochoco Creek.

Road to Shaniko

Serving as an important feeder to the wagon routes leading to Central Oregon was a road from the north, which came into existence around 1870, following a survey by The Dalles Military Road Company. This road led upland from the Columbia River, through Sherman County. U. S. Highway 97 was later to approximate the line of this road south to Shaniko, then over brushy flats to Cow Canyon. The new road from the north crossed the Steens Military Road in the Cross Hollows area, near Shaniko of a later day.

At the intersection, Cross Hollows was to have its day in the Central Oregon sun. Cross Hollows was established on May 23, 1879. There where two hollows make a perfect cross, August Scherneckau (called Shaniko by the Indians) built a store and blacksmith shop; and Jim Clark, keeper of the Burnt Ranch Stage station, built for him a sixteen-room inn. Cross Hollows was the southern terminus of Joe Sherar's toll road and part of Henry Wheeler's stage-station system.

Cross Hollows became Shaniko, which moved from its little cross canyons when the Columbia Southern Railroad came out of the north in 1900.

CHAPTER 9

Mountain Barriers

Two CHALLENGING MOUNTAIN PASSES—the lava-blanketed McKenzie north of the Three Sisters, and the timbered Santiam with its steep grades—had important roles in the early settlement of Central Oregon. Possibly the first to venture over the high passes were prospectors. But, unlike John W. Hillman and his gold seekers who discovered Crater Lake, the first persons who crossed the McKenzie lava fields and the Santiam Divide left no record of their adventures.

The first white explorer to cross the High Cascades of Oregon, west of the inland plateau, was likely Finan McDonald of the Hudson's Bay Company, in December 1825. He came over the northern Cascades, apparently between Jefferson and Hood, to join Peter Skene Ogden and his trappers at the present site of the Warm Springs Reservation Agency on the Deschutes.

Cattle had been driven eastward over the McKenzie Divide in 1859 by Henry H. Spalding, the missionary, and by Jake Guilliford. Following the mining excitement in Eastern Oregon, at least one pack train crossed the McKenzie in 1861. There is a possibility that some members of the lost wagon train of 1853 made their way over the McKenzie lava fields, headed west, but this is seriously doubted by historians.

Conquest of McKenzie Summit

In 1862 came the conquest of the McKenzie summit. That high, bleak divide is blanketed with jagged lava from Yapoah Crater, near the base of the North Sister, to Little Belknap Crater. In that same year, eastward over the rocky summit, moved a party destined to spend a winter in Central Oregon and establish what has been called the first permanent settlement of the area—the Scott party. The beginnings of the McKenzie Highway are closely interwoven with this group and also with the experiences of a pioneer who lost his life on the exposed summit—John Templeton Craig.

The unrecorded story of the conquest of the Oregon Cascades dates to the years when the Indians trailed over the mountains. The recorded story goes back to 1862. That was the year when the Eldorado-struck miners were flocking to Idaho, by way of the most direct mountain passes. Many were from homes in the upper Willamette River country. Up the McKenzie came prospectors in the rush to the gold fields, but history deals only briefly with their experiences.

In 1862, an enterprising young businessman from Eugene City, Felix Scott, Jr., made plans to supply the miners in the Salmon River country of Idaho, with the goods needed on their arrival at the "diggings." To do this efficiently, he reasoned, a direct route was necessary from Eugene City over the Cascades, to connect with roads in the eastern part of the state. The large road crew worked across the lava-blackened summit in the summer of that year. Winter overtook them on Trout Creek.

In their crossing of the lava-covered McKenzie Divide, between the North Sister and Belknap Crater in the late summer of 1862, the Scott party had eight or nine loaded wagons and sixty or more yoke of work oxen. Trailing along were some seven hundred head of loose cattle. The season was late when they reached Trout Creek, a western tributary of the Deschutes that joins Hay Creek before starting its westward race through a deep canyon. Deciding to spend the winter on Trout Creek rather than take the chance of encountering a fierce storm in the high country of Eastern Oregon, they set up quarters in a cave and built a cabin nearby—whose rotting foundation could still be seen up to ten years ago.

The first crossing of the McKenzie Divide was successful, in a rugged way. Years later, evidence was found in the lava country south of the present route of the McKenzie Highway, of the passage of the pioneers. Marks of the wagon wheels were clearly visible; even parts of wagon wheels were discovered.

The Scott Trail

The road used by the Scott party was long known as the Scott Trail. It followed up the McKenzie River from the west to Belknap Springs, earlier known as Salt Springs, which had been discovered in 1866 by John Latta. Along a part of that old road past Belknap Springs, a modern forest highway connecting the McKenzie and Santiam routes took final shape a century after Felix Scott and his brother, Marion, blazed the road. That new route, dedicated in 1962, is the Clear Lake Cutoff.

After swinging sharply upgrade on Scott Creek, from the McKenzie River, the trail of the pioneers was blazed to Fingerboard Prairie and south of Scott Lake to the present highway. Turning east again, it skirted the summit lava flows along an old Indian trail. It was a difficult route, especially on its ascent out of the Belknap Springs area and its climb into the volcanic foothills just north of the North Sister. The Scotts at times were forced to use as many as twenty-six yoke of oxen to one wagon to surmount the steep grades.

The difficult first crossing of the McKenzie Divide apparently did not discourage the Scotts for in 1865-66, they returned with about four hundred head of cattle to the same location. The historian A. L. Veazie said that a man named Ritchie brought over the McKenzie, at about the same time, a hundred head of cattle, mostly heifers. These were held in the Wilson Creek box canyon. On March 16, 1866, it is known that Marion Scott was there with Charles S. Hardisty, John B. Evans and his brother Thomas J. Evans, Lem Jones, and a man named Mills. Their camp was raided by Indians, who got away with seven saddle horses as well as camp equipment. This was a hard blow for a small party making its way overland to the gold fields of Idaho.

One of the men who came to Trout Creek in 1866 with the

Scotts returned in 1868 to settle on Willow Creek, in the present Madras area of Jefferson County. He was John B. Evans. In *Jefferson County Reminiscences,* he was quoted:

At this time the grass grew high and rank. Hay could be cut almost anywhere in the Blue Mountains. Wild timothy, pea vine, etc., grew eighteen inches high. . . . Bunch grass would make a ton to the acre. There were only a few people in the country, and practically all of these were engaged in hunting. Game was very plentiful and the skins and dried meat were sold in The Dalles. The game hunted consisted chiefly of deer, elk, and bear.

Craig Sought Better Road

Out of the successful crossing by the Scotts grew the determination on the part of John Craig to build a good road. His dream was a road that could transport settlers, supplies, and mail from the southern part of the Willamette Valley into Eastern Oregon. Old records show that others were also interested in such a plan. Between 1862 and 1871, at least five construction companies attempted the job, choosing various routes, but all failed of completion. Craig apparently was not associated with any of the companies.

Instead of joining in the various ventures, Craig settled at "Craig's Bridge," later to be known as McKenzie Bridge, on the river of the same name. From there, he directed all his efforts toward building a road, sometimes operating on borrowed funds, but always sustained by his own determination. People who knew him said he was eccentric. In one early account, reference is made to "Craig's bedroom" near the Rock House. That bedroom was in the hollow of a tree, where Craig at various times sought shelter from the storms, or "holed up" when overtaken by darkness.

He was president of the first company that succeeded in slashing and grading a road across McKenzie Pass. In 1870, the Oregon Legislature urged support of a military wagon road over the Pass. In the following year, Craig's outfit, "The McKenzie,

Salt Springs and Deschutes Wagon Road Company," filed articles of incorporation. Associated with him in the venture were M. H. Harlow, P. C. Renfrew, and A. Renfrew.

The route was to run from the end of the Lane County Road, at Park's Point, across the McKenzie Bridge and through the Lost Creek Canyon. This route, bypassing the trail used by the Scotts up the McKenzie River to Belknap Springs, meant crossing lava beds—a killing stretch for man or beast. Still, it was a thousand feet lower than the early trail. Terminus of this later road was to be the Deschutes River "near the north end of the Paulina Mountains."

Not before the fall of 1872 was Craig's road open to travel. Receipts for the first year were listed at $219.62. Disbursements amounted to $714.25. County records fail to show the toll charges. However, Robert W. Sawyer, in his *History of the McKenzie Road,* stated that the rate for a wagon drawn by two horses was $2. For four horses, the charge was $2.50 and for a man and horse, $1. The charge for loose horses and cattle was ten cents a head; that for sheep, five cents. Apparently bands of sheep were trailed over the Cascades seasonally to ranges on the grassy plateau to the east.

With the establishment of the Camp Polk Post Office, near the present town of Sisters, and the opening of the McKenzie Road, came the letting of a contract to carry the mails from Eugene City by way of Camp Polk to Prineville. At a later date, the route was extended across the Ochocos to Mitchell. One of the early-day mail contractors was A. S. Powers, who was also an officer of the McKenzie Road Company and toll collector. Whether Craig was still connected with the company in 1877 does not appear on the records; but late in the year, when he was fifty-six years old, he was employed by Powers to carry the mail over that part of the contract route lying between McKenzie Bridge and Camp Polk.

Craig died shortly before Christmas in 1877, on his first and only start as mail carrier over the high Cascade Divide. The place of death was his summit cabin, near the little lake that now bears his name. His body was found wrapped in a blanket, kneeling in the ashes of his fireplace. Later it was learned that he had been ill when he started his trip east from McKenzie Bridge, with the white barrier of the high mid-Oregon Cascades ahead. Weakened by illness or fatigued by his hike through deep snow, he apparently died while attempting to start a fire in the mountain cabin on the storm-swept summit.

On the McKenzie Divide, west of the main lava beds and adjacent to the highway, rests a slab of native rock, moulded by the fires of ancient volcanoes. It is the headstone of John Craig's grave, buried under deep snow for about six months of each year. Craig was the first man to dream of a road across the mid-Oregon Cascades into the eastern part of the state, up the McKenzie; and he dedicated his life to seeing such a road completed.

The Pioneer Wiley Trail

There was another pass over the Cascade barrier into Central Oregon, that had been used for centuries before white men came. That pass was over the divide now known as the Santiam. To the south is pinnacled Mt. Washington, to the north is Three Fingered Jack.

The Santiam was a low pass in the Cascades, known to early-day trappers before the Blue Bucket wagon train came out of the east to cross the High Desert. It is believed by some that this 1845 wagon train—while still under the guidance of Stephen L. Meek—actually was headed for the Santiam Pass. From the trappers, Meek probably learned about the comparatively low crossing of the volcanic divide.

In their early movements from western Oregon to the east, Indians apparently found some of the low passes between Mt. Jefferson and Mt. Washington among the best in the Cascades. But prior to 1840, there was a legend among Central Willamette Valley tribes that, long before, there had been a fierce battle between the Molallas of the western hills and the Paiutes from east of the mountains. According to the legend, that battle was in the mountains, along an old trail. Souls of the dead warriors entered beasts of prey, and these beasts lurked along both sides of the old battle trail that formed a natural pass up the Santiam. White men later found that Indian trails, in years following the legendary battle, bypassed the gorges where the transmigrated souls waited to make war on old enemies.

A pioneer settler of the South Santiam Country, Andrew Wiley, used one of these mountain trails in the first recorded exploration of the upper Santiam region. Actually Wiley was a hunter, not an explorer. Each season on his hunting trips he penetrated farther east into the thickly timbered recesses of the South Santiam River. In 1859, accompanied by two companions, he made his way into the high country, from where he could see Mt. Washington, the tips of the Three Sisters to the south, and the spires of Three Fingered Jack to the north. Wiley climbed a tall tree on a hill well up on the divide, and to the east sighted the open Central Oregon country. On that trip, or shortly later, he continued on east to the present site of Sisters.

Wiley was the discoverer of the famed Hogg Pass, now known as the Santiam, the location of one of Oregon's most important trans-Cascade highways. In the early years, the Santiam route was known as the Wilcy Pass, but now this name is scarcely ever heard.

Andrew Wiley is one of Oregon's forgotten explorers. He was the leader and locator of the Williamette Valley and Cascade Mountain project in 1866 and 1867. That steep, winding road approximately followed the trail Wiley blazed up the Western slope of the Cascades in 1859, on the hunt that took him from the fir forests into the region where pine, juniper, and sage took over.

Minto Route Explored

Years before Wiley found the pass that for a time bore his name, a move was launched in Salem (1845) to scout a route for a wagon road over the Cascades from Marion County. Colonel Cornelius Gilliam and Joseph Gervais, who had a rough knowledge of the region, joined a location party as guides. Nothing much came of this effort. They did, though, find a low divide, in the Minto Pass region, but gave up the project on encountering "scaley mountain rock."

One of the leaders in the effort to find a wagon route over the Cascades south of Mt. Jefferson was John Minto of Salem. He was among the first to urge the use of the North Santiam River as the site for a road. As a result of his interest in that area, his name was attached to several localities and features. One of these is Minto Mountain in Linn County. Another is Minto Pass. Minto considered the North Santiam an especially favorable route for a road over the Cascades to Central Oregon. This is now the location of the North Santiam Highway, which joins with the "Wiley Trail" route—the South Santiam—before crossing the Cascades at Hogg Rock.

This rock, the plug of an old volcano, was named for T. Egenton Hogg, promoter of the Yaquina Railroad Company, that planned to construct a line of steel over the Cascades into Eastern Oregon. At the Cascade Summit near the rock that bears his name, Hogg actually built a section of railroad, on which was placed a railroad car, but steel never reached over the divide into Central Oregon.

For many years the name Hogg Pass applied to the locality now crossed by the Santiam Highway. Santiam Pass referred to a point about three miles to the south. That was the route of the early-day Santiam Toll Road, with a station on Cache Creek, east of the divide. Eventually, in 1929, there developed a move to refer to the entire area, from Hogg Rock south to the old toll road, as Santiam Pass. Now Hogg Pass, like the earlier Wiley Trail, is almost forgotten.

Summit Challenge to Linn Residents

About the time the building of a road over the Cascades by

way of the McKenzie River was being considered by Lane County residents, Linn County was showing interest in a road over the Cascade barrier along the South Santiam River. The Willamette Valley and Cascade Mountain Road Company was formed on May 18, 1864, in Lebanon, to build such a road.

When the move was undertaken, some sort of road already existed along the lower reaches of the South Santiam and apparently for some distance east into the mountains. This is indicated by the fact that, in 1863, the McKenzie road builders, working out of Eugene, proposed to extend their road to a point known as the "Ford" on the Wiley Pass route. This "Ford" was on the Deschutes River, in the Tetherow Bridge area of later years.

The Linn County Company completed its improvement of the Wiley Pass Road in 1865 and 1866. For many years this was an important route of travel from the mid-Willamette Valley to Central Oregon and to the east. On completion of the road, it was announced that wagons could go "in ease over the mountains from Linn to the Deschutes River, and on to Canyon City and Boise." There was a tollgate two miles east of Sweet Home. In summer months, the road was used by herds of cattle, bands of sheep, pack trains, and teams.

The Wiley Road, which cut through a forest on the west side of the mountains, was just wide enough for a wagon. Trees were removed from the route, but they were not cut to ground level. The road reached over the Santiam Divide, skirted Blue and Suttle lakes, moved down Cache Creek, passed close to the base of Black Butte, and extended east to Camp Polk, facing a picturesque meadow on Squaw Creek. After crossing the Deschutes River, the road headed east into the Ochoco area.

Practically all the heavy road work ended at Cache Creek, near the eastern edge of the forest. From there to the Ford on the Deschutes, the Willamette Valley and Cascade Mountain Road virtually "wandered," following paths of least resistance around scattered trees and rock piles, or moving into new courses when ruts became too deep.

From Cache Creek east, it was said "the work consisted of a party of men, most of them on horseback, going through the country, accompanied by a wagon, at the rate of ten to fifteen miles a day, blazing trees when passing through open timber, doing a little grading at different spots, breaking sagebrush where it was too high, and putting stakes in the ground one mile apart."

For its work, the Linn Road Company received alternate sections of land. The company was capitalized for $30,000, hardly enough to pay the cost of a mile of modern highway. The road wandered from waterholes to bottom land; apparently the intent was to get as much land as possible between terminal points.

Tetherow Crossing Favored Camp Site

In 1878, Andrew Jackson Tetherow and his wife, Sophronia, came to Central Oregon from Polk County and built a home on the east bank of the Deschutes River near the historic ford, the main crossing of the stream on the Santiam route, where the river is swift and shallow. A. J. Tetherow was the son of Solomon Tetherow, a captain of the lost Blue Bucket wagon train of 1845.

At times, fording of the river was difficult, because its flow had not yet been diverted into irrigation ditches. Sometimes whole outfits floundered in the swift water and lighter vehicles were overturned. Tetherow solved this problem by starting a cable ferry in 1879, which he continued to operate for six years. "Tetherow Ford" later became a favorite camping spot. Here settlers from western Oregon gathered around campfires in the evening to tell of their experiences while crossing the Cascades, especially their woes when ascending steep, sandy Seven Mile Hill.

A bridge was constructed at that site in 1885, and opened to travel on July 6. For years the east-west road over the bridge was the main artery of travel through Central Oregon. The Deschutes crossing was about halfway between Cache Creek of the Sisters country and Prineville.

Guy W. Jordan of Corvallis had vivid recollections of the rugged Santiam route, prior to the turn of the century. He recalled that his father erected a cabin that was still standing on the Cache Creek toll station site up until 1961, when it fell in a storm. Jordan said:

It was common in those days for the settlers to go to the Willamette Valley from Central Oregon to trade, and especially to get fruit. It was a journey of three and a half days, either by the McKenzie or the Santiam routes. My travel from Sisters was over the Santiam Pass, and it was a big day's drive to Fish Lake. The second day we passed such landmarks as Tombstone Prairie, Sand Mountain, and Seven Mile Hill, with the second night stop either at Mountain House or Upper Soda. Sand Mountain was one of the rough spots, and it was a stretch of road with few places wide enough to pass another wagon. It was very rocky and steep in places.

The third day out on our trip west from Sisters, we followed the Santiam River over dirt road. The third night was spent in the Lebanon area.

Like the McKenzie, the Santiam was a seasonal route, closed through the winter by snow. In those long months, the mid-Oregon Cascades were effective barriers to travel, and they remained barriers until the era of modern highway construction and the re-routing, in 1962, of the highway from its McKenzie-lava-field divide to the lower Clear Lake Cutoff.

All three of the mid-Cascade routes of pioneer days—the McKenzie, the South Santiam, and the North Santiam—now cross the mountains at the same place, the Santiam Pass. The pioneer McKenzie Road, blazed over the lava fields by John Craig and his associates, remains as an alternate route for summer use.

Part Three

THE RANGE LANDS

CHAPTER 10

Settlers of the Open Range

NEAR THE GEOGRAPHIC CENTER OF OREGON is the great sagebrush plateau that comprised the open range of pioneer days. Grassy lands reached from the Cascade timber line east to the pines of the Blue Mountains. The northern boundary was the Shaniko region, with its mounds covered by brush and grass. To the south was the old lake country with the interior drainage.

This is the region geographers inappropriately call the High Lava Plains, but lava is little in evidence, aside from volcanic areas east of the Sisters and in the Paulina foothills. Rock of the range country is blanketed with soil. In the Bend-Redmond-Prineville triangle of the present, and reaching into the High Desert, are forest-like stands of juniper. In early days, bunchgrass grew tall in the area. Sage of several types, including the fragrant Big Sage, still covers much of the surface.

Water is not abundant in this country that was once an open range. Streams—mostly in deep canyons—and springs are the sources of range water, with the exception of playas that fill in damp weather or in spring thaws.

Young Land, Geologically

The open range country is a young land, geologically—the least eroded part of Oregon. Cinder cones in the Newberry

Crater area near Bend still retain their steep slopes and yield little nourishment for plants attempting to gain a foothold. Canyon walls of many streams, such as Crooked River, are nearly perpendicular, scarcely changed by weathering. Many volcanic buttes have craters unfilled by the drifting dust of centuries.

The open range of interior Oregon is not a monotonous plain. This is part of the interior country, where faulting has thrust land masses into high horizons. In places, these skylines are from two to three thousand feet above adjacent basins, elevations ranging from thirty-five hundred feet in the Deschutes River bed to more than six thousand feet in the higher buttes. The general level is around four thousand feet. The interior plateau is so young that parts of the region have no well-developed drainage.

This open range country, that was to lure families interested in stock raising, was once part of colossal Wasco, created January 11, 1854. Wasco then included all of the Oregon Territory between the Cascade Range and the Rocky Mountains, with its northeast corner near Butte, Montana. The total area of the original country was some 130,000 square miles.

Settlement of Central Oregon was slow in starting. To the north, a beginning had been made in 1838, at the Methodist Mission at The Dalles on the Columbia. That was thirteen years after Ogden's party headed up the Deschutes country on the first recorded exploration of Oregon's inland region.

The tide of immigrants, beginning in 1843, had swept past Central Oregon in two great floods. The main stream of westward migration poured over the Oregon Trail along the Columbia and past The Dalles; first, down the river, then over the Barlow Pass. Lighter streams of immigrants moved through Southern Oregon. Few of these broke away from the wheel-rutted Oregon Trail to attempt the "shortcut" across Central Oregon. Not until 1863 did the first settlers come into the little-known interior country.

Indian Raids

The government at first strongly discouraged settlement east of the Cascades because of the trouble with Indians. On August 7, 1856, General John E. Wool, commander of the Department of the Pacific, U. S. Army, issued an order to Colonel George Wright at Fort Dalles, forbidding immigrants to locate east of the Cascades. Colonel Wright considered the Cascades a "most valuable separation of the two races." The non-settlement order was revoked by General William S. Harney on October 31, 1858, after it became apparent that it would be more difficult to keep the whites out of the region than to keep the Indians under control.

Aside from the venturesome gold seekers, there was no heavy movement of settlers into Central Oregon, even after General Wool's orders were lifted. The greatest hindrance to the settlement of the area was fear of the Indians—and this was well founded. Back of that fear were some provocative statistics: from the first settlement of Oregon to June 1869, the number of persons killed in Indian raids, not including battles, was reckoned in government statistics at about 1,040. Not until 1873 did the Modoc War come to its bloody end in the Klamath lavas.

Then there was a lack of roads; those left by the immigrants who crossed the High Desert were without value. And, blocking easy approach to Central Oregon from the earlier-settled upper Willamette Valley, was the great barrier of the Cascades. In their crossing of the McKenzie lava wilderness in 1862-3, the Scotts made a start in the conquest of the Cascades. Their winter stop on Trout Creek has frequently been referred to as the first settlement in that region later embraced by great Crook County, but that winter encampment could hardly have been called a settlement. It was little more than a winter camp, with a cabin and a cave for shelter, and a corral for stock.

The first settlers faced stern frontier conditions, but they had their choice of fine grazing lands, cold springs up near the head of green valleys, and mountain streams. The first to file on lands in the Clarno area and on Ochoco meadows found ideal conditions for ranching. Most of them built their homes near big springs, and some of them planned their farmsteads so that cold spring water would flow through small buildings to cool milk and butter and keep vegetables fresh. The Cold Camp Ranch, ten miles east of Antelope, was one of the places where chilling spring water was used for refrigeration. It was a place youngsters from Antelope liked to visit, to admire the food-filled shelves close to the bubbling water.

Livestock men filed on 160-acre claims with an eye to the surrounding government range that would be utilized in ranch operations. On bottom lands, hay was grown and placed in big stacks for winter use. The acreage actually owned by many of the first ranchers was not great, but their "spread," including the free range, was extensive. Eventually, land seekers filed on the open range. Stockmen watched their coming with fear that the era of free land was past. They called the homesteaders "scissorbills" and referred to the land on which they filed as "Starvation Flat" or "Squatters Gulch," but the homesteaders came in ever-increasing numbers. To protect home ranches, owners occasionally had their hired help or members of their families "take up" adjacent lands. It was not uncommon to see daughters and sons of ranch owners ride away from home ranches at dusk, to spend nights in their homestead cabins, then return to the central ranches on the morrow. In this manner, homestead residence requirements were filled.

Homestead Law, 1862

Under the Homestead Law of 1862, a citizen of the United States could acquire 160 acres of the public domain providing he met certain requirements: he must live on the land five years, make his home on it, cultivate the ground, and pay a fee of about sixteen dollars. However, he could gain title after only fourteen months by paying a minimum of $1.25 per acre. There were also other land laws under which public domain could be acquired. They included the Mineral Land Act of 1866, intended to spur the exploitation of minerals; and the Timber Culture Act of 1873. The Desert Land Act of 1877 offered land at $1.25 an acre to the settler who would irrigate it. Then came the Timber and Stone Act of 1878, which resulted in Oregon's land fraud cases of 1905.

Numerous homesteaders of the 160-acre era, and the 320-acre desert land claims that followed, built up small ranches, raised their families, and established schools and churches. Many hamlets, towns in name only, were established in the new homestead country.

The first actual settlers in Central Oregon were persons who, in the early 1860s, located beside The Dalles-Canyon City Road, to cater to traffic moving to and from the gold diggings in the upper John Day River area. One of the earliest of these settlers was Christian W. Meyer. Born in Germany in 1819, Meyer was a pioneer of the California gold rush in 1849. With his partner, Frank Huat—also known as Alkali Frank—he set up a home on Alkali Flat, in 1863, about five miles east of Mitchell of the present. The men kept a stage station and an eating place, and provided overnight accommodations for travelers.

Meyer possibly was the first person, south of the John Day, to divert water from a creek to irrigate an acreage. He developed a producing farm with a garden, a fine orchard, and a grain field. The acreage was high in Bridge Creek, which flows through a canyon, narrow in the Mitchell area, to join the John Day River in a region of gaily colored hills—the John Day hills with their entombed fossils of mammals that ranged over that region some forty million years ago. Dipping to the edges of Meyer's irrigated farm were the tilted beds of Cretaceous oceans with their marine shells and the stony bones of flying reptiles— the pterodactyls of primordial seas.

Clarno, on the John Day River

Meadows of the John Day River, some twelve miles east of the Maupin Stage Station in the Antelope Valley, early attracted ranchers seeking home sites from which stock could be ranged in grass-covered hills. To that area in 1866, Andrew Clarno brought his family from California, following a stop in Eugene City. The Andrew Clarno Ranch was the first real ranch operation in the area known as Central Oregon. The post office of Clarno was named for him.

In 1867, Clarno arranged to have lumber sawed at a mill at Cascades on the Columbia. The lumber was moved to The Dalles on a scow. From there, John Clarno, seventeen-year-old son of Andrew Clarno, hauled the lumber single handed, a hundred miles to the homestead. Using wagons drawn by twelve yoke of oxen, it took thirty days to make the trip.

When Andrew Clarno came to Oregon, he brought from California more than three hundred heifers. The herds rapidly multiplied until Clarno cattle covered the John Day hills. For a time, Clarno's partner in the livestock operation was William Snodgrass. Cattle were sold in Portland, or to buyers who trailed them to the Union Pacific Railroad in Utah. Steers brought $18, and feeders were worth about $10 a head. The cash received for the animals was kept in a buckskin purse, the Clarnos' only bank.

Andrew Clarno was a friend of the Indians who seasonally moved through the John Day basin, close to the great mesa east of the river, the mesa that was to be known in later years as Iron Mountain—a lava-covered upland overriding colored strata of the John Day formation. Frequently the Indians visited the Clarno ranch house.

Clarno also served as a Federal agent while the government was attempting to put the Indians on reservations. The only trouble he had with them occurred when Paulina's raiders stole his saddle horse and milk cows while he was making cheese for the army at Camp Watson, and later when tribesmen stole a herd of his cattle and trailed them west to Trout Creek.

Ochoco Settlements

First attempt at settlement in the Ochoco country was made in the fall of 1867 by D. Wayne Claypool, William Smith, Captain White, Raymond and George Burkhart, and Elisha Barnes, all of whom came to the area over the Cascades from Lebanon in Linn County, traveling the old Wiley Trail. The group spent the winter hewing logs for frontier cabins, only to see their first cabin, that of Wayne Claypool, go up in smoke during an Indian raid in the spring of 1868. At the time of the raid, only three of the first settlers of the Ochoco were in the valley, the others having returned over the Santiam to make ready to bring their families to the new Oregon frontier. The three remaining were Captain White, E. Johnson, and George Barnes. Their food, bedding and guns were all stolen by the Indians.

The men were in a field when the cabin was burned. After making certain the Indians had left the burning cabin, they fashioned make-believe guns from sticks of wood and bravely marched to the ruins of the Claypool home. But where to go? The men were afoot, without food or rifles. If they decided to cross the Santiam they faced a hike of some thirty miles over snow. Years later, George Barnes, historian of the first attempt to settle on the Ochoco meadows, wrote:

In fact, to attempt to cross the Santiam Pass seemed so hopeless that we finally concluded to try to find the Canyon City Road, which we knew lay somewhere to the north of us. . . .

We perhaps looked very brave as we marched down the valley with our make-believe guns on our shoulders, but we did not feel that way. Two days and a half later we found the Warm Springs Agency, by accident. Our course was guided by canyons and ridges. At the Agency we were welcomed by one of the best women Oregon ever knew, Mrs. John Smith (wife of the superintendent of the Warm Springs Reservation). We were fed and made to feel at home. Two days later Johnson and I started for home. . . . We hired an Indian guide to take us to Cache Creek.

Captain White remained at the Agency as the two men started their hike over the Santiam Divide. Apparently the raided Ochoco settlers stayed at the Agency for some time, because when they reached the divide, the snow pack had dwindled. On the Santiam summit, Barnes and Johnson met James M. Blakely, who was moving a herd of cattle over the Cascades from Linn County to Wild Horse, in Umatilla County. Blakely gave the men their supper and breakfast. Next day, the two men reached their homes in Linn County, "safe, sound, and hungry," and carrying the word that Indians had raided the Ochoco settlement.

In their 1868 sweep into the Ochocos, the Indian raiders overlooked a new log cabin on Mill Creek, built on the land of William Smith. There a broad canyon, opening into a wide meadow, cuts its way from the pine-covered Ochoco hills. Swampland, with willows and tall grass, was the choice of Elisha Barnes when he staked out his claim in 1867.

The Indian raid on the settlement did not halt the eastward movement of land seekers across the Santiam to Crooked River. Most of them settled on McKay Creek, north of the green Crooked River Valley, but some filed on land up and down Crooked River; and some crowded into the bottom lands of Ochoco Creek. Others staked claims up Mill Creek to the timber edge.

Hardships of the pioneers of the Ochoco were many. In the first years of settlement, there was a great fear of prowling Indians, and even isolation imposed severe hardships. In the range country, especially near the head of Crooked River and in the highlands of Camp Creek, neighbors were few and generally far apart. Since roads were seasonally impassable in parts of the area, because of drifting snow or deep mud, ranchers had to move in supplies when roads were not muddy or snow covered.

Crops were cut by hand, and boards for homes were shaped from pines with a broad axe. Conditions along the Ochoco in the first years of settlement were little different from those of Colonial days on the eastern seaboard, and in timbered valleys of Kentucky and Ohio. Grain was threshed with a flail, or tramped by horses, to be winnowed in the air as autumn breezes swayed grasses in bottom lands. Wheat was ground in mortars in much the same manner as Indians crushed seeds and roots. In most cabins there were candle molds, but occasionally a rag in a saucer served as a lamp to light a cabin. Coal oil, in bulky five-gallon cans, was available in Oregon at the time, but it was difficult to transport over the mountains.

Mrs. Reason Hamilin was to win recognition as the first white woman to live on the Ochoco, where her husband built a home close to a creek that flowed out into green meadows. Mrs. Hamilin, however, was not the first white woman to call the area her home. That honor goes to the hospitable wife of Captain John Smith, who in 1865 was appointed superintendent of the Warm Springs Indian Reservation, about thirty-five miles to the northwest of the Prineville site. The Smiths demonstrated good-neighbor hospitality in various ways, even sending mail from The Dalles to the new Ochoco settlement, by friendly Indians.

Central Oregon's First Schools

Women brought their Bibles and their faiths into the timber-fringed Ochoco Valley when they came over the high Santiam Divide from Linn County settlements. In the new lands along Crooked River and its tributaries, they saw to it that a school was erected before a town was founded. The school was built in the fall of 1868 on the Claypool claim, about eight miles upstream from the Prineville site. The one-room school was constructed of logs. There were no nails, and seats were made of hewn puncheons, with no backs. The roof was of shakes.

William Pickett was the first teacher in that school—the first in all Central Oregon. Funds for the operation of the school—which in its first year had seventeen pupils and was in session only three months—were raised by public subscription. Each family provided a different set of books, but despite lack of uniformity, Pickett managed to teach. Once, when Indians moving through the Ochoco country caused some concern, the school served as a stockade. Breastworks and trenches were prepared, but never used.

The Ochoco school continued late into the fall, and the helping hands of the youngsters were missed on the farm where so much work had to be done. Men were busy making rails and shaping boards, hewing house logs, and caring for their stock. On the Lower Ochoco and in the Prineville area, tall ryegrass, abundant in the bottom lands, had to be cut and the ground plowed. Men hunted in the woods. Generally they did not have to go far: deer came out of the pines to graze on meadows close to the new homes.

From a log-cabin start on Ochoco Creek, Central Oregon schools were at first slow to expand. As communities gained town status, grade schools were founded, but for many years the only high school in the region originally encompassed by Crook County was in Prineville. Not until 1908 was a high school established in Bend, with Redmond served by a high school two years later. As early as 1906, Redmond had a grade school, established by the Townsite Company and with parents hiring the teacher.

Isolated ranch communities established their own schools, frequently in homesteaders' cabins, and paid their teachers through subscriptions. Most of the teachers came from the east, and were "kept" by ranch families, with a small charge for board and room.

In at least one instance, a teacher held classes in an old sheep cabin. The district was No. 51 of old Crook County, and the place was Axehandle, where a cold spring bubbled from the earth, to send its flow into a tributary of Currant Creek. The community that was to become Madras did not have a school until 1902. Residents of the area built the small structure, with funds for materials obtained from donations, pie socials, dances, and other community projects.

Religious Efforts

Horse-riding and buggy-driving missionary ministers and priests were the first to serve the scattered families of the region; and Bishop Robert Paddock of the Episcopal Church was likely the first bishop to visit the area. He drove south from The Dalles, stopping en route at the home of parishioners. One of the stops was with the H. C. Rooper family in Antelope. Another was in Bend at the A. M. Drake home. It was Mrs. Drake's wish to see an Episcopal Church built at the foot of Wall Street, as in New York. Later, she donated a lot at the foot of Wall Street, overlooking downtown Bend, and there Trinity Episcopal Church eventually was built.

The Reverend A. Bronsgeest, a quiet, friendly priest, driving a two-horse buggy and carrying a small box camera to take pictures of the children of parishioners, also visited the interior country at about the same time that Bishop Paddock did. Seasonally he sent word of his coming, and asked that members of the Catholic faith meet at a certain ranch on a set morning for Holy Communion. There Father Bronsgeest set up his altar, said Mass, spoke to the small group of ranchers, then went on to other communities.

One of the first churches in the interior country dates back to the days of the gold rush into the John Day country. This is St. Thomas' Episcopal Church in Canyon City, built in 1876 under the supervision of Dr. Reuben Denton Nevius, who had organized a congregation of Episcopalians in Canyon City, in 1876. The church is still in use.

Baptists were early in the Central Oregon field and took the lead in establishing churches. One of the first of these, in Prineville, was established in 1873. It was the first church to serve the little community taking shape under the Crooked River rim, close to converging Ochoco Creek.

Wheel Ruts Become Roads

The first roads to serve the inland region that was to become a range empire were little more than wheel ruts, out of the north from The Dalles and over the Santiam from Linn and Benton counties. A military route, blazed by supply wagons, earlier had taken tentative shape east from Crooked River into the Harney Valley, and a road that was to be well-used in the 1870s came out of the Klamath basin, through a forest of jackpines and past the Farewell Bend ranch on the Deschutes.

In early years, travel was light, and largely seasonal. The road over the Santiam Divide to Cache Creek was blocked at least six months out of each year by snowdrifts which at times remained as travel barriers until mid-June. The road from California and the Klamath Basin was not usable in winter, and remained in that condition until the early 1920s.

The supply road from The Dalles was intended for year-around use, but it was virtually impassable for heavy wagons in the winter months. For this reason, ranchers moved in their supplies before winter storms came. Generally, these supplies were brought to interior towns and ranches on wagons that had taken loads of wool to The Dalles, then the end of the rails. Horseback travel was heavy, with riders using shortcuts—trails over high mountain passes and rugged uplands that could not be used by wagons or buggies.

Teamsters calculated well in determining the best and shortest routes through the inland country. When the state highway system was established, many of the major highways closely followed the routes of the pioneers. One of these highways is U.S. 97, which was routed down Cow Canyon—a rugged path for pioneer teamsters. Another is U.S. 20, across the Santiam Divide past Hogg Rock, not far from the road used by the Ochoco settlers in their eastward migration over the Santiam.

The first sawmill in the Ochoco-Crooked River Valley was built by Ole Swartz, on Mill Creek. It was a small, steam-operated plant of limited capacity. This was not a commercial venture—it was more of a community service plant. The region's first commercial sawmill was established on upper Willow Creek, east of Madras of the present, by C. C. Mailing, who came to Central Oregon in 1877. Boards from the Mailing mill were used in many cabins and homes of the region prior to the turn of the century. Timbers for the first bridge over Crooked River, at the Trail Crossing site, were hauled from the Mailing mill in 1890. The mill obtained its timber from a fine stand of pine that reached well to the foothills of the western-sloping Ochocos.

Madras Plateau Challenges

Homesteaders on the gently sloping Madras plateau, with giant Mt. Jefferson on the volcanic skyline in the west, gambled with the elements in attempting to raise dry-land wheat during the early years of the twentieth century. Except in a few winters, only light snow fell on the plateau. Rainfall was slight. There was little surface water, with the exception of springs up close to the Ochoco timber to the east. There was water deep under the surface, but drilling was costly. Farmers, most of them attempting to grow wheat, looked at the blue skies and prayed for rain when clouds appeared. Most of them hauled water a considerable distance up steep grades out of the Deschutes canyon—or drilled wells.

Deep in the Crooked River Gorge west of Culver were giant cold springs that flowed into turbulent pools filled with gem stones. These were the Opal Springs. James Henry Windom and G. Springer were the first to utilize the water from the big springs near the bottom of the deep, rocky canyon. In 1898, joined by other ranchers, they installed a water wheel and pump to raise water to the first bench above Opal Springs, a height of about five hundred feet. The water was then placed in troughs for cattle. In 1914, E. A. Thompson installed an engine to force water out of the gorge through pipes to residents of the Culver community. Later, Opal Springs provided water for an area system.

High Desert Lures Land Seekers

With the coming of the railroads in 1910 and 1911, attention centered on the High Desert lands to the east of Bend. Promoters predicted that the sage country would become far famed for its wheat. A few homesteads had been filed prior to 1900, around the head of Crooked River, high in the Bear Creek country and in the Millican Valley, but most of the plateau remained in government ownership. Virtually all lands were homesteaded in the 1906-1916 decade. Families moved to the bleak, waterless land, to live in small cabins and to found new communities. Persons ill-prepared to struggle with the grim, lonely sage country came from many parts of the United States. They paid land locators, who took them into the High Desert by team and buggy and showed them section corners of land open for filing. The land seekers paid $100 or more for this location effort. Homes and barns were built with lumber hauled from Bend. Part of the homestead improvement work consisted of the erection of barbed-wire fences, to keep range stock out of cultivated areas. But the fences failed to protect green fields from inroads by rabbits, thousands of which scampered throughout the sage.

It was a grim life that families of the desert faced: winters were cold on the high plateau, more than a mile above sea level, and in the spring and summer, dusty winds whipped across the high country. Dust drifted into the cabin homes. Gardens greened in the spring, then wilted under summer heat. Water for domestic use was scarce. Generally it was pumped from some distant well, drilled to a depth of from 250 to 400 feet through the plateau lavas, and hauled to ranch homes in barrels. Precious rain water was caught in barrels placed under the eaves of cabins—but rains seldom came to this high land where the annual precipitation is only about eight inches.

Ice as well as water was obtained the hard way by residents of the area. Homesteaders in the northern Fort Rock country found plenty of ice in a lava cavern they named the East Ice Cave. There they gathered on warm summer Sundays for picnics—and plenty of ice cream. Residents of pioneer Bend found it more difficult to obtain ice. It was quarried from the Arnold Ice Cave and hauled to town in great chunks piled on a horse-drawn wagon. Pioneers would cut the ice with saws and lift it to the lip of the cave with block and tackle. Ice from that cave was used occasionally over a period of about a decade, and was brought to town when ice failed to form on the Deschutes.

In 1910, when a warm summer followed a mild winter, ice sold in Bend for forty dollars a ton, and about the only ice available was that harvested from the Arnold cavern. In the cold winter that followed, ice sold as low as five dollars a ton.

Social Life in Sage Country

There was considerable social life in that stern, raw land, just as there was on the Ochoco in earlier days, and at stage stations on the long haul from The Dalles to Canyon City in the early 1860s. On the desert, the homesteaders, many from cities, attempted to reclaim a stubborn, semi-arid domain, working long hours in the effort, but they found time for some social activities. Most of this centered in the small, one-room school buildings that served as community centers. Dances and socials were common, and occasionally home-talent plays were presented. Basket socials were the most notable functions. Both mother and daughter put forth their best culinary art, and hoped that some certain young man would have enough money to buy the gay basket filled with goodies. The bountiful basket suppers were served at midnight, but these did not mark the end of dances which generally continued to daylight. While their elders danced, youngsters slept on coat-covered benches. At least once a month in the long winters, the "Literary Society" arranged debates, some of which concerned the need for better roads to serve the new homestead era, while others touched on national and international topics as a world war brewed in Europe.

The High Desert social picture was typical of the social life in other parts of inland region, from Bridge Creek near Mitchell to the Opal Springs community near Juniper Butte in the country that was to be Jefferson County.

Homesteaders Lose Struggle

By 1911-12, the High Desert was thickly settled. At night, kerosene lights blazed in the small windows of scores of cabins. Old-timers recalled that from the top of Pine Mountain, a high landmark overlooking the plateau, the lights looked like twinkling stars. They were stars that were to disappear, one by one.

It soon became evident to the homesteaders of the High Desert that their attempts to convert the plateau into a second wheaty Palouse were a losing struggle. Crops failed. Only rye thrived under the desert sky that was so stingy with its moisture. Stock ranged into the rim country, and many horses and cattle disappeared.

For several years, High Desert homesteaders clung to their early hopes of reclaiming the brush plateau. There were rumors that a railroad was to be built across the high country from Bend to Burns. Also, there was a proposal that the volcanic rim of Newberry Crater be tapped, to spread East Lake water over desert farm lands. Hope was held that juniper forests could be converted into pencil wood. That hope was high when a pencil factory was established in Bend, but the new industry failed.

There even appeared a possibility that jackrabbits, pests that destroyed crops, could provide valuable fur for the eastern hat industry. A rancher, Charles H. Bishop, received from a New York hatter a check for $500, in payment for rabbit skins. Bishop shipped the pelts east in a great bale. Eventually he received a fine sombrero made of rabbit fur, but the industry failed to develop.

Looking south from Fort Rock Cave of Northern Lake County. This rocky shelter—formerly called Cow Cave—is the oldest known habitation of ancient hunters in Oregon. Sagebrush sandals unearthed from this cave have a radio-carbon date of around nine thousand years.

One of the top tourist attractions in northern Lake County is the Fort Rock formation, a great amphitheater on a plain once flooded by an Ice-Age lake. The huge rock crescent is a tuff ring.

In early days, Indian writings covered the rocky walls of this gorge near Millican, on U. S Highway 20, east of Bend. Many artifacts were found at camp sites, but vandals have destroyed most of the writings.

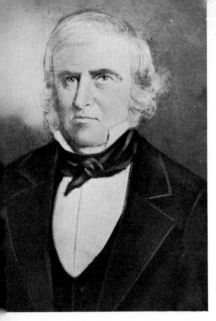

Oregon Historical Society

Left: Peter Skene Ogden was the first to explore Central Oregon and leave a diary of his journey. Ogden and his trappers made their way into the Crooked River region in 1825, crossing the present site of Prineville. Right: The first white man to cross the Bend site and leave a record of his explorations was Nathaniel J. Wyeth. Heading up the Deschutes River, he visited the Bend area in 1834.

Left: Many geographic features in Central Oregon have been named for the Snake Indian Chief Paulina, who was shot and killed by a rancher on Trout Creek in 1867, near the present village of Ashwood. Right: Howard Maupin, who operated a stage station on Antelope Creek in the Canyon City gold rush days, was one of three men who followed Chief Paulina to the cove on Trout Creek, where Paulina was shot and killed. Paulina's death virtually ended Indian depredations in Central Oregon.

Peter Britt—Portrait and Landscape Photographer

Left: John Y. Todd, a colorful figure in early Central Oregon history, built the first bridge over the Deschutes River at the Sherar site, and later founded the Farewell Bend Ranch, which gave the city of Bend its name. Right: Robert W. Sawyer, Bend publisher, was the area historian in early years. A Harvard graduate, he came to Bend in 1912, and in his later life played a prominent role in state affairs.

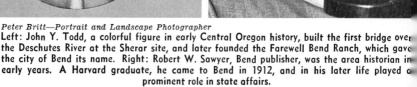

Left: John Diamond, Lane County pioneer, was in the group that located a wagon road up the Middle Fork of the Willamette. He himself named Diamond Peak, a prominent Cascade land mark. Right: Alexander M. Drake, who platted and founded the City of Bend, is shown with his wife in Venice in 1907, during their extended European travels.

When World War I came, many of the ranchers left their desert claims to accept jobs in war industries. Bend received its full share of disenchanted homesteaders, who obtained employment in the new pine mills erected at the edge of the Deschutes.

Pioneers Tapped Streams

The earliest pioneers to settle along the river basins and creek bottoms in Central Oregon saw the need for irrigation in the warm summers if winter feed were to be raised for stock, and gardens cultivated for family use. Those pioneer settlers, on choice lands along stream bottoms, were the first to divert water, generally to irrigate alfalfa patches or small gardens.

There is no record of the first attempt at irrigation in the inland region. Possibly it was on Andrew Clarno's ranch, close to the John Day River, or on Mill Creek or Marks Creek. Maybe it was near Mitchell, on the old stage road to the Canyon City gold mines, where Christian W. Meyer cultivated a garden to provide vegetables for his wayside stopping place. As early as 1872, A. J. Shrum turned the flow of Cherry Creek onto his lands just south of the John Day River. That was the first recorded use of water in the area now in Jefferson County. However, Shrum, Tom Connely, and Pat Fagan discovered that Cherry Creek could be unruly at times: occasionally cloudbursts sent great heads of muddy, boulder-laden water through the creek, to destroy crops, carry away buildings, and spread rocks over fields.

Irrigation use of the spring and early summer runoff from Antelope Creek started around 1870, not long after Joseph Sherar blazed a trail for a pack train through the area to Canyon City. Howard Maupin, who lived at the Antelope stage station, used the creek's flow. Irrigation along Trout Creek, near Ashwood of later years, took place about the same time.

Apparently the first diversion of Deschutes water for crop purposes within the present boundaries of Deschutes County was on the roadside ranch of Andrew Jackson Tetherow, in the present Tetherow Bridge area. A. J. Tetherow, son of Captain Solomon Tetherow of the Lost Wagon Train of 1845, established a home on the Deschutes near the Santiam-Prineville road crossing in 1878. In the Metolius River country, where giant cold springs bubble from the earth, irrigation of the D. W. Allingham and Dan Heising places started in the early eighties.

But the pioneer irrigation efforts were puny compared with those that followed, which impounded winter runoff along the upper reaches of the Deschutes River, Ochoco Creek, and Crooked River to provide water for 160,000 acres and create for the region a multimillion-dollar industry.

CHAPTER 11

Era of Cattle Barons

BEFORE THE FIRST HOMESTEADERS FILED in the Bend area, stockmen had for a number of years been using the upper Deschutes country with its lush pastures in the pines as summer range for cattle. Some of the herds were brought over the Cascade Divide from Western Oregon, by way of the Scott Trail or over the Willamette Pass. Occasionally early-day stockmen of the Deschutes "harvested" the high desert pasture to the east by moving their stock into the Millican Valley and the Pine Mountain foothills. This was done seasonally when weather conditions permitted.

No fences were built, even on the home ranches, until about 1885. Previous to that year, the only enclosures were corrals, built at various locations on the range, though there were a few fences along bends of the river where calves were kept. Cattle were usually branded where they were found—on the open range; but sometimes stock was overlooked because of no fall roundup for checking brands. This once led to trouble. In the mid-1880s, for the first and only time, the Crooked River, Trout Creek, and Antelope ranchers held a roundup, which took in the upper Deschutes River country. During the roundup, some unbranded cattle were found. The ranchers decided to sell the unbranded stock and divide the proceeds. However, this plan did not please the Deschutes stockmen, who were certain the unbranded animals were from their herds, but they were in the minority and abided by the vote of the majority. They then had to watch their own cattle being sold to the visiting riders. After that there was no invitation from the Deschutes ranchers to others from remote areas to join in roundups.

Stockmen of the timbered upper Deschutes country were never bothered by Indians, but once a rumor reached the Prineville setttlement, off to the east on Crooked River, that all the stockmen of the upper Deschutes had been killed in a raid. Ochoco ranchers, fully armed, went over to investigate, only to find the rumor was without foundation.

Harsh Winters

Range feed was abundant in the Central Oregon cattle country prior to 1900, though seasonally stockmen faced the fear of a hard winter and the loss of animals. No great amount of hay was harvested in earlier years, making the hazard of loss of stock in severe winters very great. The region is believed to have suffered a bad winter in 1861-62, but there were no permanent settlers in the area at the time. Evidence of heavy snow in the uplands came in the spring when a flood swept through the lower Deschutes Gorge—noted for its even flow along the upper reaches—and carried away Sherars Bridge, even though the span had been built well above the level of the river.

Probably the worst winter in white man's early-day occupancy of the interior range country was in 1883-84, usually referred to as "the winter of 1884"; but the storm really started with an unprecedented chill as the year 1883 faded. In the Camp Polk community, six feet of snow covered the region for ninety days. When the long-awaited spring breakup came, bands of horses and herds of cattle were dead on ranches, or in the hills and valleys where they had been trapped by the heavy storm. Weather records were not kept at the time, but old-timers said thermometers "froze."

Residents of the Squaw Creek country recalled riding the ranges the following spring and finding the carcasses of some animals under trees, where they had starved and died in the intense cold. On Ochoco ranches, settlers built trails and tunnels through the deep snow to reach farm buildings. In the Prineville area and on Trout Creek, stock fared much better because considerable hay had been cut and stacked the previous summer, but the loss was heavy in the Sisters and Metolius River areas. Ranchers recalled that the December cold preceding the storm was terrible—easily thirty-five or forty degrees below zero. Then came the heavy snow. There was little drifting, yet the snow piled into a mass that covered almost everything, partly burying farm buildings. It remained on the ground until mid-March. Stock caught in the hills, away from home ranches, suffered a heavy loss. Carcasses of horses were found with tails and manes missing—eaten by other starving animals. Bark was chewed from juniper trees. For years, the girdled, dead trees remained as lifeless range memorials to that terrible winter.

The bitter cold caused no loss of life among settlers, but it did result in much suffering and near-starvation conditions. It was also a severe blow to the young livestock industry of the region, grimly proving the necessity of having plenty of hay in stacks for cattle, horses, and sheep.

Cattle Drives

Central Oregon had no Chisholm Trail in its cattle era, but drives over unmarked range routes to market centers were not uncommon. Even before big herds were established on the grasslands of the Ochoco and adjacent areas, drovers moved herds eastward over the Deschutes plateau. Cattle from western Oregon ranches were moved over the Cascades, then trailed to new mining communities of Eastern Oregon and Western Idaho. Some of the cattle trails led north to the Okanagan valleys of British Columbia. Thousands of California cattle were in these herds moved into the north country. There was a heavy movement of cattle from California in 1864, when that state enacted its "herd" law. Finally, cattle migrations through Oregon from outside states resulted in the Oregon Legislature in 1864 enacting a law calling for the taxation of all livestock "driven through this state to a market in any other state or territory."

Routes of cattle drives north from California through Oregon varied. One of the most popular trails was from Red Bluff past Goose Lake to the Boise basin. Some of the moving herds grazed over the southeastern fringe of the Central Oregon country.

Eventually, when Central Oregon herds increased in number, drives originated in this region, herds being taken from the interior country to the railhead at The Dalles on the Columbia. In these unhurried drives, cattle were permitted to graze leisurely as they slowly headed north over an unfenced domain, on a route largely dictated by water holes, springs, and streams. However, the drives to The Dalles and the movement of smaller herds over the Cascades to the rapidly settling Willamette Valley were short compared with the big movements of cattle out of the range country east of the Cascades.

Huge, widely scattered herds were driven into the east as early as 1868, over mountains, deserts, and rivers to Council Bluffs, Cheyenne, and other good markets of the time. In some of the drives there were up to five thousand cattle. Even larger herds were driven from the green slopes of Steens Mountain. Frequently, the big herds that were rounded up for the drives bore a number of brands and represented the stock of several ranches. Watering places and range feed generally guided the drovers as they pushed their fat herds eastward, hopeful that market conditions would be favorable when they arrived.

Cattlemen sometimes found that the market shifted sharply during the course of even a fairly short drive. Such was the case with Robert Mays, early-day Eastern Oregon stockman. Mays had a string of five ranches. One was near Dufur and one was at Tygh Valley. A third, the Horse Ranch, was seven miles from Bakeoven. Still another was in the Antelope area, and the fifth was on Muddy Creek where a high, black mesa forms the eastern skyline. It was during the hard times of the nineties. Mays was getting along in years, and his sons decided to quit the stock business. They sold two thousand cattle for $15 a head, with delivery to be made in The Dalles two months later. By the time the cattle were delivered, value of animals had increased $5 a head, representing a loss of $10,000.

Teal & Coleman

One of the greatest cattle ranches of Central Oregon was that of Teal & Coleman in the 1870s. Joe Teal of Portland was in charge of the ranch, with Henry Coleman, his brother-in-law, as his partner. Another of the firm was Barney Goldsmith of Portland. Henry Coleman and his brother, Frank, actually operated the big ranch, with Teal and Goldsmith spending most of their time in Portland.

Home ranches of the spread were in the valley bottoms of Jefferson County of the present. The acreage sprawled across Trout Creek—an easterly tributary of the Deschutes River that has its source in springs in the pine-covered Blue Mountains, about eighteen miles above Ashwood. This meandering stream, seasonally dry in places, cuts through a rocky barrier at a point where Little Trout comes in from the north. Flowing into the Trout Creek basin from the northwest is another historic stream, Antelope Creek. The vast holdings of Teal & Coleman were later broken up into "smaller" ranches, one of them the ranch of Bidwell Cram, who at one time ranged his cattle over some twenty thousand acres. Another part of the Teal & Coleman spread became the historic Priday Ranch, founded by A. J. Priday and increased to some seventy-two thousand acres.

Motorists driving south over U.S. Highway 97 enter the pioneer Teal & Coleman ranch country as they reach the foot of Cow Canyon, at Willowdale.

In 1880, the country was overstocked with cattle, markets were poor in the west, and severe winters were taking a big toll. Overgrazed ranches were deteriorating, some water holes were drying, and shipping points were distant. Under these conditions, Teal decided on a long drive to Cheyenne, Wyoming, to clear his range of some of the cattle.

Teal should have been forewarned of the difficulties ahead because in the winter of the previous year, 1879, Clarence King had such bad luck while driving twelve thousand head of cattle from the Steens country of Southeastern Oregon, to Medicine Bow, Wyoming. Winter caught one of King's herds near Fort Hall. Indians pestered the drovers and their herds, and many of the cattle died in the chilling wintry blasts and deep snow. Eventually, only some five thousand steers reached Medicine Bow. Some of the cattle, mostly Durhams, had been bought from Pete French; others from Henry Miller.

Nevertheless, Teal decided on a drive that year, 1880. He induced John Y. Todd, veteran rangeman and operator of the Farewell Bend Ranch, to be drive boss. Together they rounded up about three thousand cattle, including their own stock and smaller herds of other ranchers of the area. As drive boss, Todd took the lead on the long trail east, with his fifteen hundred cattle. The Teal herd followed. Teal had assembled his herd on Trout Creek; Todd had taken his cattle from the Farewell Bend Ranch and upper Deschutes country. Trails of the herds did not merge until the eastern part of the state was reached. There is no known written record of that big drive or the exact route followed, though it is assumed that the trails were primarily dictated by range feed and watering holes. Apparently the Teal and Todd cattle did not swing as far north as the Lander cutoff.

Disease struck the herds, resulting in heavy losses on the trail. At Cheyenne, Todd turned his cattle over to Teal for marketing, while he himself headed back to his ranch on the Deschutes. Having failed to receive any money for his cattle by the following spring, he returned to Cheyenne. There he learned about the fate of the drive and the loss of his small fortune. Under marketing arrangements, the cattle had been sent to Nebraska to be fattened. While being moved across the Platte, most of the cattle had broken through the ice and drowned. As a result, Todd, the original drive leader, was now bankrupt, and the Teal outfit nearly so. Because of the financial loss he suffered, Todd sold his Farewell Bend holdings to John Sisemore for $14,000. Most of this went to pay the small ranchers who had placed their cattle in the drive herd. Todd retained only a squatter's right to some Squaw Flat holdings near Sisters. Later he did acquire range in the Ochoco country, but not until a Portland man, Arthur Johnson, gave him sufficient funds for a new start in business.

The Teal & Coleman empire, with headquarters on Trout Creek, started to shrink, following the Cheyenne trail and other cattle losses, but a number of other ranches developed into large operations shortly after the turn of the century. These included the Prineville Land & Livestock Company, widely known as the Muddy Ranch because of its headquarters on a creek of that name, a short distance south of the John Day River. This ranch practically ruled the ranges of the John Day slopes along Muddy Creek and its tributaries.

There were other large spreads along Trout Creek and the John Day River; in the Prineville country, Antelope Valley, and along the northern rim of Central Oregon. To the south in the broad Chewaucan Valley were additional huge cattle spreads, including the famous "ZX" ranch, adjacent to the Fremont Highway of the present. Farther south, in 1869, John S. Devine arrived in the White Horse country, close to the Steens, to found a spread that was to become part of the Miller & Lux empire. In 1873, Pete French established headquarters for his cattle domain a short distance to the north, where lush meadows were watered by miniature rivers pouring from the Steens slopes. It was the middle of the twentieth century before a new stock empire began developing—that of the Hudspeth Land and Livestock Company. By 1960, cattle had again taken their place in the Central Oregon economic picture—but now they graze within fences, not on the open range.

CHAPTER 12

Sheep in the High Country

LIKE CATTLE, sheep in early days were trailed to Oregon from the east and from the south—but the first sheep arrived by sea, not over a dusty trail. They were aboard the *Tonquin* when that ship, from New York, arrived off the mouth of the Columbia, on March 22, 1811. These first sheep were to serve as the foundation herd for the Astor colony. Soon other small flocks were trailed to Oregon missions. As early as 1842, Joseph Gale herded a band of sheep north from California. The first sheep to reach Oregon, by crossing the plains, were those of Joshua Shaw, who arrived in Polk County in 1844. On the long trip west from Missouri, the sheep fell into daily movement with the Shaw cattle.

There were sheep drives as well as cattle drives out of the area to points as distant as Nebraska. Stockmen trailed sheep east to feeding areas in the corn belt, as near as possible to the Old Oregon Trail. First drives of sheep east from Oregon were well to the north, over the Blue Mountains and southeast to a crossing of the Snake River. Idaho was entered at Old's Ferry, near Weiser. Later the sheep trails bent to the south, to follow the Malheur River out of Central Oregon, and cross the Snake at Nyssa. As late as 1882, more than twenty thousand sheep in three bands were driven from Eastern Oregon to Laramie, Wyoming. In charge of each band was a foreman with three helpers and a cook, who drove the cook wagon. Coordinating the daily movement of the three bands was a supervisor.

Eastward drives of sheep, and also of cattle, continued out of the area until railroad steel bridged the range gap between the region and the Union Pacific railhead in Utah. Prior to the construction of the railroad to Wallula and The Dalles—Kelton,

Utah, generally was the terminus of the long drives from Oregon, all of which were history by the time The Dalles, on March 16, 1883, observed its great Railroad Day. By December 1, 1884, trains were operating between Portland and Omaha, Nebraska.

Hard Winters Take Toll

Some of the hard winters of early years took a heavy toll of sheep, as well as of cattle and horses. In the early eighties, snow fell to a depth of four feet over most of Central Oregon, trapping bands of sheep in corrals, or in range country distant from home ranches and hay. Some two thousand sheep in one band died on Upper Willow Creek, east of the Madras site of a later day. A sheep herder known only as "Whispering Smith" lost his life in the storm.

Many of the old-time residents of the range region recalled winters when it was necessary to break trails with strings of horses, to get sheep into the home ranches with their stacks of hay. Crusting of deep snow occasionally resulted in great suffering to stock. Feet were cut by the icy edges that formed when rain fell on deep snow, then froze, leaving bloody trails.

Stockmen suffered loss of sheep in hard winters, but not disastrous losses. Mid-Oregon sheepmen evidently realized that winters could be severe, and that plenty of hay would be needed. This was raised in abundance in the Ochoco country, on Hay and Trout creeks, and in other places that served as centers of the stock-raising industry. Also, sheepmen realized the importance of having good herders. Some of the earlier flockmasters were from Australia. Then came a hardy group of men from the highlands of Scotland. Some of these, who started as herders in early days, became independent operators and, in a number of instances, owners of some of the big ranches of Central Oregon. Scottish names on mailboxes along the John Day River, adjacent to the big spreads, tell part of the early immigration story.

The Lonely Sheepherder

A man with one of the loneliest jobs in the world is the sheep-herder, and there were many of these on the Central Oregon ranges. Their pay was low even for those days—$35 or $40 a month. Bunk and board were provided, but there were no vacations or vacation pay. Through most of the year their homes were outpost cabins on ranges far from home ranches. From a small cabin with its nearby panel corral, sheep and herder moved before sunrise each morning, remaining in the hills until shadows of the rim country grew long and dusk came. By lantern light, the herder prepared his meal—mutton, beans, potatoes, bread, and prunes—and shared his leftovers with his dogs. The herder's bed was a straw-filled mattress, on which he slept while pack-rats often scampered around his cabin.

Seasonal Moves

Winter generally found the flocks moving toward the home ranches, where hay was available in hundred-ton stacks. Winter days were short for the herders; generally their flocks never left the feeding grounds. Springs and summers, though, were different. First came the season of lambing on open ranges. At night-fall, lamb-drop areas were circled with lanterns and flags, to scare away predators. In later years, portable corrals were set up in the lambing areas. In these miniature corrals, ewes and lambs were placed at night. On some ranges, at night the ewes and lambs were moved to sheds or central locations in wagons, where such vehicles could be used in the generally rocky or hilly range country.

Occasionally at lambing time, wintry weather slipped over the open ranges to pile up snow in the grass country. At such times, crews worked to save new-born lambs from chilling to death in the cold blasts. It was not uncommon to find more than a dozen lambs, wrapped in sacks, inside one small cabin, where half a dozen men cooked their meals, ate, and attempted to sleep.

The summer season provided a new routine for herders, as flocks were trailed to distant mountain ranges in the Ochocos or the Cascades. Across part of the route, the sheep grazed on lush range, as they were slowly urged toward the mountain pastures. In other areas, the animals were virtually flogged through brushy lands, along fenced lanes, and over the streets of Prineville, Redmond, Sisters, and Bend. The task of moving them through lanes became even more difficult when the first automobiles appeared on Central Oregon roads, around 1905. Once a flock reached a mountain allotment, the work of the herder slowed a bit. In some of the forests there were green meadows through which meandered cold streams, and occasionally deer grazed near meadow edges. Herders and their camp tenders were assured fresh meat through the summer, even in the hottest of weather—the alchemy of the high, dry air making that possible. In the hours of sunshine, the carcass of a deer or sheep, hanging from a limb of a tree, remained covered with a wool sack to keep away the flies; but when night came, the sack was removed, to permit the meat to dry and cure in the mountain air.

In most stock communities, sheepmen used central shearing sheds to which big bands of sheep were trailed each spring for the removal of fleeces. Operating in the pens were men skilled in the use of hand shears—usually crews of Mexicans, moving north with the season. Before the coming of power shears, pay was by the fleece, eight or ten cents apiece. As each fleece was removed, it was quickly tied, then tossed by a corral assistant to a man packing wool into a huge sack which dangled from a circular metal rim at the top of a frame. The wool packers lowered themselves into the sacks and packed into place the fleeces as they were tossed in by helpers. Once filled, the bags, each weighing around five hundred pounds, were sewed closed, then rolled out to be loaded on freight wagons and hauled to Shaniko.

Dreaded Scabies

Early in the history of the sheep industry in the region, the dreaded scabies appeared. Many of the pioneers believed that scab was on the range even before sheep were brought in from other areas. Old-timers said that the original bighorn sheep—native to the region as attested by their twisted horns weathering on range hills—were afflicted with the scabies.

Regardless of the manner in which it was introduced, scab was a serious problem for pioneer sheepmen. On many of the big ranches, ingenious dipping vats were constructed. Sheep were moved from corrals through narrow chutes, at the end of which were "curtains," usually strips of old gunnysacks. Beyond the curtains were long vats filled with vile-smelling "dip," holding a solution of sulphur, creosote, lime, and other ingredients. Racing after each other, the sheep plunged through the curtain and found themselves in a vat. While swimming across the long vat to a gentle incline leading to the open range, they received a complete saturation of the wool from the scab-killing solution. Dipping took place immediately following the shearing of flocks in the spring.

Long after sheep disappeared from the Central Oregon ranges, some of the old vats remained, their repulsive odor still noticeable. So powerful was this sheep dip that it preserved the wood in some of the vats for several decades.

One of the greatest fears of stockmen was that of losing sheep through smothering, resulting from a pile-up of animals in a corral at night. A sudden scare by prowling coyotes occasionally caused such a pile-up. Huddling during storms and severe cold also took its toll of sheep. From such losses, only pelts of the smothered animals could be salvaged. It was not uncommon to see scores of pelts drying on fences following the "spooking" of a flock of sheep.

By the turn of the century, open range was rapidly disappearing east of the Cascades, and watering places were passing into private ownership. With the coming of the railroads, it was no longer feasible to make the long drives of Oregon sheep to the Midwestern corn belt, to be fattened for the Chicago market; but there were smaller drives, mostly to Shaniko, where sheep were loaded on double-deck cars for the trip east. By 1950, Oregon's sheep population center had shifted over the Cascades to westside pastures, only a few bands of sheep remaining in the far reaches of Central Oregon, which once had produced range and hay for tens of thousands of these animals.

Jack Edwards of Hay Creek Ranch

The open-range country of Central Oregon brought to the state one of its most colorful figures of early days, John Griffith Edwards, a native of Wales and a veteran of the grim range wars of Utah, Colorado, and Wyoming. Edwards developed the nationally-famous Hay Creek Ranch, in the high country between Madras and Ashwood. He lived in a colorful era of American history—an era that witnessed the growth and fall of huge cattle and sheep empires covering millions of acres. In his own varied career he managed a sheep empire and won international recognition for fine stock.

Edwards' first holdings were in Wyoming, and it was there that he earned the enmity of cattlemen who vowed to get him off their ranges. But Edwards refused to move. Eventually homesteaders filed on the open range from which cattlemen could not drive him. Then the sheepman looked west.

One of the big ranches of inland Oregon, at the time, was on upper Hay Creek, then in Wasco County. It was established in 1873 by Dr. David Baldwin of Oakland, California, who had been lured to the region by the fine grass in the high country near the Ochocos. Later, Baldwin sold the ranch to C. A. and J. P. Van Houten and H. Loneoy. They were owners of the spread when Edwards arrived and purchased a half interest, sharing ownership with J. P. Van Houten and C. M. Cartwright. Seven years later, Edwards gained full control of the company. In that short time, the ranch had been developed into what John Minto,

Oregon historian, called "the greatest Merino breeding station in the world." The ranch boasted a sale of 500,000 pounds of wool each year; some 50,000 sheep grazed over a thousand hills and many valleys; and seasonally, 2,500 tons of alfalfa was produced on the ranch. Jack Edwards became world-renowned for his fine flocks.

Jerry Schooling, who worked on the ranch for many years, helped design and build a three-story home for Jack Edwards' bride, the former Elizabeth Justice Bell of Yorkshire, England. Soon this fine home in the Central Oregon highlands became the center of Oregon hospitality. E. H. Harriman, railroad builder and father of a son later to be governor of New York, was an occasional visitor; so was Samuel Hill, the road builder for whom a bridge over the Columbia River near Biggs was to be named in 1962. Governors and mayors, magnates and nobility also found their way to the beautiful home up near the head of Hay Creek, where green hills face the distant Cascades.

The Hay Creek flock of Rambouillet sheep was the largest in the world, and buyers came even from Russia to purchase rams. By 1910, Jack Edwards, a veteran of two livestock frontiers, decided to sell because of a reduction of summer range in federal forests, and also because grazing regulations had reduced to forty thousand the number of sheep he could place on forest range each summer. Edwards decided that his big Hay Creek sheep-breeding plant could not be profitably operated under such a reduction. He sold the spread to L. F. Menefee of Portland and Henry L. Pittock, publisher of the *Oregonian*. They were owners until 1922, when they sold out to W. U. Sanderson, who in turn traded the spread in 1937 to Fred W. Wickman, for an island in Hawaii. Wickman sold the holdings to A. J. Smith and Sons of Kalispell, Montana, who were owners from 1952 until 1954, when Wickman again resumed operation.

The big ranch was in the Pacific Northwest news again in 1963, when it was announced that the current owners, Curtis Martin and his sons, William F. and Curtis W. Martin, of Portland, had sold the spread to J. W. Chase & Sons of California. The price paid was in excess of two million dollars.

The Hay Creek Ranch—which has one of the most colorful histories of all Oregon livestock operations—continues as one of the big spreads of the interior country, in the range region that gently slopes west from the timbered Ochocos.

CHAPTER 13

Range Wars

THE OPENING SKIRMISH of the four-year range war occurred in 1902. Not until 1906 did the bitter struggle end—unique in the history of the West for its ferocity and its loss of livestock.

Events that led to the outbreak of the Central Oregon range war had their beginning many years before the slaughter of sheep started. Early settlers found that the interior Oregon country was well adapted to the raising of cattle, sheep, and horses. Cattle rapidly increased in the late 1860s, after the first pioneers came over the Santiam and McKenzie, to establish ranches along rivers and streams or near cold springs. Flocks of sheep appeared in the same areas where cattle grazed. Soon, some of the largest cattle spreads and sheep ranches in the West were established. A few, such as the Hay Creek Ranch, were to become nationally known.

Some of the stockmen specialized in cattle, others in sheep. On the open range, cattle and sheep did not mix. Cattlemen charged that sheep were destroying the range, trampling out the native bunchgrass and pulling forage out by the roots. They also charged that cattle refused to graze on lands over which sheep had passed.

Flocks and herds were wintered in the lower country, near the home ranches. As weather and grass conditions permitted, the stock seasonally was moved to mountain pastures, mostly in the open pine country of the Ochocos, where water was abundant and grass was good. Thousands of cattle and hundreds of thousands of sheep competed for the same range in the high country. Sheepmen from half a dozen counties—Wasco, Crook, Gilliam, Umatilla, Sherman, and Morrow, not to mention Lake and Harney

—drove their flocks in to the Blue Mountains or the Cascades each summer as early as possible. The slowly moving flocks in some instances grazed to the doors of established ranches, especially along tributaries of the Ochoco, Crooked and Deschutes rivers, and Trout Creek.

Sheepmen not only competed with cattlemen for the uncontrolled mountain ranges, but frequently they competed among themselves for the same choice lands. It was not uncommon for sheepmen to remove their bells from flocks, then, especially on moonlit nights, push toward the timbered mountains past other flocks that were bedded down.

Izee Sheep Shooters

It was inevitable that range trouble should brew. In fact, there was a flare-up even before the end of the nineteenth century, that resulted in cattlemen of the Izee area organizing to offset the inroads of sheepmen. The cattlemen formed a group they named the Izee Sheep Shooters—a group that set the pattern for the Crook County Sheep Shooting Association of later years. The Izee flare-up was primarily over Snow Mountain summer range. Cattlemen felt that their only protection was to organize against the ever-encroaching herds of sheep. On the other hand, sheepmen thought they had as much right to the government range as did the cattlemen. Sheep shooters followed a rather simple plan of attack: they first captured herders and their camp tenders, blindfolded them, and lashed them to a tree or fence post; then they proceeded with their mission, the slaughter of sheep.

Crook County Association

The second organization formed in the area to combat sheepmen was in the Paulina country of eastern Crook County. At the request of this group, a representative of the Izee cattlemen rode west from Grant County to help them organize. The meeting was held in late July of 1896, under a lone pine tree on Wolf Creek, about six miles from the hamlet of Paulina on Beaver Creek.

Cattlemen arriving at the designated tree found a large bonfire surrounded by more than thirty men, their horses tethered nearby. One late arrival recalled that it was 11 p.m. when he reached the tree and that the meeting was still in progress. Meanwhile a roll call had been taken and the following stern agreement had been submitted for consideration:

If in the accomplishment of a mission—the killing of sheep—it becomes necessary for the group to shoot a herder or camp tender, the victim is to be buried where he falls. Should any member of the sheep-killing group fall in a range battle, he is to be brought home for burial, and nothing is to be said about the manner in which he met death. In the event any member of the association is brought to trial for sheep killing, other members must be willing to go on the witness stand and swear to lies to obtain an acquittal.

Three of the men refused to go along with the group's mandates, but the association carried on. The remaining men swore themselves to secrecy, approved the compact, and decided on "deadlines." Over these deadlines sheep would not be permitted to pass; those found across the lines would be slaughtered and their herders would face possible death. The deadlines were marked with huge blazes of the "saddle blanket" type, cut on trees. Half a century later, the blazes were still visible in the Ochoco country, when loggers started the harvest of pines.

Slaughter at Benjamin Lake

The greatest of all sheep slaughters was at Benjamin Lake on the High Desert in 1903, near the Crook-Lake line. These two counties, Crook and Lake, were the scene of most of the range skirmishes in Central Oregon, and Benjamin Lake was near the center of them.

In July of that year, a group of sheepmen from the Silver

Lake area separated their wethers from their winter flocks, put a herder and camp tender in charge, and moved them into the Benjamin Lake area. The sheepmen had been in camp at the lake for only a few days, when early one morning eleven masked riders galloped in from the east, out of the Paulina basin in the high country southeast of Prineville. Armed with rifles, pistols, and clubs, the riders said they had been invited to make the visit —in fact they said they had been dared. Sheepmen later insisted they had not dared the cattlemen to drive them out. Regardless of invitation or dare, the cattlemen moved into camp with their faces blackened, determined to kill anything that had wool on its back.

On the desert, some 2,700 sheep were grazing on greening uplands where a moist winter had revived the playa lakes that served as watering places for flocks.

Before starting the near-annihilation of the big Lake County flock, the sheep shooters made certain that their work would not be observed. The herder was taken prisoner, bound, then tied to a tree, with a sack over his head. One man was left with the captured herder while the others headed into the sage country to search for the camp tender, who was then captured, bound, and blindfolded. The slaughter that followed was probably the most methodical of all killings of sheep in the western range country. Before the armed riders headed back for their ranches in eastern Crook County, more than 2,400 sheep lay dead in the sage near Benjamin Lake.

Gruesome tales of the slaughter circulated through the stock country for many years, some of the persons telling them providing such graphic details that there was little doubt of first-hand information. They described bleaching bones of sheep—scattered widely through sagebrush and junipers by predatory animals—which marked the scene of the slaughter for many years.

Silver Lake Killings

In February of 1904, approximately three thousand sheep

owned by Guy McKune of Silver Lake had been placed in a corral for the night, when five heavily armed men, all masked, rode into camp. One man guarded the herder while the others killed the sheep, using guns, clubs, and knives. Before leaving, the sheep shooters warned the herder that other bands using that range would receive the same treatment, unless moved at once.

On May 5, 1904, more than 2,300 sheep owned by Grube and Parker were killed, forty miles south of Silver Lake, when the two herders were overpowered and bound by ten masked men.

Some of the raids on flocks occurred at dawn; others took place in the evening. Most of the killing occurred in corrals, but occasionally flocks were crowded over precipices. As far as known, no herder or camp tender fired on the sheep shooters in Central Oregon. However, in Baker County on July 21, 1904, G. W. Brooks, a herder, opened fire on six masked men when they started shooting into his flock of 2,300 sheep. After being shot at and pursued by the raiders, Brooks managed to escape. Little Summit Prairie, in the Ochoco forest, was the scene of a sheep slaughter on August 4, 1904, when horsemen killed more than a thousand sheep owned by Morrow & Keenan. Thirty riders armed with rifles and pistols moved the sheep over the deadline into an open prairie where they were killed. The mission was completed in about two hours.

During the range war years, considerable hay was burned in stacks. In some cases, pressure was brought against ranchers not to sell their hay to sheepmen. A Wheeler County sheepman suffered a heavy loss of sheep one winter because the rancher who had promised to provide hay had been threatened.

As range wars made heavy inroads into the region's main industry of stock raising, a group of sheep owners from Antelope called a meeting of stockmen from southeastern Crook County, hoping to work out with cattlemen an agreement for the division of the Blue Mountain range. However, no agreement was reached. Hardly had the sheepmen returned to their homes when sheep shooters shot and killed sixty-four sheep of the Allie Jones flock on Mill Creek, about fifteen miles east of Prineville. This occurred on June 13, 1904, and was the first slaughter of sheep in Crook County.

Wool Growers Meet

On June 21, 1904, a meeting of the Central Oregon Wool Growers' Association was held in Antelope, with a large attendance. Principal discussion concerned the spreading range war. Growing out of that meeting, rewards aggregating $1,500 were offered "for information leading to the arrest and conviction of any person or persons guilty of shooting, killing, or maiming any member of the Oregon Wool Growers' Association, or any employe of such member while engaged in his duties." A committee composed of J. D. McAndie, H. C. Rooper, and Joe Bannon was named to visit the scene of the trouble in the Blue Mountains, to confer with the cattlemen relative to establishing lines for summer range; but the slaughter of sheep went on. In January, 1905, some five hundred sheep were killed near the ranch home of Fred Smith of Paulina. The masked riders bound and blindfolded the herder, then six riflemen opened fire on the sheep—not quitting until around five hundred animals were killed. As sheep were moved toward summer range in the mountains, there were various harassment tactics—attempts were made to "spook" flocks on night bed grounds, riflemen on cliffs shot into moving bands, and camps were destroyed.

Finally, on July 16, 1905, the indignation of the entire state was aroused to white heat when a group under the name of the Crook County Sheepshooters Association sent to the editor of the Portland *Oregonian* a "report of proceedings for the past year." Writers of the letter suggested that the governor of Oregon attend to his own business, adding:

We recently extended our jurisdiction to cover a wide territory of the desert heretofore occupied by sheepmen, and we expect to have to sacrifice a few flocks of sheep this coming winter . . . Our annual report shows that we have slaughtered between 8,000 and 10,000 head the last shooting season. We have burned the usual number of camps and corrals this season, and also sent out a number of important warnings which we think will have a satisfactory effect. We have just received a shipment of ammunition that we think will be sufficient to meet any shortage which might occur on account of increases of territory requiring general protection.

Authority for the letter was never established, but the given number of sheep killed up to that time was about right. The letter succeeded in arousing the wrath of state officials and many laymen—out of which grew a general demand that state action be taken to halt the range war.

One of the most costly of all these struggles occurred in Lake County during April of 1906. The stock firm of Parker and Green had moved a band of sheep into the area, north of the early community of Lake and east of Fort Rock. The herder was Phil Barry, only recently arrived in the United States from Ireland. One day Barry was visited by a group of masked riders who advised him to remove the sheep from the range at once. Thinking that the visit was just a bit of drama of the western range, Barry paid little attention to the visitors.

In two weeks the masked men returned. They drove part of the band of 2,200 sheep over a steep cliff, watching while the woolly animals plunged to death on the rocks below. Unable to crowd all the sheep over the cliff, the riders opened fire with rifles. Altogether about 1,800 sheep were killed that day. Apparently stung by demands from Salem that some action be taken to end the range struggles, investigators managed to learn that the sheep shooters had earlier obtained rifle shells from a Silver Lake store. A short time later, the storekeeper, Creed Conn, disappeared. His body was found several miles from town. He had been shot to death. Some investigators believed that this killing was a move to block any effort to identify the men who had bought the ammunition.

At the time of the slaying of the Parker and Green sheep, the owners were in San Francisco, isolated from the rest of the world by the 1906 earthquake and fire. Not until they returned did they learn of their loss.

The slaughter in Lake County brought to an end the era of Oregon's grim range wars, but their termination was directly due to the action of forest officials in assigning summer range in the Federal reserves and marking the boundaries of that range. Up until 1905, there had been considerable opposition to the creation of the forest reserves, authorized by the bill of July 28, 1902. For many years stockmen had used forest pastures seasonally, feeling it was their right to continue such use if the stock industry were to prosper. However, the sheep killing and range struggle pointed to need of supervision of grazing and the allotment of rights on forest ranges.

On April 11, 1906, the forest supervisor at Prineville received from the national forester in Washington, D. C., a letter outlining provisions that had been made for grazing permits and allotments. At a meeting held in Canyon City, November 15, 1906, each stockman with a prior history of grazing in the Blue Mountains was assigned an allotment with boundaries shown on maps.

From 1902 to 1906, range wars were responsible for the destruction of more than ten thousand animals, the burning of countless sheep sheds and hay stacks, and the forming of a strange organization—the Crook County Sheepshooters Association, whose leaders and members to this day remain unknown.

CHAPTER 14

Horses on the Desert

CENTRAL OREGON HAS LONG BEEN FAR FAMED as a range country that produces fine horses and cattle. It is strange that history has almost bypassed the story of one of the greatest of the "horse kings." William Walter Brown, though he is scarcely known, was likely the most colorful of all figures who controlled a range empire in the sage country, where he ruled for half a century. At one time Brown owned 38,000 acres of land; 22,000 sheep, and 10,000 horses.

A native of Kenosha, Wisconsin, where he was born July 15, 1855, Bill Brown came to Oregon with his parents in 1869—the family settling near Oregon City. Brown, with his brothers, George and Robert, first visited Central Oregon in the late seventies, en route to California to look over range opportunities. They noted the great expanse of open range east of the Deschutes plateau, with its fine native grasses. Not finding California to their liking, the brothers returned to Central Oregon in 1882, and made homestead entries near Wagontire Mountain. At first they raised sheep, but Bill Brown soon added horses and established Buck Creek, in the High Desert region, as the center of his empire.

To the south were the big cattle spreads of the Miller & Lux people. To the north were the Ochocos, where sheep and cattle grazed dangerously near "deadlines." To the west were the frosty Cascades. A part of the Bill Brown spread of early days was the Gap Ranch, now adjacent to U. S. Highway 20, between Bend and Burns.

122

Bill Brown's Giant Spread

Hidden away in the interior highlands, the giant spread of Bill Brown—much of it government land but with springs and streams in the rancher's name—was virtually unknown to the outside world. There had been limited settlement of the interior range country since 1880, but ranches were far apart and separated by huge blocks of government land. Because of the large Federal acreage, the 1880-1890 decade was the heyday of the big livestock operators, typified in Oregon by Pete French, John Devine, and Bill Brown. By 1909, two events occurred that were to change the land-ownership picture of the inland country: two railroads started building south through the Deschutes Gorge, centering attention on government land available for homesteaders; and, in 1909, a new homestead act was passed, allowing a homesteader 320 acres of non-irrigable land. In 1916 this acreage was increased to 640.

The number of land seekers in the range country was also increased by advertisements in eastern papers calling attention to Oregon's public lands available for homestead entry. Railroads even offered special rates to land seekers. One advertisement read: "A feature of the plateau lands that makes them attractive to wheat growers is that moisture stands close to the surface." (Wells were vainly drilled later in that area to a depth of three hundred feet in a costly search for water.) The result of these events was a great rush for land in the High Desert and the end of Bill Brown's long-time range empire.

Some part of Bill Brown's story has already passed into the realm of legend—yet this legend is based on fact. The stories about Brown of Buck Creek, Fife, and Wagontire increase as the years pass. Nowadays they greatly outnumber those of his famous range neighbor to the south, Bill Hanley. Brown herded sheep, hiked as many as twenty miles between ranches of his spread—even when horses were available—operated a ranch store, amassed a fortune, then watched that fortune shrink.

Bill Brown entered the horse business at the time when the demand for such animals was low. He paid from $2.50 to $10 per head on a dull market and soon established a brand that was to become well known on ranges spreading over four counties. Though he owned a number of other brands that he had purchased from other horse raisers, his own brand was the Horseshoe Bar, and he made it a rule never to sell any of his horses in areas where his stock grazed. A confusion of brands would have resulted.

It was near the end of World War I when Brown won recognition as the region's horse king, the owner of one of the largest herds of horses in the West. There was a big demand from Canada, France, and other allied countries for horses for remount services. Later the United States bought Brown's tough, well-bred, High Desert horses for cavalry use. In 1917, during one of the largest sales on the Brown ranches—when war had improved the market—geldings were bought at $100 a head and mares at $85. There were more than 1,000 animals in that sale.

Then came the era of armored warfare. The demand for horses dropped, and Bill Brown's fortune on the hoof became a liability. Finally only one market remained: packing plants where the High Desert horses were slaughtered and their meat canned. Reluctantly, Bill Brown of Buck Creek, Wagontire, and points between and beyond, sold his fine animals to those plants. On the high ranges of Central Oregon—land of artemisia, bunchgrass, and rimrocks—were held some of the last big roundups of horses in the western states. The animals were herded to railroad points and shipped to packing plants where they were converted into cured meats for foreign markets or for chicken feed.

Horse Trader Tactics Used

Confidence in his fellow man was one of Brown's strongest characteristics. In the early years of his half century of stock operations, Brown maintained the "Horseshoe General Store" at his Buck Creek Ranch for the convenience of his many employees and his neighbors. The store carried a stock worth about $15,000, but Brown had no time for merchandising jobs, such as marking prices on goods or checking invoices. Like a good horse trader, he preferred to bargain and then set a price on some article. Bookkeeping details bothered him. He used a box instead of a cash register, and jotted down accounts of sales on whatever was handy—a cigaret paper, the end of a shoe box, or the side of a paper sack. Naturally the store did not prove profitable.

Brown's checks were unique. They were written on the backs of labels of canned goods, the corner of a newspaper, or torn pieces of tablet paper—and they were always honored.

Throughout his long rule as "horse king," he depended largely on big springs and a few good streams to consolidate his empire. By controlling these watering places, Brown was able to expand his bands of horses and his herds of sheep. He built his big spread slowly, acquiring forty acres here, a small tract there, and a section of land along a creek bottom somewhere else. Eventually he owned some sixty sections of range country, controlling much of the adjacent government range land.

Bill Brown weathered many winters of deep snows and seasons of prolonged drouth. Once he was forced to fight for his open range, and in a duel in the sage downed his opponent, William Overstreet.

The feud involved early acquisition of land and water in the Wagontire country in 1885. At the time there was a bitter feeling between sheep and cattle interests. Overstreet drifted in from Texas and hired out as a sheepherder for Joe Foster, who had contested in court one of Brown's claims. The duel in the sage, in which Overstreet died, occurred a short time later, after sheep had grazed on Brown's cattle range. The two men shot it out at a distance of eighteen paces. Brown immediately reported to T. J. Shields, Silver Creek justice of the peace. A Lake County grand jury refused to indict him. Though the defense of his home range was all part of a day's work, the shooting weighed heavily on the rangeman in later years.

In earlier years, when Brown centered most of his range activities on raising sheep instead of horses, wool was freighted from the inland ranches to The Dalles. Freight strings moved around Hampton Butte, down Bear Creek to Prineville, then over the long drag to the Shaniko flats and Bakeoven, and across the Deschutes at Sherars Bridge. It was a long, tough road. One year Brown freighted 32,000 pounds of wool to The Dalles and received only six cents a pound. Returning freight strings brought supplies for the Brown spread and for the store on Buck Creek.

Bill Brown was graduated from San Jose Normal School in California before moving to Central Oregon at the age of twenty-seven. He spent most of his long life in the interior range country, remaining there until he retired; his holdings liquidated and his big spread gone. In his declining years, he saw men fight for the flow of Wagontire Springs, water of which he had left open to the public. Brown died at the age of eighty-six in Salem, in a home he had endowed in the heyday of his rule. Though he remained a bachelor throughout his life, he often spoke about a family and his aspiration to marry a strong young woman "whose offspring would be a credit to the human race."

Men who worked on the Brown ranches added to and possibly enriched the many stories of the "horse king." These stories have been incorporated in the saga of William Walter Brown. One of them is that Brown built up a resistance to strychnine, fearing he might be poisoned. Another story is that the resistance was developed because of Brown's habit of carrying raisins and strychnine in the same pocket, and nibbling on the raisins when he became hungry on desert rides or hikes. He sprinkled strychnine on desert carcasses, as bait for coyotes. On one occasion, his former workers recalled, Brown went into a drugstore in Prineville, purchased a bottle of strychnine, removed the top, and tasted a bit of the poison he had placed on the blade of his pocket knife.

Bill Brown's Empire Gone

The ultimate shrinkage and breakup of Bill Brown's range empire, that covered parts of Crook, Harney, Lake, and Deschutes counties, was primarily due to the heavy influx of land seekers following the expansion of desert claim acreage. Other big ranches that depended on open range for their cattle, horses, and sheep, severely felt the loss of "government land" they had used for years. There was evidence of hard feeling in the range country. Fences were frequently cut and cattlemen suffered heavy losses of range stock. Homesteaders charged that their access roads were being blocked and took their cases to court. The limited water holes on the plateau were drying, or were being barred to long-time users. Bill Brown was still watering his horses, sheep, and cattle at springs around Wagontire Mountain, and George Millican was drilling deep into old lavas to obtain water for his stock.

By the middle of the twentieth century, most of the big ranches in Central Oregon had disappeared, or had dwindled—taxes making it necessary to break up the stock empires of earlier years. The center of sheep population had by now shifted west of the Cascades, and cattle had taken over where sheep once grazed. No longer was government land available, except under the Taylor Act or Bureau of Land Management regulations and supervision.

Part Four

A COUNTRY TAKES SHAPE

CHAPTER 15

Growth of Towns

THE HORIZON-BOUNDED RANGE COUNTRY east of the Oregon Cascades was still without a town in 1870—yet the seed of a hamlet that was to grow into a thriving city had been planted. The site of this future town was mainly a large meadow, covered with tall ryegrass and willows. Only a few years before, placid Chief Ochoco and his small band of Paiutes had followed trails through this grass but had left unanswered the question: Was the Ochoco area named for the chief, or was the chief named for the *ochocos?* This is the Indian word for the willows that fringed both Crooked River and its tributary, Ochoco Creek. The Chief receives little mention in pioneer history, but for a time his name was given to much of the land now in Crook County. His range was east of the Sisters and into southeastern Oregon, yet he refused to join tribes taking part in the Bannock War of 1878. He later backtracked to the land of his fathers, in the Fort Bidwell area of Nevada, eventually dying there.

Barney Prine

Barney Prine and his wife Elizabeth were part of the first rush of settlers to the rich Ochoco lands after a wagon road had been cut across the Santiam Divide. In 1868, they established squatters' rights to a home on the bank of Crooked River. There

Prior to the turn of the century, Prineville was still a rangeland village. The bridge in the foreground spanned Crooked River, a stream which occasionally flooded.

Deep in Bridge Creek Canyon, the little town of Mitchell has suffered from floods as well as fire through the years. The view here is upstream on Bridge Creek.

Bend was receiving attention throughout the West, as a new Oregon town, when this picture was taken in 1905. Freight teams are shown resting in front of a building under construction in this view north along Wall Street.

The modern City of Bend grew from this mountain lodge—the A. M. Drake home facing the Deschutes River from the east. It was built in 1900. When this picture was taken, about 1912, the building served as the home of the Bend Emblem Club.

Horse racing was a common sight on Bend's one main street in pioneer days. This picture was taken in 1909, at the height of a Fourth of July celebration. Bucking contests were also held on this street.

The original Pilot Butte Inn, a famous historic landmark of early-day Bend. Freight teams plodded past over the dusty street, and automobiles later pulled up at the boardwalk curb. The old building was moved to another location in later years, to make way for new Pilot Butte Inn.

Shaniko was probably the destination of passengers on this stage, in front of a wayside stop early in the century. At Shaniko, price of meals at Columbia Southern ranged from thirty-five to fifty cents.

Shaniko became one of the largest wool-shipping centers in the world after the railroad arrive in 1900. This is a view along Shaniko's main street in 1910, when the Hill and Harriman system were building railroads in the Deschutes Gorge to the west.

Prine built a cabin of juniper logs with a thatched roof of rye-grass and willows, to be followed soon by other buildings: a small home, a blacksmith shop, and a store with a keg of first-rate whiskey in the front room. This became a popular stopping place on Crooked River for men who rode the open ranges.

The Prine buildings were not impressive—in that little clearing on the edge of the ryegrass where rim shadows in the early afternoon reached out over Crooked River. A writer of the day commented, "I believe Prine was all of one day building them." It was said that Prine's first invoice of goods for his store amounted to $80 and that his first stock of liquor consisted of a case of bitters. With its combination store, saloon, post office, and blacksmith shop—not to mention a stable for the convenience of rangemen—Prine's pioneer establishment was a sort of supermarket for ranchers in the Ochoco country. The iron that Prine used in his blacksmith shop was obtained from one of the immigrant wagons abandoned by the ill-fated train of 1845.

In addition to his saloon-store-shop venture, Prine also laid out a race track that ran from the bank of Crooked River toward the center of the present city. It was a level course, fast and at times dusty.

Village Starts in Horse Trade

A horse trade indirectly figured in the start of the village of Prineville. In the fall of 1870, a young rancher, Monroe Hodges, traded a pony to Barney Prine for Prine's rights to the land under the rimrocks where Crooked River cuts its way to the north. Twenty dollars was thrown in to bind the contract. However, the name Prine was not erased from the locality. When a post office was established on April 13, 1871, it was given the name Prine, Oregon, located near the center of the range country eventually to become Crook County.

The land involved in the Hodges—Prine trade was the same as that which Monroe Hodges later acquired as a donation claim. It reached from Prineville's main streets of the present, to the steep, lava-rimmed hill just west of town. Here, north of Crooked River, Hodges built a large log house which was later to become a familiar hotel where "Old Pete," the Indian chef, became famous for his fine dishes.

Later that year when Hodges brought his family by saddle horse to the Crooked River Valley, he began to realize the possibilities of the range country for raising horses. Years afterward his son, L. M. Hodges, became an exporter of horses from Crook County, and his corral was long used in early-day roundups. One of the younger Hodges' companions on rides over the rangeland was Billy Foster, both of whom were well acquainted with riders of the era of unfenced ranges—including Pleas Cheny and Bill Doran. This was the Doran of the range country who was never known to admit that a horse was too mean for him to ride. Other famous riders of the Crooked River ranges were Raleigh Thorne, Elam Faught, Columbus Friend, Henry Hackleman, Bill Vanderpool, Jud Hall, and Dave Prine. This hard-riding crew and their companions played an important part in the conquest of the unfenced frontier.

Old buildings and corrals of that long-distant range era can still be seen in many places: on Camp Creek, where Maury Mountain timber reaches to meadows; along Marks Creek, where a skeleton barn holds memories of yesteryear; and along Trout Creek, where thousands of sheep and cattle once grazed.

First Hotel

After making his trade with Prine to clear the way for the claim, Monroe Hodges hired two men to erect buildings so that he could "keep travel." This business thrived as more and more people came to this region that was now winning recognition as one of Oregon's outstanding stock centers. Hodges eventually erected a stable, and after that a meat market, to provide for his prospering hotel. Six years later, in 1877, he rented his hotel to "Shoe Peg" Hamilton and built a house in "uptown Prineville." There, Hodges—who had established the first hotel, the first meat market, and the first livery stable in Prineville—spent the rest of his life.

Prineville—First Town

By 1877, Prineville was definitely a town, the first in Central Oregon; but it was December 22, 1880, before a city council was named. At that time, Prineville was one of Oregon's most isolated communities—it was 120 miles from railroad and telegraph communication, at The Dalles on the Columbia. Not until 1900 did a railroad come to Central Oregon—and then it stopped at Shaniko. However, Prineville was beginning to take its place on the map of Oregon, a map largely blank near its center; and this rangeland town was soon to become the county seat of newly formed Crook County.

Prineville was more than thirty years old before Bend was founded, and a bit older when Redmond came into existence, a short distance to the west of the Ochoco. Prineville's rival towns in those early years were the busy community of Antelope, on the old trail to the gold mines at Canyon City; the village of Mitchell, across the Ochoco summit to the east; and the hamlet of Ashwood, on Trout Creek, not far from the rock-walled basin where Paulina died under gunfire on an April morning of 1867.

Gold Created Ashwood

Ashwood, some twenty miles south of Shaniko and forty miles from Prineville, dates its history to the 1870s when the Whitfield T. Wood family settled on Trout Creek, close to rhyolite-tipped Ash Butte. The town was platted by James and Addie Wood, in June of 1899, and took its name, Ashwood, from the Wood family and from the ashy volcanic butte overlooking Trout Creek. Early settlers of the area included Thomas H. Hamilton, a pioneer of 1874, who grazed as many as 7,500 sheep on his extensive holdings. His more than two hundred cattle were scattered over the Hamilton hills and valley pastures, with fine summer range available in the adjacent Ochoco timber to the east. In the higher country to the west was the far-famed Hay Creek Ranch, and on Lower Trout Creek were the holdings of Howard Maupin.

Ashwood, however, was not established as a range center, but as a mining town. On March 27, 1897, Thomas J. Brown was tending sheep on a ranch near Trout Creek when he picked up a piece of quartz which proved to be rich in chloride and free gold. Within a short time, 480 ounces of gold and 6,000 ounces of silver were mined from the "grass roots," in a high, lush canyon facing from the east the theater-like cove across Trout Creek.

Brown staked his claim and called it the "Oregon King," but within a short time the ground was restaked by Charles Cartwright of Hay Creek. Brown sued Cartwright in district court. The question involved was whether Brown had properly and legally located the claim and whether he had complied with filing laws. The case was moved to the circuit court of appeals, then retried in district court. Finally it was recommended that the case be settled out of court. Thomas Brown, largely destitute because of a railroad accident in which he had lost a leg, settled his claims against Cartwright for $20,000. The "Oregon King" operated sporadically through the years, with work once carried on by the Alaska Juneau Mining Company.

Early in the twentieth century, Ashwood became a busy mining town, with two hotels, and several stores, saloons, and livery stables. It had grown along both the east and west banks of Trout Creek. East of the stream—turbulent in spring, nearly dry in summer—was the fine home of the town's founder. Limbs of big apple trees spread over the narrow road that led to the highlands around Axehandle, a community eight miles to the east. Youngsters from the range country found the short ride under the cool trees enticing, and in the autumn they emerged from the shadowed lane with pockets well filled with apples.

Search for Gold Expanded

Ashwood's growth was due not only to the "Oregon King"

operations in the westward-sloping hills some three miles distant, but to the search for gold in the old hills facing Trout Creek, and in the ancient lands sloping up to the Ochoco timber. Several good prospects were located and mined. One of these was the "Morning Star," facing Trout Creek canyon from the north. Stock in this mine was widely sold in the United States around 1905. High in Long Hollow near the road to the Donnybrook community was located the "Red Jacket." Prospectors seeking silver and gold in that deep shaft cast aside reddish ores that gave the claim its name. Many years later it was discovered that the red ore was cinnabar, holding riches in mercury used in two world wars.

As mining operations along Trout Creek expanded, workers swarmed into Ashwood on Saturday nights. Saloons were kept busy, but Ashwood was never a brawling town on the Central Oregon frontier. Possibly it was too close to its quiet, rangeland background. To the west, dark basaltic cliffs nearly encircling Paulina Basin served as a reminder of grim frontier history.

No one knows when the Ashwood country was first traveled. Possibly a member of Nathaniel J. Wyeth's party made a detour into the region in 1834, or maybe some of Peter Skene Ogden's trappers scouted Trout Creek on their 1825-1826 trip through the canyons of the Deschutes. However, miners on their way to the Canyon City diggings in the early sixties were likely the first to explore the area and hastily examine the sulphide ores later found to hold gold and silver.

Like a number of other communities in the area, Ashwood, now in Jefferson County, originally was in Crook. When Ashwood was a precinct of big Crook County, most travel between the mining village and the county seat, Prineville, was across the Ochocos and down McKay Creek over a road that was rugged most of the year. Travel over the timbered divide in winter was by horseback.

Antelope, on the Gold Trail

On their way to the John Day country in the early sixties, packers, prospectors, and adventurers passed across the head of a broad valley in the high country, about sixty-five miles southeast of The Dalles. Named for the fleet-footed animals that early-day explorers saw in the area, Antelope Valley meadows were green in the spring months, from the rim country on the west to the rounded hills on the east. On the western skyline loomed Courthouse Rock, a sort of beacon pointing the way for the slanting evening sun.

Up near the head of the valley, Antelope took shape beside the trail first used in 1862 by the party of Joseph H. Sherar, when he moved supplies from The Dalles to Canyon City. Howard Maupin settled in Antelope Valley in 1863, beside the Canyon City trail, to become caretaker of the stage station established by Henry H. Wheeler. Second arrival in the green valley adjacent to the Wheeler stage station was Nathan Wallace. He moved to Antelope Valley in 1870, acquired Maupin's holdings, and operated the stage station, a small store, and a blacksmith shop. About a year after Wallace acquired the "town" of Antelope from Maupin, he became the hamlet's first postmaster.

First buildings at the Antelope site included a small stockade for protection against Indians. This stockade in later years became a frequent rendezvous for the few settlers of the region.

New Antelope Founded

The Dalles-to-Canyon City stage route was changed in 1881 from the Maupin-Wallace Stage Station to a point about two miles west. At that time the town of Antelope was moved from its old location, with only the graveyard on the hill left to mark its pioneer site. New Antelope had about all that a community required in pioneer times.

There was a blacksmith shop, where horses were shod before starting the long trip into the John Day basin, across canyon-furrowed hills and rocky gulches. For miners moving to the gold diggings there was a store with varied supplies. The Union House Hotel provided accommodations for weary travelers, and a big livery stable provided for horses. Soon the new Antelope even had a community center—Tammany Hall.

By 1887, Antelope was no longer a mere watering and feeding place for teams and a wayside restaurant for travelers. Pioneer H. C. Rooper, who lived to be a patriarch of the community, wrote in 1887: "There is enough of a town so you can see it with the naked eye." In 1892, the *Antelope Herald* reported that Antelope was enjoying a great boom, with a school being planned. Four years later, residents petitioned for incorporation as a city of Wasco County, claiming there were 170 people within the proposed boundaries. At last Antelope was officially born —a town founded on the gold trail to the John Day country.

Through Antelope's main street plodded slow-moving freight teams, headed for The Dalles, bells on their leaders musically jingling. Ranchers from communities as distant as Mitchell and Silver Lake, Fossil and Burns, rode over Antelope's "Main Street," placed their horses in livery stables, or tied them to hitching posts—then visited their favorite saloons: the F. W. Silvertooth, McLennan & McBeth, or McKay & Tunny "emporiums." In those saloons, trail-weary men gathered and talked, argued, and at times killed. Sheepmen intermingled with cattlemen in those taverns of long ago, but on their timbered summer ranges, grazing boundaries were marked by "deadlines."

Away from the noisy saloons were many fine homes, under rows of poplars that lined both sides of the main street and some of the side streets. There were also a number of churches in pioneer Antelope, and on Sunday mornings the sound of gently tolling bells carried across the valley to ranch homes, echoing from high rims to the northwest. In later years when the town became the trading center of an inland empire, it had its gay social set. There were special dinners, parties, and "formals." On Christmas Eves, community programs were held in one of the churches, or in the community hall, and presents were stacked high at the base of the town's yule tree. Gaslights illumined "downtown" Antelope, guiding pedestrians across boardwalks over which freight outfits rumbled on dusty days and cool nights.

Behind Antelope is a typical pioneer story—the history of a frontier town that might have developed into a major city east of the Oregon Cascades. Primarily, Antelope's fate rested with Oregon's permanent highway development. For years, all traffic into Central Oregon, and east to Burns and south to Lakeview, was funneled through Antelope—down a steep grade from the Shaniko plateau and through lower Antelope Valley to the inland region. For a time, in 1917, the future of the town was in the balance, with the route of U. S. 97 tentatively set through Antelope Valley. Then came the choice of the Cow Canyon grade and the bypassing of Antelope. In the following years, Antelope lost population, as it had to a lesser degree in 1911, when trains started operating through Deschutes Gorge.

By 1960, Antelope, of gold-trail fame, had won wide recognition as one of Oregon's best-known "ghost towns," and was making an appeal to tourists. Part of that appeal was lost when the far-famed museum of John Silvertooth—housed in a building which had its start as a saloon in 1898—was destroyed by fire in 1964.

Mitchell's Career Turbulent

A Central Oregon town with a history similar to that of Antelope is Mitchell, in the deep upper canyon of Bridge Creek, Wheeler County, where warped, elevated beds of ancient seas shape part of the skyline. Prineville, Antelope, and Mitchell together formed a large triangle on the frontier map of Oregon.

Like Antelope, Mitchell was a town that came into existence to provide for the need of travel—men with packstrings and teams moving over the "gold trail" between The Dalles and Canyon City. The town was named for a former U. S. Senator from Oregon, J. H. Mitchell. When the town was platted in 1885, it had two stores, a blacksmith shop and a hotel. Nearly all of the early-day buildings were crowded in the narrow bottom of Bridge Creek, through which destructive floods occasionally tore.

Over the years, Mitchell suffered from fires as well as floods, the town having been both burnt out and washed out, several times. Few Oregon towns of pioneer days had a more turbulent career. The first flood of a series struck Mitchell in 1884. That summer, a sudden storm sent a roaring head of water down the narrow confines of Bridge Creek, and water tumbled over a nearby bluff in a brown, destroying cataract. Houses were washed away, and boulders and other flood debris were dumped onto the town's one street.

Then came the terrible flood of July 11, 1904. Residents fled to the hills when heavy rain, dropped from thunderheads, funneled into Bridge Creek. The roar of the oncoming flood could be heard in advance of the appearance of a wall of water, but not all escaped to the hills that sloped sharply to the bottom of Bridge Creek. Two lives were lost, and twenty-eight buildings were swept down the canyon. Those who escaped to the hills watched the heavens blaze with lightning and heard the crash of thunder echoing from cliffs that were once ocean ooze.

Flash floods have been part of the history of Bridge and Cherry creeks through the years, especially in places where slopes of steep canyons are rocky and barren of vegetation. Floods from sudden electric storms form muddy torrents which quickly converge into valleys and destroy everything in their paths. Before the destructive power of the floods was known, pioneer ranchers built their homes in valley bottoms. Some of these homes were carried away by floods and dumped into the John Day River. Even stacks of hay were floated out of fields.

Twickenham and Spray

Fourteen miles north of Mitchell, close to colored hills entombing bones of prehistoric animals of the John Day epoch, was one of the many "stage towns" of interior Oregon, Twickenham

—formerly called Contention. The early name apparently com-
memorated a quarrel between pioneer residents, "Pike" Helms
and Jerome H. Parsons. Parsons' daughter Frankie—fresh from a
girls' finishing school where she had been impressed by Theo-
phile Marzials' poem "Twickenham Ferry"—decided the name
Contention was undignified and managed to have it changed to
Twickenham. On June 6, 1896, Twickenham Post Office succeeded Contention, established ten years earlier.

Nowadays neither office exists, mail for the area coming
through Fossil. Twickenham was never considered a real town
though—it was merely a stopping place on a stage route, in a
broad canyon flanked by green and gray hills capped by massive
layers of lava. This is the old land slashed by the John Day
River as it flowed north for a junction with Bridge Creek. Sepa-
rating Mitchell on Bridge Creek and Twickenham on the John
Day River is a high mesa.

Although Twickenham was only a range hamlet, it was one of
three communities aspiring to be the county seat, when the question was placed before voters of slicing parts of Gilliam, Crook,
and Grant, to create Wheeler County. Seeking county seat status
were Fossil, Twickenham, and Spray. Fossil was the choice, by
a big vote; Twickenham ran second.

East of Mitchell, on the John Day River, was Spray, settled in
the 1860s, and named by its platter, Mary E. Spray. In early days
the John Day River was crossed by a ferry at the Spray site. In
more recent years Spray has become a community center on Oregon Highway 19, on the twenty-two mile stretch between Service
Creek and Kimberly.

Richmond, Waterman, and Caleb

Other Wheeler County hamlets of early days included Richmond, one of the "business centers" of a well-populated range
area known as the Shoofly community. Also in Wheeler County
in range days was the hamlet of Waterman, better known as
Waterman Flats, a village that has disappeared from the Central

Oregon map. Nearby was a post office called Caleb. South of Richmond, some sixteen miles, was the community of Antone, on the old Mitchell-John Day Road, not far from the fringe of the Ochoco Forest. The Antone Post office, established in 1894, was bypassed when the new U. S. Highway 26 was constructed from Mitchell to the John Day.

Burnt Ranch

Burnt Ranch, a community on the south bank of the John Day River at the western edge of Wheeler County, earned its name during the days of Paulina's raiders. Before that it was known as Grade, because of being in the area where The Dalles-Canyon Military Road cut through the soapy shoulder of a steep hill as it dipped to the John Day bottom lands. Grade was a place detested by pioneer freighters because of the gumbo that accumulated there on wagon wheels in wet weather. A short distance west of Burnt Ranch in early days was the James Connolly ranch, where a fine orchard reached to the river's edge. Past here moved heavy traffic in the years when The Dalles, and later, Shaniko, was the end of the rails.

Gold Mined in Howard Area

Another small "pocket of civilization" that had a pioneer history was Howard, a post office that was to migrate from place to place through the years and eventually disappear. The original Howard was on Ochoco Creek, about twenty-eight miles east of Prineville, at a location later known as the Ochoco Mines near the mouth of Scissors Creek—a stream that held golden flakes and occasional nuggets. Named for a rancher and prospector who in 1872 found gold on Scissors Creek, Howard was an active mining community for many years; not until the nineties did the mining boom fade. Though long missing from the Oregon map, old mines on the route of the early Ochoco Highway section show Howard's pioneer location.

A number of other communities in Crook County experienced a fate similar to that of Howard, their names and locations being unknown to the younger generations. Grass grows on trails that converged on the little hamlets which served ranchers and miners of another era.

Old Camp Polk

Close to the eastern foothills of the Cascades, Camp Polk, ancestral to the Sisters community, had its start in 1866, the year Captain Charles LaFollette and his First Oregon Volunteer Infantrymen came over the Cascades to the edge of Indian country. Later, after the soldiers hiked back over the mountains without firing a shot at an Indian, Samuel M. W. Hindman and his family settled in the Squaw Creek area near Camp Polk. There in 1875, Hindman established a post office and set up a store. At that time, the area between the Deschutes River and the Cascades was a lonely no-man's land, but eventually the region thronged with cattlemen and sheepmen who had used the Santiam Pass in moving their stock to Central Oregon.

Sisters Replaced Camp Polk

Meanwhile, nearby Sisters was growing from a ranch to a town; by 1888 it had taken over the Camp Polk post office. The townsite plat of Sisters was filed on July 15, 1901, when the community on the upper Deschutes that was to be known as Bend was still called Farewell Bend. Not until some forty years later, however, was Sisters incorporated as a city, to win recognition as the eastern gateway to two major Oregon Cascade passes, the timbered Santiam and the lava-blanketed McKenzie. Sisters has a logical name; on the western skyline, seemingly only a stone's throw away, is the grand trio of peaks known in pioneer days as Faith, Hope, and Charity.

Stock traffic over the Santiam Road was largely responsible for the town's first growth. Shortly after 1880, big flocks of sheep from interior ranches were driven past there, en route to summer pastures in the High Cascades. At that time, Sisters was the "last chance" town, the only settlement between Prineville and the mountains, so early merchants did a good business in the summer months. By 1908, the heyday of sheep traffic through Sisters, bound for Santiam and McKenzie ranges, had passed, and mountain allotments had been reduced.

Black Butte Ranch

One of the big stock operations was the spread of the Black Butte Land and Livestock Company, which included a ranch at Grandview, the pioneer A. S. Holmes Ranch at Long Hollow, and the Black Butte Ranch, west of Sisters and adjacent to the present Santiam Highway. Lige Sparks, a member of the Black Butte firm, obtained the ranch under terms of the Swamp Act; he was to drain the acreage—a beautiful, open meadow facing the Three Sisters. Sparks' name has been perpetuated in Sparks Lake, in the Cascades Lakes Highway country west of Bend.

Camp Sherman

Not far from Sisters is another community with a long history—the Metolius River country, named for the cold springs that flow from the western base of timbered Black Butte. First to discover this recreation center, homesteaded many years before, were Sherman County farmers. Following the hot harvest seasons, many of them camped along the Metolius. For this reason, the area later became generally known as Camp Sherman. With buggies and wagons, the farmers from Sherman County crossed the Crooked River-Deschutes country at the Cove, in the area where old John Buchanan with pick and shovel built a road down the west side of the Deschutes. They then made their way past Green Ridge to the Metolius. But long before the Sherman County farmers found the restful beauty of the Metolius, ranchers had filed on land in the area. Apparently the earliest homestead filed in the region was the Allingham Ranch, a mile downstream from Camp Sherman of later years. The filing was by David Warren Allingham, a "short whiskery man everyone called grandpa." After Camp Sherman was established as a post office, use of the old community name Metolius began to fade. Originally this had been spelled "Matoles," the Indian name for white fish or spawning salmon.

By the 1960s, the Metolius recreation area, with the jagged spires of Mt. Washington as its backdrop, was attracting visitors from many parts of America.

Millican

When rangeman George Millican left the verdant Crooked River Valley to graze his stock in the open country east of Farewell Bend, he gave his name to a region, and then to a town which became well known in the range era, and even better known in later years when the fast, modern highway, U. S. 20, was built across the plateau. A native of New York, Millican came west as a small boy and visited mining camps up and down the West Coast. He reached the Ochoco country as early as 1863, after a ride over the McKenzie Pass from Linn County. In 1868, he moved his cattle to the Ochoco, extending his range southward into the area known to pioneers as the "Great Sandy Desert," where he became widely known as the raiser of fine stock. A crater high in the Cascades, near the North Sister, bears his name. Walterville, in the Eugene country, was named for his son Walter, believed to have been the first white child born in Central Oregon, by 1870.

When settlement of the country east of Bend started with a rush in the homesteading era, this valley became generally known. There P. B. Johnson established a store on the dusty Bend-Burns road, and became the first Millican postmaster in 1913. Shortly after 1920, W. A. Rahn, a bachelor, took over the operations. In a short time the hamlet gained considerable attention as western America's "one-man town." When it was featured in one of Ripley's "Believe It or Not" cartoons, mail poured in from all parts of the country and the Millican cancellation stamp on letters became widely sought.

After the Oregon State Highway Department constructed U. S. Highway 20 across the valley on a new line in 1930, Rahn had to move his "one-man town." Twelve years later, Billy Rahn retired and left the Millican Valley. A family then moved into the village to make Millican a one-family town.

Brothers

East of Millican on U. S. Highway 20, in Deschutes County, is the small town of Brothers, once a busy trading center for homesteaders; later the headquarters for a state highway department maintenance crew and a stopping place for east-west travel. It is generally assumed that Brothers was named in contradistinction to Sisters, but old-time residents of the area maintain this is not true.

Brothers, they say, was named because of the many brothers who had homesteads on the High Desert and adjacent valleys in the land-rush days. In 1913, P. H. Coffey filed a claim where the town of Brothers was afterwards located. On becoming the community's first postmaster, he proposed several names for the new office, established to serve homesteaders whose cabin lights on winter evenings glittered like fireflies in the sagelands.

One of the names he suggested was Brothers—and he did not intend that the name should be in contrast to the older town of Sisters, well to the west. The reason was obvious. In the sage-covered valley and plateau were two King families. In one family there were three brothers and in the other four. There were also four Stenkamp brothers, two Varco brothers, two Kruse brothers, two Gutfleisch brothers, and two Hague brothers.

Imperial, Dream of Promoters

Beyond Brothers and just west of Hampton in Deschutes County is the site of the ghost town of Imperial, where not even the foundation of a building is now visible. Imperial was largely the dream of a promoter of the homestead days who was certain that eventually the High Desert would bloom like the Imperial Valley in California. Imperial never materialized as a city, but for years residents of Bend got inquiries about the town, its status and its future. Lots had been sold widely throughout the country. Now Imperial has returned to the sagebrush from which it came.

Laidlaw

In 1904, the same year the townsite of Bend was platted, a little hamlet was established on the Deschutes River about six miles downstream. This was Laidlaw, named for W. A. Laidlaw, who was active in the promotion of the new town, confident that it would grow into a city and that some day a railroad would come over Hogg Pass from Western Oregon. He was also sure it would be the center for one of Oregon's largest irrigation areas. Besides, Tumalo Creek would serve as a natural flume, to move logs from the eastern Cascades to mill sites adjacent to the town. Actually it did have a good chance of becoming the big town of the country just east of the Sisters, and would possibly have attained that status if Alexander M. Drake had not arrived in his covered wagon to build a mountain lodge that became the nucleus of the upriver city of Bend.

At first, Laidlaw was headquarters of the Columbia Southern Irrigation Company, which was succeeded by the Tumalo Irrigation District. The Columbia Southern had purchased interests of the pioneer Three Sisters Irrigation Company, which diverted water from the Deschutes River south of the Bend site.

The Laidlaw Post Office was established in 1905. A few years later, when the State of Oregon was active in the development of the Tumalo Irrigation Project, Tumalo post office was set up near the construction camp, southwest of Laidlaw. The camp was a busy center while work was in process; this included a storage reservoir in the Bull Spring basin. However, when water was turned into the basin after a dam was completed, it failed to hold storage; the water escaped through rock fissures. On failure of the project and abandonment of the camp in 1914, the name Tumalo was transferred to Laidlaw.

Tumalo, erstwhile Laidlaw, was frequently in the limelight as Bend struggled to survive. There were rumors of a railroad coming over the Cascades that would make Tumalo its terminus, or at least would serve the town when rails were extended across the state. It was believed that this line would be the Corvallis & Eastern. Bend pinned its hopes on a north-south railroad through interior Oregon, but pioneer Tumalo was confident an east-west line would tap the region and bypass Bend.

After W. P. Myers established his *Chronicle* at Laidlaw, a bitter editorial feud developed between the villages of Bend and Tumalo, at the time still known as Laidlaw. Editor Myers claimed a circulation of about four hundred, a number that almost equaled the entire population of Bend. Both towns had fine agricultural possibilities, and there were many who believed that Tumalo would win in the race to become the metropolis of the huge upper Deschutes basin. However, the cards were stacked against the community that lost its original name. Railroads eventually came from the north, not the west, and Bend was the terminus. In 1911, the year the railroad reached Bend, the *Chronicle* suspended publication and one more ambitious town faded into a quiet community. The Corvallis & Eastern became a lost cause.

La Pine

Around 1910, when the railroads pushed up the Deschutes gorge and Bend was in the national limelight, a number of towns in Central Oregon were mapped. One that materialized was La Pine, then in southern Crook County, and now in Deschutes, not far north of the Klamath line. The town was platted near the center of the Deschutes Land Company's segregation, which was to receive water from Crescent Lake, as well as other sources.

The La Pine Townsite Company was pledged to develop a big town in the heart of a 28,000-acre segregation, and the nucleus of the town was to be a fine hotel "planned for the main street in the center of the townsite." Lots were set aside for the hotel, stores, stables, and other facilities. John Uhlman of Scappoose—a Swiss dairyman who had won a medal as the best butter maker at the Lewis and Clark fair in Portland in 1905—was to operate a dairy in the new town.

The birth of La Pine marked the death of nearby Rosland, with a post office dating back to 1897. La Pine, which first moved to be on the line of a projected railroad, found itself by chance on the route of U. S. Highway 97, after the Oregon Highway system took form in 1917. When this highway was modernized years later, it cut through the eastern edge of town, paving a wide street in its wake. Through the years, La Pine has grown steadily. The highway department has established a maintenance station there, and motels for tourists and fishermen have been built. In the early 1950s, it was designated as headquarters of the Mid-State Electric Cooperative, which brought Bonneville power into the region.

Desert, Lamonta, Forest, and Carmical

One of the missing towns is Desert, a post office in the Haystack area, established in 1882 about twenty-five miles north of Prineville. Lamonta—site of which was marked only by a windmill in later years—was a little town as well as a post office in early days, halfway between Prineville and Madras on the stage road from Shaniko. Forest, on Crooked River, was a "town" well known to early-day freighters, at the point where teams made the crossing of the river on the long haul from Shaniko to the new Bend country. The Forest Crossing was at the south end of the Lone Pine flat, a short distance north of the pioneer community of O'Neil.

In the O'Neil-Forest area was another place familiar to freighters of yesteryear. This was Carmical, named for Philip G. Carmical, who settled in the area and constructed a cabin in 1872. Carmical was on the main route of travel and became known as the Carmical Station. Later a bridge was constructed over Crooked River near the crossing.

In the desert country east and southeast of Bend and in northern Lake County were many post offices that were abandoned when homesteaders left. They included Rolyat (Taylor spelled backward); Sink, Held, West Branch, Brookings, Woodrow, Connolly, and half a dozen others. Heisler, a stage station and post office, was an important stopping place on the Shaniko-Prineville-Bend Stage Line in pioneer times. One of Central Oregon's post offices of early days was Maude, in the Pony Butte country west of Ashwood.

Opal City, Horse Heaven, and Kilts

One of the better-known communities in the years when railroads were being built was Opal City, north of Crooked River Canyon. For a time, while a bridge was being constructed over Crooked River by the Oregon Trunk in 1910-1911, Opal City was the end of the rails into Central Oregon. In the high country south of the John Day, where a big mercury-mining operation was to be carried out over a period of years, Horse Heaven Post Office was founded; and not far away was Kilts, which largely served the Donnybrook community east of Ashwood.

Not to be overlooked in the story of Central Oregon towns is Hillman, ancestral to Terrebonne, and named after James J. Hill. For a time, Hillman was a name that blazed in promotion literature in an appeal to land seekers. However, in 1909, it was announced that the promoters were in trouble, charged with gross misrepresentation in advertising. The town of Hillman died while being born, and the little town of Terrebonne (good earth) took its place to serve the north rim of Deschutes County.

Four miles from Redmond, Cline Falls long struggled for a

place in the sun, hoping for a railroad and water from the Deschutes. The town was platted on a high western bench of the Deschutes River, overlooking spectacular falls. Several business buildings were erected there, and a number of fine homes were built. One of the homes belonged to a dentist, Dr. C. A. Cline, for whom the town was named. Near the old townsite—from which all buildings have been stripped—are Cline Buttes, scene of a short-lived gold strike in 1904, and many years later the location of radio beacons guiding planes through aerial lanes. Cline Falls was intended to serve as the center of an irrigation area, but when water failed to come to the western Deschutes benchland, the town disappeared. Redmond, to the east, grew.

CHAPTER 16

New Counties Are Formed

ABOUT THE TIME PRINEVILLE set up its city government, there was talk about a new county that would include practically all of Central Oregon. The September 16, 1880 issue of *The Dalles Times* carried this news note from Prineville: "The question of the division of Wasco County is generally being agitated here."

Primary reason for the move to create a new county was the great distance of Prineville and its neighboring communities from the county seat at The Dalles, where all legal business had to be transacted and all court cases tried. Also, the road between Prineville and The Dalles was virtually impassable in the winter months. Residents of the Ochoco—practically all from communities west of the Cascades— never became attached to The Dalles; and residents of The Dalles, still the central city of a western empire, were only remotely concerned with the new settlements in the Ochoco country. About the only interest was on the part of the merchants of The Dalles, who, in an effort to get business from the interior country, contributed funds for road improvement.

Apparently without any great opposition, Crook County was carved from Wasco on October 24, 1882. Wasco originally encompassed nearly all of the region now known as Central Oregon. The John Day River, gnawing its way north to the Columbia, formed part of its boundary; the jagged ridge of the Cascades marked another. Until the breakup came, it included the present counties of Jefferson and Deschutes, as well as a section of Wheeler County.

New counties, however, were not a new idea in the region that was once part of huge Wasco County from which several

149

counties had already been carved. In the early 1890s, new counties "which would have left Wasco nothing but The Dalles and
the cemetery beside it" were even proposed. Cascade County
had been sought to the west of Wasco, where Hood River County was created later. Stockman County and Tygh Valley County
—never created—were sought south and east of Wasco.

The bill creating Crook was introduced in the legislative assembly by Frank Nichols, a representative from Wasco County,
but a resident of Prineville. Nichols went to the legislature
pledged to work for the creation of a new county from the southern part of Wasco. He was also pledged to oppose John H.
Mitchell as U. S. Senator from Oregon. The county-creation
measure went into the legislative hopper early in the session as
House Bill 65. In the House, the measure passed by a large majority, but in the Senate it was tabled without discussion. This
was done in an effort to force Nichols to vote for Senator Mitchell. Nichols refused and started a backfire in the house against
the Senate's tabling the bill that would create Crook.

Crook County Created

Prior to the session, the state treasurer had an opportunity to
pay off about $100,000 of the state's indebtedness, thereby sav-
ing a sum of interest that was large in those days. When the
legislature convened, a bill was introduced in the lower House to
legalize the payment. Through the efforts of Nichols, it was
tabled, in retaliation to the Senate's tabling of the county-creation bill. The stalemate was broken only when the Senate finally
voted for the creation of Crook, which was named for Major-
General Crook of the U. S. Army, who made a brilliant record
in the Civil War. Prior to the Civil War, he served on the western frontier. When the Williamson-Abbot party headed north
from California, in 1855, to seek a possible railroad route through
the Deschutes country, Crook headed a military escort of a hundred men.

The bill designated Prineville as the temporary seat, with the permanent location of county government to be selected at the next election. At that time, Prineville became the permanent county seat.

Three other communities—Cleek, Mill Creek, and Mitchell—had also been suggested. Cleek, which is recalled only by old-timers, got its name from the Henry E. Cleek Ranch on which it was established. It was one of the points on the stage run to Prineville in early days; horses were changed there. Cleek was never a serious contender for the permanent county seat of Crook, but if it had been selected it would have been within "seeing distance" of Madras, a county seat of later years. As for Mill Creek, it was not even a town. It was just a small community on a creek which drains from the high Ochocos to Ochoco Creek, its recognition based mostly on the fact that it was the location of a sawmill, the first in Crook County.

Nichols: "Lost Man of History"

Frank Nichols not only played the leading role in the creation of Crook County, but was once sheriff of a vast segment of the Oregon country, a strip that reached from the Pacific to the summit of the Rockies. A native of Missouri, he crossed the plains by ox team and spent the winter of 1844 and the spring of 1845 at the Whitman Mission. He attended school there for about two months, and that was the extent of his formal education—yet he came to be recognized as one of the region's best-informed men.

After leaving the mission, Nichols went to the Willamette Valley and visited Portland, which at that time was a mere handful of cabins. In territorial days, he was appointed the first sheriff of Polk County, when he was not yet twenty-one years old. "I had a pretty big territory—many times more than I could handle," he once said, adding: "I never saw more than a small section of my bailiwick, but I did the best I could to perform my duties as sheriff, the principal one being to collect taxes."

In 1879, at the age of fifty-four, Nichols moved from Polk

County to the frontier village of Prineville, where he studied law and was admitted to practice. His knowledge of law and his leadership in the inland stock country—of which Prineville was the center—won Nichols a place in the state legislature from Wasco County.

Nichols lived in Prineville during the reign of the Vigilantes. There he saw Prineville grow from a hamlet to a busy range town that boasted of being America's last frontier. In his later years, "Uncle Frank" Nichols, still seeking new frontiers, moved to the little community of Tumalo when the site was known as Laidlaw. Frequently he visited nearby Bend, to meet Marsh Awbrey and other old-timers and talk of the days when Laidlaw vied with the village of Bend to become the metropolis of Central Oregon. At the time of his death in 1920, he was the only surviving appointee of the old Provisional Government of Oregon.

Frank Nichols has been forgotten in Crook County, which he helped to create. No prominent landmark in the range country he knew so well bears his name, but in Deschutes County there is a "Nichols" market road.

Wheeler County Created

Wheeler County was created on February 17, 1899, but not until considerable opposition had been overcome in the counties from which it was formed—Grant, Gilliam, and Crook. As early as 1895, an effort was made to form a new county in the area. The name suggested was Sutton County, which would have honored a pioneer rancher, Al Sutton. Sutton Mountain, overlooking his pioneer ranch on Bridge Creek, now bears the name of the family. The county was eventually named in honor of Henry H. Wheeler, whose narrow escape from death in an Indian attack became part of the region's history.

Gold lured Henry Wheeler west from his native state of Pennsylvania. Eventually he reached The Dalles from Yreka, California, where he had made more money in the lumber business than in mining. In the early 1860s, The Dalles was the gateway to the newly discovered upper John Day River gold fields. Wheeler saw the need of a stage line connecting The Dalles and Canyon City. He prepared an outfit and, in early May 1864, began his first stage trip from The Dalles, with a four-horse team, a lever coach, and eleven passengers. The route led over Sherars Bridge, through the Antelope Valley, and into the John Day country. He made three trips a week, changing horses eight times on each run, at stage stations he had established along the route. On the long trips inland or return, the fare for each passenger was forty dollars.

Wheeler also handled the Wells-Fargo business and had a contract to carry the U. S. Mail. For the mail contract, which he obtained in the spring of 1865, he received twelve thousand dollars annually. In his four years of stage operation, Wheeler lost eighty-nine horses to the Indians; also a stage, and even a stage station at the stop later known as Burnt Ranch. For a time he was with the Ben Holladay firm, but later he entered the stock business in Wheeler County, and for many years lived in Mitchell, beside the road over which he had driven stages in Indian days.

A memorial standing close to U. S. Highway 26, near Mitchell, recalls the place where Wheeler was attacked and shot through the cheek by Indians on September 7, 1866, while he was carrying the mail.

CHAPTER 17

Rule of the Vigilantes

ON A MID-MARCH DAY IN 1882, a rider raced into Prineville from Willow Creek to spread the news that two men had been killed in a property-line dispute. The men were A. H. Crooks and his son-in-law, S. J. Jory. Named as the slayer was a neighbor, Lucius Langdon. Out of that incident developed a dark chapter in the history of Central Oregon, right on the eve of the creation of Crook from Wasco and at the time new Crook County was in its formative stage.

Over a period of two years, before officers were named by a vote of the people in a general election, a group of men, self-styled Vigilantes, rode over bloody trails and through dusty streets. Before this sorry reign was over, nine men were either dead or missing. One died hanging from a juniper, his body riddled by bullets. Two died dangling from bridges. One died as he was dragged through Prineville streets behind a racing horse. Two died under gunfire, with death in one case coming through a window from outer darkness. Six-shooters were heard in the night. One man died at his ranch home; a rancher disappeared and was never found. Threats of death were sent through the mails.

Vigilantes Take Over

The rule of the Vigilantes started on the day Crooks and Jory were killed near a disputed fence line, in the range country northwest of Prineville. It continued until the new county held its first election, on June 2, 1884. That was an election which apparently repudiated the rule by masked riders.

154

Much has been written about the Vigilantes of the Ochoco, but few stories are the same. Some do not agree in any detail. Each side—one represented by the Vigilantes, the other by those who opposed government by six-shooter and rope—had its own version of the killings. The main sources of the history of the short and bloody era were men directly in touch with many of the frontier incidents. One of these was Colonel William Thompson, historian for the Vigilantes. His book, *Reminiscences of a Pioneer*, published in 1912, contains a detailed account of the rule of the masked riders. Another valuable source was James M. Blakely, Crook County's first elected sheriff, who rode on the side of law and order. Blakely, who later served as sheriff of Wallowa County, lived to be over a hundred years old. F. A. Shaver and others who compiled the *History of Central Oregon,* published in 1905, obtained some of their information from men such as these.

The Blakely Story

In 1939, many years after the masked men had made their last ride, Jim Blakely gave to Herbert Lundy of the *Oregonian* an eye-witness story of the stirring days when guns and ropes, not the law, ruled early Crook County. The Blakely story reconciled many of the conflicting versions of previous accounts, especially those dealing with the slaying of Crooks and Jory on a fence line between Willow Creek ranches beyond Grizzly Mountain.

Because spring comes early to the Central Oregon range country, Crooks and his son-in-law, Steve Jory, decided in mid-March 1882, to blaze lines on some government land near the western edge of the Ochoco timber in the Grizzly area, up near the head of lava-lined Willow Creek. This line-blazing work was near the ranch of Lucius Langdon, and already a hard feeling existed between Langdon and Crooks about the property lines. Crooks and Jory worked through the morning. When noon came, they left their axes leaning against a tree near the Langdon barn, and went home to lunch.

"Langdon was waiting when they came back," Blakely recalled. "He shot and killed them both. Then he got on a horse and lit out."

Later that same day, a Trout Creek rancher, who happened to be riding by the Willow Creek ranches, found the bodies. The man was Garrett Maupin, son of the pioneer Howard Maupin, who was in on the killing of Chief Paulina years before. It was Maupin who rode into Prineville to spread the word that Crooks and Jory had been murdered. At the time, the area was still a part of Wasco County, with Deputy Sheriff J. L. Luckey of Wasco representing the law. Working for Langdon when the two ranchers were shot was young W. H. Harrison. Blakely, later to serve as Crook County's first elected sheriff, said Harrison was in Prineville that day and had nothing to do with the murders.

Within minutes after Maupin brought the news that two men had been killed on Willow Creek, a loosely-organized posse, including Harrison, rode out from Prineville, following shortcuts to the Langdon ranch. There they found the bodies on the ground, each apparently instantly killed with rifle fire. Langdon, the man accused of the double murder, was not in the vicinity.

As darkness enveloped the ranch country, a posse was organized on the Langdon ranch, and out of that posse grew the Vigilantes who were to rule the region for about two years. Some of the leaders of the group suspected that Langdon might have gone to the home of his brother on Mill Creek, seventeen miles north of Prineville. Part of the posse went there that night, returning with the word that Langdon had run away from the house and disappeared in the darkness when a barking dog warned of the approach of riders.

On the following night, Blakely and some companions rode to Langdon's ranch home. In the darkness, a dog barked again, Blakely reported, adding, "I saw Langdon mount a white horse in front of the house, jump the horse over a ditch, and start for the road. We carried rifles and pistols, but there wasn't any occasion for gun play. I called out for him to stop and he rode right up to me. Mrs. Langdon was at the door of the house, screaming."

Blakely identified himself to Mrs. Langdon. Then Langdon and the men went into the house, where Mrs. Langdon prepared supper. After supper, Blakely notified the Crooks and Jory families that Langdon had been taken prisoner. A warrant had been issued for Harrison, but he was not arrested as Blakely vouched that the man had been in Prineville at the time of the shooting.

The posse returned with Langdon to Prineville after midnight, following a long ride around the slopes of Grizzly. There the prisoner was turned over to Luckey, who took him to a hotel. Meanwhile Harrison had been arrested. At daylight on March 17, 1882, the wild ringing of the Prineville school bell awakened people of the village. Shortly before the bell sounded, the Vigilantes had seized Harrison, dragging him through the streets behind a galloping horse, while people watched in horror from doors and windows. The race ended at a bridge, from which Harrison was hanged. Langdon had already been shot and killed in the hotel by masked men.

Sheriff Luckey's Story

In a letter to Sheriff Storrs of Wasco County, Deputy Sheriff Luckey gave his version of the double lynching:

. . . Blakely woke me up (about 2 a.m.) saying they had captured Langdon and wanted to turn him over to me. I went down to the stable office where they had him, put the shackles on him, took him into the hotel, had a good fire built, and told Langdon to get some sleep on the lounge. I sat down by the stove to guard him. The town was soon aroused. Quite a number of men came in to see Langdon, I suspect through morbid curiosity. W. C. Foren, deputy marshal, came in and stayed with me. Harrison went to bed, and about 4 a.m. got up and sat by the stove.

As I was sitting at the stove with my back to the front door, the door was suddenly opened and I was caught and thrown backwards on the floor and firmly held while my eyes were blindfolded. Immediately a pistol was fired rapidly five or six times.

I heard someone groan, and at the same time the firing ceased. Harrison was hurried from the room. I could tell it was him by his cries. The doors were closed and I was allowed to get up. I went to Langdon and found him dead. I looked around and saw a masked man standing at each door, warning by ominous signs that no one was to leave the room. As soon as they were satisfied that Langdon was dead, they left.

At daylight I took some men to help search for Harrison, and found him hanging from a banister of the Crooked River iron bridge. The town is quiet today . . . I feel conscious of having done my duty as an officer, so there I let the matter rest.

Actually there were three versions of the slaying of Crooks and Jory and the lynching of Langdon and Harrison. One was the brief written report submitted by Deputy Luckey to Sheriff Storrs of The Dalles a few days after the deaths of the four men. The second was a reference to the killings by Colonel Thompson in his book. The third was that of Blakely in the *Oregonian* on March 12, 1939. Primarily the accounts vary in reports on the search for Langdon following the shooting of Crooks and Jory, and events that took place just prior to the lynching of Langdon and Harrison.

In his version, fifty-seven years after the shooting and lynching, Blakely cast doubt on many of Colonel Thompson's statements. He also questioned part of Luckey's report to Sheriff Storrs, but basically the facts are these: Crooks and Jory were murdered while they worked on line fence, and Langdon and Harrison were lynched by a mob. Out of these events grew the Crook County Vigilantes.

Vigilantes Strike Again

Unified by the lynchings on that bloody night of March 16-17, the Vigilantes banded together to become a powerful force in Crook County. They organized formally as a "stock association," but generally continued to dictate frontier rule from the saddle. They struck violently again on the night of Christmas Eve that same year, killing Al Swartz in the Burmeister saloon while he was playing cards. The bullet came through a window from the outer darkness. Swartz reportedly had defied the Vigilantes. On that same night, masked riders went to the home of W. C. and J. M. Barnes, where they hanged two young men, Sidney Huston and Charles Luster. The Vigilantes charged that one of the youths was planning to steal some horses, but opponents of the Vigilantes had a different explanation for the lynchings. They said that Luster, a jockey, had agreed to throw a race, but instead had bet sixty dollars on his own horse, which he rode and won.

Not long after this episode, Steve Staats, a member of a pioneer family, was shot under mysterious circumstances at his ranch near Powell Butte, about ten miles southwest of Prineville. Staats had openly condemned the Vigilantes for lynching Harrison. The Vigilantes were also blamed for the death of Shorty Davis, who lived on a small ranch near Prineville. He disappeared about the time that Staats was killed.

Shortly after Huston and Luster were lynched, Mike Mogan was shot to death in the Burmeister saloon. This possibly was not a direct act of the Vigilantes, for the slayer was known. Then came the death of Mogan's brother, Frank Mogan, on December 18, 1883. He was shot by Colonel William "Bud" Thompson. In his *Reminiscences of a Pioneer,* Thompson later attempted to justify his shooting.

The slaying of the Mogan brothers finally brought things to a head. The break came when some men, headed by Jim Blakely, openly defied the Vigilantes. The Vigilantes warned, "If Jim Blakely doesn't watch his step, he will be going up the hill feet first some day." The "hill" was the pioneer cemetery on a flat just north of town, overlooking the green Crooked River Valley. Blakely and his men adopted the name "Moonshiners" because they kept lookout stations at night when masked men rode. Old-timers said that one of these stations was on top of an early-day flour mill in Prineville.

The Moonshiners were not a gun-slinging, night-riding outfit. Most of them were established residents of Prineville, whose leaders realized that new Crook County was off to a bad start in law enforcement and was remiss in its obligations to the state which had just approved its creation from Wasco. Soon the Moonshiners had expanded into an organization of about seventy-five, and all were men who had played a part in shaping Oregon's new Ochoco frontier.

One day when the Moonshiners were sufficiently strong, they decided to make a show of force. Fully armed and astride fine horses, they rode down Prineville's main street. The little community had never seen such a display of power. Here, they agreed, was a militia with law on its side and determined men in the saddle. Furthermore, the men were unmasked, and all were known to their neighbors.

In one of the saloons, when the "cavalry of Crooked River" rode past, was a group of Vigilantes. The Moonshiners dared them to come out, but they remained in the building.

End of the Vigilantes

That ride by Jim Blakely and his armed men through the dusty streets of Prineville ended the rule of the Vigilantes. When the first regular election was held in Crook County in June 1884, practically all who opposed the Vigilantes were elected, most of them sworn to rid the area of the masked riders.

Because of the deaths with which they were charged, the Vigilantes did not dare to apologize openly for their short rule; yet in later years through unsigned letters and remarks to friends, they let it be known that they considered their stern rule necessary because of the lack of law and order prior to the June 1884 election—when voters had a chance to name men with community backing. Backers of the Vigilantes also noted that, in its pioneer days, Prineville had only deputies as county representatives.

Sherars Bridge was the gateway to Central Oregon from the early 1860s until a railroad was built to Shaniko in 1900. Pictured downstream here, under the bridge, is the narrowest defile in the entire Deschutes Canyon. The old 33-room hotel of Joe Sherar is shown at the left with barn at the edge of the river. State Highway 216 now crosses the Deschutes at this point. None of the building remains.

etherow Crossing on the Deschutes River was well known to families of pioneer days who rossed the Santiam Divide en route to Prineville. The A. J. Tetherow ranch, in background, was a night stopping place for many on the long drive.

On the long drive from Bend to Shaniko in pioneer days, it was not uncommon to meet freight teams like this one, bound for the interior. This eight-horse rig, with its three freight-laden wagons, was photographed in the timber south of Bend.

Freighters frequently found it necessary to "double teams" in the long haul into Central Oregon from Shaniko. In this scene south of Bend, fourteen horses teamed up to draw the wagon through the snow.

Shaniko was the end of the rails in Central Oregon for ten years before the railroads came, first to Madras, and later to Redmond and Bend. Two stages are pictured here, crossing Grizzly Mountain, on the route to Prineville.

Antelope, on the old gold trail between The Dalles and Canyon City, was a small town when this picture was taken in 1891. The view is north toward the high country, where Shaniko was later to take shape. Note the cattle wandering through the street.

This store-hotel is one of the few business houses remaining in the "ghost town" of Ashwood. During the boom days on Trout Creek, this was a busy center. Ash Butte, overlooking the creek was on the range of Chief Paulina.

Madras was awaiting the railroads when this picture was taken in early 1910. One line came out of the gorge through Gateway, the other up Willow Creek. The Hill and Harriman system ended their struggle for right-of-way a short distance south of Madras, at Metolius.

Even when Crook County was created in 1882, its only law officer, with the exception of a marshal in Prineville, was a deputy. When Crooks and Jory were murdered and Langdon and
Harrison were lynched, this information did not go to Sheriff
Storrs in The Dalles by telephone, telegraph, or express rider.
Deputy Luckey reported the events in a letter that took two
days to reach The Dalles.

In the few years that Crook County was ruled by Vigilantes,
Prineville was a village—a town of one dusty main street near
the banks of the Ochoco. There were four saloons. Til Glaze
operated one and Dick Graham another. Then there were the
Kelley and the Burmeister establishments. Incidentally, Dick
Graham was the coroner, most of whose business developed in
competitive saloons.

Crook County needed strong law enforcement in those early
years, but two men carried the load—a town marshal and a
deputy whose superior officer was in The Dalles. After the
Vigilantes made their last ride, Crook again became a rapidly
developing stock country, its serenity disturbed only by a brief
range war. Residents of Prineville were proud of the vast ranges
beyond the hills, referring to the region as "the West's last frontier."

CHAPTER 18

Tombstone Tells Story

Silver Lake is a quiet village in a broad valley—a great bowl in northern Lake County fringed by timbered mountains and tilted rims. Its main street is part of a fast, modern highway, the Fremont. Not so many years ago, that highway was a dusty road, part of the early network that had distant Shaniko, then the end of the rails, as its center.

A community known to few Oregonians, Silver Lake is surrounded by the open range, part of it in the timber, part in the sage country. Outside Silver Lake, ranch homes are scattered. To the south and east of the town is the lake from which the community gets its name. Size of the shallow lake varies from year to year, depending on weather conditions. Geologists say that it is a mere remnant of a much larger body of water—an ancestral lake of the pluvial days following the last of the ice ages. Old Silver Lake joined vanished Fort Rock Lake; it spread northeast to form a giant embayment known as Christmas Lake, and flooded Thorn Lake basin. In that large but shallow lake of the Pleistocene, the now-arid Connley Hills were islands.

Old Silver Lake was an imposing body of water, deeply flooding the site of the town that bears its name. Over it flocked many waterfowl, and on its shores grazed two species of camels, a tribe of horses no longer represented, and herds of bison. One of the old arms of Silver Lake bears the name Fossil Lake—a name significant because of the discoveries of bones of animals and birds found there through the years. The lake is now dry, and on warm summer afternoons, sun devils twist across its surface as thunderheads appear over the southern rims.

162

Thomas Condon was the first to trace the ancient story of Silver Lake. He found many fossil bones there, "black and glistening" in the dry bed of the old lake. Among them were some arrowheads, but these apparently were not of the same age. They probably settled down among the older fossils as winds whipped away the silts and sands.

The first settlement of the Silver Lake country occurred in the early 1870s, on the road between Lakeview, near the California line, and The Dalles far to the north. There were already a number of ranchers in the basin when Condon arrived to search for the black bones of elephants, sloths, giant beavers, and camels. A post office was established in December of 1875 in this range-land outpost, sometimes called the "gateway to the desert." The office was in a small log cabin, nine miles east of the town's present site. In 1884, H. F. West homesteaded the site under Preemption Claim laws, and four years later he platted the town of Silver Lake. Estimating that the new town would require about fifteen blocks, he set these aside—but they were never fully used.

Establishment of Central Oregon towns closely followed the same pattern; they were all in the range country, where horses had to be shod, farm machinery repaired, wagon wheels tightened, and plow shares sharpened, so—one of the first businesses set up was a blacksmith shop. This pattern held true for Silver Lake. In 1888, the year Silver Lake was platted, Sam Allison opened such a shop, beside the road that swung in from the north and headed south over Picture Rock Pass into the Summer Lake country.

By the beginning of 1894, Silver Lake, founded close to Buck and Bridge creeks, had grown to a town of about fifty people and served a region that reached up the valley into the Fort Rock area, east past Thorn Lake, and south toward Winter Ridge.

In this village, on Christmas Eve, 1894, occurred Oregon's worst fire tragedy. Forty-three people died or were fatally burned, trapped in a second-story auditorium-dance hall above the F. M. Chrisman store. The fire started when a hanging kerosene lamp was accidentally tipped by a man who stood on a bench, better to see the Christmas program being presented by youngsters in the high-windowed room.

Fire Tragedy Described

On the evening of December 24, about two hundred people, most of them from the surrounding range areas, gathered at the J. H. Clayton hall for the Christmas party. Most of the program was presented on a stage at the end of the big rectangular room. Downstairs, the store was busy because of the many people in town, many of them doing their Christmas shopping. Survivors recalled in later years that everybody within riding distance was there.

The big Christmas tree, covered with cotton, was not on the stage, but between the only two windows in the room. Board benches had been placed so everybody could sit down. George Payne, though, stood on a bench for a better view. When his head hit a coal-oil lamp suspended from the ceiling, the tipped lamp immediately became a torch, starting a fire that claimed the lives of forty-three persons, including entire families. Many of the victims were children.

When the lamp fell to the floor, the flames quickly spread and the cotton-decorated tree caught fire. As panic spread through the hall, many of those outside tried to get in to help. People blocked the one exit of the auditorium, and the outside balcony, at the top of the wooden stairs, gave way under the great weight. All those on the balcony plunged to the ground. About a dozen people clambered through a broken window, from which billowed heavy smoke. The door, which opened inward, soon jammed. A ladder was placed against one of the windows, but few escaped that way.

Even as flames were still sweeping through the building and rescue attempts continued, Ed O'Farrell raced south to get medical help. The nearest physician was Dr. Bernard Daly of Lakeview, about one hundred miles away. While changing horses on his ride to Lakeview, O'Farrell arranged to have others ready for Dr. Daly. The story of the doctor's ride through the lonely range country to the fire scene is a saga of western medical history. On his arrival at Silver Lake, he cared for a dozen seriously injured people, and some twenty others with slight injuries and burns.

Only charred skeletons remained in the ashes and embers when they cooled. A community funeral was held, and burial was in a common grave. In the Silver Lake cemetery, adjacent to the Fremont Highway a quarter of a mile south of town, stands an impressive granite memorial to mark the site of the grave. Sand-blasting winds have whipped through the little cemetery in many storms since the Christmas Eve tragedy, but the names of those who perished can still be read.

The town of Silver Lake did not die in that terrible fire of long ago. In the timber rush and homestead era following the turn of the century, it became a busy place, serving both the old, established ranches and the homesteaders. Gradually most of the homesteaders left, and for a decade or more, Silver Lake was a quiet village—only to enjoy a new prosperity when the Fremont Highway was routed over its main street prior to World War II. In the late 1950s, Bonneville power began providing electricity for the operation of irrigation pumps.

Small pine mills have also come to the area, and over the Fremont Highway come tourists, many of whom stop to hunt Indian artifacts around the shores of old lakes or to hunt for fossils in the sage country off to the east. Over Silver Lake's main street, the route of Oregon's Highway 31, occasionally move herds of cattle, reminding residents of the town's pioneer past.

Fort Rock

Near the northern edge of the old lake basin is the village of Fort Rock, named for the nearby spectacular landmark of the same name, an isolated landform whose origin has long mystified geologists. It is a steep-walled semicircle rising 325 feet above the desert floor at its highest point, and measuring about three-fourths of a mile in diameter. Sage plains reach away from the formation in all directions. It got its name in 1873 when a Lake County rancher, William "Yankee" Sullivan, rode into the area on a cattle roundup, noted the landform's similarity to a huge fortress, and called it Fort Rock.

Fort Rock stands as one of Oregon's most interesting volcanic phenomena. Some geologists believe that volcanic mud, spraying from deep central craters, formed it. They call it a tuff ring —one of many in the area. Apparently it is an eroded remnant of a giant tuff ring which built up in the basin when a lake still covered the area. Its story is probably this: a volcano began in the shallow lake, hurling up fine ash and rock fragments which fell back to earth in a rim surrounding the crater. Volcanic explosions were followed by a slumping of crater walls, with rock rolling back to the vent to form a plug. Water rushing into the crater and the volcanic throat provided steam for other explosions. Waves of the old lake apparently had a part in sculpturing the present formation.

Attempts have been made through the years to attach a legend to the unique formation; and it has been said, without any historical backing, that the fort-like landmark was a scene of a battle long ago between Indians and whites. Arrow points and spear tips have been found in the area, but it is likely that they were used by ancient hunters, not in a battle lost to Oregon history.

Fort Rock was a busy village in homesteading days, when bottom lands that are now dusty were grass covered, and dairy herds grazed in the area. Now it is only a small trading post for nearby ranchers and for the visitors who drive in seasonally from the Fremont Highway to view the historic landmark.

Fremont

About five miles from Fort Rock, westerly across the sage, is the site of Fremont, one of the basin's "ghost towns." This was a busy village for a time, when it appeared that Fort Rock and the adjacent valley would become an important dairying center. Fremont even had a cheese factory. The vanished town was not far from Fremont National Forest, from which it apparently got its name. The forest, of course, was named for Captain John C. Fremont, who explored Central Oregon in 1843 and discovered Summer Lake from heights of Winter Ridge, south of Silver Lake.

Only a few posts today mark the site of Fremont. On the now-barren site, a notched stump remains a tourist attraction. The stump, with the notches serving as stairs, was used by women of the village to mount their horses, in the era of side saddles.

Fort Rock, Sink, Wastina, and other towns of the basin were the result of attempts to farm the valley, near the end of an unusually wet cycle. Some good crops were produced and meadows cultivated in years of high moisture, but then came a period of dry years when it became evident that crops could not be grown without irrigation.

CHAPTER 19

Farewell Bend

SPRAWLED ACROSS THE DESCHUTES, directly east of the Three Sisters, is the young town of Bend, founded in 1904. Its site was marked by only a few scattered cabins when Vigilantes rode the Central Oregon ranges, yet the site of this city has a history dating back to a stormy December day in 1834. At that time Nathaniel J. Wyeth, trader, trapper, and patriot, passed through the present location of Bend and headed up the Deschutes to make the first recorded passage of white men through the area. Nine years earlier, Peter Skene Ogden and his trappers had ridden upstream on Crooked River over the Prineville location.

In 1843, came explorer John C. Fremont, toting a cannon across Tumalo Creek to the west of Bend. The next recorded visit was that of the survivors of the Clark massacre in the fall of 1851. Other wagons, some of them from the "lost train" of 1853, in attempting to follow the new Elliott cutoff, rumbled out of the junipers and sagebrush to the east. They halted on the Deschutes River, while scouts tried to find a pass over the Cascades in the Three Sisters area. Finally they discovered blazes that led them south to Diamond Peak.

Eventually came the hunters, the stockmen, and the ranchers. There is little record of the activity of early hunters in the upper Deschutes country until the arrival of the first stockmen. Stockmen found weathered cabins and lean-tos of hunters in the up-river country and reported hearing stories that some of the hunters obtained as many as five hundred deer hides in a single season.

Indians Lived on "Bend of River"

Long before the first whites reached the upper Deschutes country, Indians lived near the "bend of the river." Called by tribesmen the Towornehiooks, the stream was apparently a favored camping spot for natives of the region, being easily accessible from the antelope country to the east and from the pine country to the west. Small meadows along the river, open glades, and riverside vegetation provided feed for the ponies, and deer and antelope came in from the desert to water at the river.

Obsidian spear points and beautifully shaped arrowheads marked the site of old camps in the Bend area. Caches of skinning knives, shaped from volcanic glass, have also been found there—some under three feet of dust. This volcanic glass—obsidian—possibly was brought from Newberry Crater, some forty miles to the south, when that high caldera was free of snow. Another likely source of obsidian was Glass Buttes, seventy miles to the east. Other possible sources were in the Three Sisters area. In 1932, a cache of perfect spear points was discovered in a rocky ledge close to the Deschutes in Bend. The abundance of chipped obsidian indicates that Indians made their homes here seasonally over a long period.

Upstream on the Deschutes, one of Oregon's present big irrigation reservoirs—Wickiup of the North Unit District—got its name from old wigwam poles. These wickiups—frames of which were fashioned from willows and lodgepole pine—stood on low grounds adjacent to the river. Even after the first hunters and ranchers came, the bleached-pole skeletons of the wickiups remained to tell their story of the past. At summer camps, the first people of the basin ground roots and seeds, skinned deer and antelope, and lived the carefree life of Indians who shifted their hunting grounds as seasons changed and game moved. To the east of Bend is a cave that possibly served as winter quarters for the first "permanent" residents of the area.

Wagons from the North

In the late fall of 1867, a caravan of wagons laden with supplies for the Indians on the Klamath Reservation is the first recorded passage of vehicles over the full length of the region now crossed by U. S. Highway 97, from the Columbia River to the Klamath Basin. That caravan traveled a largely unmapped route from Fort Dalles to Fort Klamath. Heading the train was J. W. Perit Huntington, superintendent of Indian affairs in Oregon. The wagons circled into formation in camp at or near the present Bend site on the evening of November 4.

With the supply train were some seventy men—Warm Springs scouts, United States soldiers, teamsters, and a group of Klamath and Modoc scouts. As provided under the Indian Treaty of 1864, the wagons were carrying to the agency supplies for the Modocs, Klamaths, and a small band of Paiutes. Feeding on range grass as they moved south with the wagons were sixty head of beef cattle.

Captain O. C. Applegate of Klamath Falls, a member of the party that met the train near the Madras location, recalled long afterward that the Bend camp site was a busy place on that November night in 1867. In the west, the Cascade peaks were already white with snow. Campfires blazed in the junipers and pines; teamsters watered their stock in the Deschutes and fed them under the trees. Cooks were busy around their fires. Indian scouts set up their own camps, apart from those of the whites. Out in the marginal pines, where Bend homes later were to be built, guards were on the alert, fearful that surviving small bands of Indians might attempt a raid on the stock, especially the fat cattle; but the night passed peacefully.

Winter gripped the Klamath basin when the Huntington supply wagons finally pulled into Fort Klamath. The journey from the Bend site had taken nearly a month, and much of it had been over an old Indian trail.

Ghost Rider of Ranges Arrives

Passage of the supply wagons through the Deschutes country was followed by seven quiet years. Young jackpines quickly grew to hide the paths chopped for the wagons on that first recorded north-south passage, part of it over the route of the Elliott train of 1853. Then, on a fall day in 1874, came the "ghost rider of the ranges"—the first person to file on land now within the city limits of Bend. His name is unknown, but he is not mythical. On October 21, he filed for and received General Land Office No. 2896, Oregon City series, with settlement alleged as of July 11, 1874. There is a possibility that this rider, Bend's first legal settler, never spent a night in the area, unless he spread his blankets under the stars and listened to the Deschutes as it slipped past willows fringing the bank of the stream. Part of the area he filed on is now covered by Bend's far-famed Mirror Pond. On March 10, 1880, S. S. Splaun, who is believed to have been a representative for a Crooked River stockman, filed on practically the same land on which "Homesteader No. 2896" had filed in 1874. Splaun did not make final proof.

Three years later, in 1877, another rangeman rode into the Bend area, a man who was to play an important role in the pioneer history of this region during the closing decades of the nineteenth century. This was John Y. Todd, the man who built the first bridge across the Deschutes at the Sherar site, in 1860. He had tired of carrying supplies by pack train between The Dalles and Canyon City and had returned to ranching. Todd rode into the upper Deschutes country to look over the range. He liked this region where pines from the eastern Cascades reached across the river to intermingle with junipers, where abundant grass grew in the marginal timber, and where cold springs fed the Deschutes in the high country. Todd bought the relinquishment of Tom Geer on land near the southern edge of the Bend site, a place that was becoming known as the Farewell Bend Ranch. For the ranch rights, Todd gave Geer $60 in cash and two saddle horses. U. S. Land Office records show that the place was not filed on again after the relinquishment until 1878. The new filing was by John T. Storrs, a friend of Todd's and later sheriff of Wasco (1880-1884). Apparently Storrs filed on the land to hold it until Todd could take over.

To that ranch on the east side of the Deschutes, in a cove with a meadow reaching to the water's edge, Todd moved his cattle from the Warm Springs Indian Reservation and the Wapinitia ranges. In a big fall roundup, in 1877, Todd and his riders gathered some twelve hundred head of cattle. After moving the big herd across to the east side of the Deschutes from the reservation, the riders permitted the cattle to range widely, but always kept them pointed for the upper Deschutes basin. To keep up with his shifting stock operations, Todd established headquarters at Squaw Flat, north of old Camp Polk in the Sisters country.

In the following year, 1878, Todd made a final cleanup operation on the Wapinitia range, gathering about eight hundred more cattle. These he drove directly to the Farewell Bend range. He also moved his ranch headquarters to the Deschutes from the temporary location on Squaw Flat. His cattle covered the country from the Grandview and Metolius River areas south to the Farewell Bend Ranch on the Deschutes. They ranged no farther south than the Big Meadows, primarily because a little range war had developed between Todd and Joel Allen. Mostly it was a war of words, an attempted stampede of cattle by "spooking," and a lawsuit. Actually, both men were fighting over government range.

A cabin was built by Todd in 1879 on the forks of the Big and Little rivers in the upper Deschutes basin. The old building later became known as the Dorris cabin. Felix Dorris was Todd's cattle foreman in the Big Meadows district.

Cattle Brought over Cascades

In 1879, Barney D. Springer and Douglas Strope brought a herd of cattle over the Cascades from the Willamette Valley, to get some of the fine range in the upper Deschutes country. Todd eliminated competition by buying the cattle and hiring Springer to ride for him. At this point, John Storr's name disappeared from official records as legal owner of the Farewell Bend Ranch. Springer made the new filing, to hold a strategic ranch for Todd. In later days, especially in the upper Crooked River region, this practice was known as "government land frauding," but it was a common practice in early days. Filings were made under the Pre-emption Claim Land Act. To get title, a person was required to pay the government $1.25 an acre.

Todd's son, John C., once wrote:

John Y. Todd made quite a place out of the Old Farewell Bend Ranch. He raised feed for the horses and milk cows, furnished hay for the teams and saddle horses, and kept a man on the ranch at all times. Most of the time that Todd controlled the place, a man named Smeltzer worked for him.

Smeltzer used to get up mornings, light his fire, go the short distance to the Deschutes, catch enough trout for breakfast, and be back by the time the frying pan was hot. Old-timers said Smeltzer did not hunt deer; he just waited for them to come down to the river to drink, then knocked them over. A person did not have to look for horns before shooting in those days. The deer season was always open, and the early residents had fresh venison whenever they wanted it.

Old-timers said that this cattle baron of the interior country, John Y. Todd, had slept under the stars more than any other person in Oregon.

In the summer of 1881, John Sisemore, a Kentuckian who had spent most of his youth roaming the West, unpacked his mule and pitched camp at the Farewell Bend Ranch. John Y. Todd, operator of that ranch, and Sisemore greeted each other in typical western fashion. They joined in an evening meal; then, late into the night, the two men sat in front of a stone fireplace in the ranch house discussing the merits of stock raising on the Deschutes.

The following day, Todd showed Sisemore around the ranch.

Among other details, Sisemore noted that the "back wall of the fireplace was 35 miles thick." It had been built against a rocky rim facing a meadow on the Deschutes.

The Kentuckian was impressed with the possibilities of grazing stock on the High Desert to the east in the winter months and early spring, and on the lush meadows of the Cascade forest in the summer. The vastness of the adjacent government range also interested him. Besides, Todd was ready to sell because of the failure of his cattle drive in 1880. The result was that John Sisemore purchased Todd's relinquishment and acquired the Farewell Bend Ranch.

Returning to Fort Klamath, where his stock were being pastured, Sisemore—assisted by Jack Pelton, Pete Barneburg, and Henry Ward—started trailing his stock north to the new range. It was already late in the season. As the drive finally got well under way, a severe snowstorm occurred. Cattle scattered widely in the stormy night as heavy winds whipped the new snow into drifts. Only with the help of Klamath Indians were the riders able to round up the herd and move the cattle back to Fort Klamath, where they spent the winter. Some animals were lost.

In the spring of 1882, Sisemore drove the depleted herd to the Deschutes range. Soon his family joined him, to become one of the first families of Farewell Bend. All but Sisemore himself moved back and forth between Sams Valley, their earlier home in Jackson County, and Farewell Bend; Sisemore lived at the ranch winter and summer to take care of the stock. When the community became "thickly settled," his family moved permanently to the ranch.

Later, the old Sisemore place became the site of the Farewell Bend Hotel, a stopping place for travel through the region, competing with the W. H. Staats' stopping place for the patronage of travelers. The two places were only about a mile apart, on the east bank of the Deschutes. Competition finally reached the point where Sisemore, at his own expense, constructed a bridge across the Deschutes in front of his place—then presented the span to the county, which was Crook at the time. It was a move to pull travel that way, past or to the Sisemore Farewell Bend Hotel.

This bridge, the first ever constructed for public use in the immediate Bend area, was 285 feet long and cost Sisemore a dollar a foot. It was placed in use in 1904. Since Sisemore was then Crook County's road supervisor in the Farewell Bend precinct, he was authorized to collect personal poll taxes to pay most of the cost of the bridge.

That same year, 1904, Sisemore sold the historic ranch to Dr. W. S. Nichols, from Oklahoma. Dr. Nichols paid $6,000 for the 240-acre ranch, which in pioneer days had been purchased for $60 plus two saddle horses. Dr. Nichols immediately made plans to convert the bottom land along the Deschutes into a fruit farm, selling the timber on the land to the Pilot Butte Development Company. He planted some two thousand strawberry vines and many apple, prune, and other fruit trees. It looked as though the Farewell Bend Ranch, long headquarters for riders of the Deschutes ranges, was to become the first fruit center of the upper Deschutes; but Nichols failed to take into consideration the cool climate of the plateau that pushes into the Cascade foothills. Only the strawberry plants bore fruit.

Such is the varied history of the Farewell Bend Ranch—first the headquarters of John Y. Todd and his riders; later, the home of John Sisemore and his family; still later, the approach to the first span over the Deschutes in the Bend area, and finally the center of an orchard that never bore fruit. Eventually it was to have a significant industrial history—location of the multimillion-dollar Brooks-Scanlon pine manufacturing plant.

Bend's first school was on the Farewell Bend Ranch. It was taught in a log cabin, erected in the autumn of 1881 by George, Charles, and Walter O'Neil, under the supervision of their father, E. M. O'Neil, whose wife was the first teacher. Five children were enrolled that first year.

Not a scrap of sawed timber was available when the O'Neil boys started construction of the school. Logs were hewn for the foundation, and other logs were cut to the required length for the walls, and chinks were filled with clay, mixed with hair and grass. Classes were taught in the pioneer school more than twenty years before Bend was incorporated. In 1877, the school moved "up town," to another log cabin, which for many years stood in Bend's Drake Park.

In the 1890s, the little outpost community on the Deschutes had a sort of dual personality. By some it was known as Farewell Bend. How the Farewell Bend name originated—a name later given to a city after the U. S. Postal Department lopped off the "Farewell" part—John C. Todd explained:

The major part of the travel through the Bend country in early days was headed north. These people followed down the upper stretches of the Deschutes, through the meadow country, and saw many bends in the river. To avoid the lava areas, they traveled northeast past Lava Butte, striking the river again at another large bend. When they headed northeast from this bend toward a crossing of Crooked River upstream from Smith Rock, they knew they would not see another bend. Instead of saying "goodbye river," they said farewell to the bends of the river. This was how the old ranch got its name, Farewell Bend.

To others, the little community was known as Deschutes, again because of its location on that stream. Some called it Staats' place. Still others called it Pilot Butte, because only a stone's throw to the east, at the edge of the High Desert, was an old volcanic cone named Pilot Butte. Close to the Farewell Bend Ranch was the stopping place of William H. Staats, serious competitor for the trade in the area.

The Staats trading post, though, did have one advantage: in the summer season the Staats store was in a position to offer patrons from the hills and dusty roads, the fresh vegetables grown in his fine, irrigated garden on the bend of the river. This was the first irrigated garden on the Deschutes in Central Oregon, aside from the one on the Tetherow ranch downstream some twenty-five miles. Water was raised from the river through a bucket mill. Circling buckets on a big, rotating wheel dipped into the river, carried their water to the level of the garden, then dumped the flow into irrigation ditches.

Staats' place was patronized by riders of the sage country, sheepmen en route to Cascade camps, hunters, and anglers. Business was brisk most of the year, except during the winter months, despite the competition of the nearby Farewell Bend Ranch and its facilities for travelers.

"Farewell Bend" Shortened

In 1886, Sisemore decided that there were enough people in the community to warrant application for a post office. It would be an office that provided service for the entire Deschutes basin and would bring trade to the stopping place. Naturally he favored Farewell Bend as the name for the office. True, there was a Farewell Bend in the far eastern part of the state, on the old immigrant road leading from the Snake River to the Blue Mountains, but that place was not even a community and had no post office. However, postal officials in Washington, D. C., knew nothing about Farewell Bend or the proud history of the old ranch—or the role it played in the north-south sweep of travel through the region.

Deciding that the name Farewell Bend was too long, they marked out the "Farewell" and notified John Sisemore that the official name of the new post office was Bend. The Bend office was opened for business on January 18, 1886. Its location was the Sisemore cabin, back a short distance from the Deschutes River, and John Sisemore was its postmaster.

The little post office had its ups and downs, and was discontinued on May 1, 1899, apparently because William H. Staats, in his nearby stopping place on the Deschutes, had appeared in the picture. Staats was named postmaster on April 18, 1899, shortly before Sisemore's office was discontinued. Records covering the history of the post office are a bit confused for this period, but apparently some persons desired to change the name of the office to Pilot Butte. This was ordered on May 13, 1901, yet for some reason the name was never used.

Bill Staats had platted a townsite right under the nose of his neighbor and competitor, John Sisemore. The new townsite was named Deschutes, Oregon, on December 30, 1902, when the village of Bend, still not sure of its name, was taking shape under the guidance of Alexander M. Drake.

After Staats obtained the change in the name of the Bend Post Office to Deschutes, the office continued under that name until June 30, 1906. However, comparatively few referred to the slow-growing community as Deschutes, It was called "Staats," "The Bend," "Farewell Bend," or "Bend." A few residents of the range community asked that their mail be addressed to "Pilot Butte, Oregon."

Mail Brought from Prineville

Staats' trading post had a typical western frontier background. Stages from Prineville in early years of the century swung in there on a dusty road, over a low, rocky rim just east of the river. From the Staats place, those same stages headed south for Rosland, on the long drive into the Silver Lake country.

A number of stockmen purchased their summer supplies at the little store on the Deschutes and got their mail at the Staats Post Office, officially known at the time as Deschutes. Mail was brought to the Deschutes Post Office from Prineville, over a wagon road that wandered through sagebrush and around old junipers. Prineville was the nearest town—capital of a range country that reached from the Cascade crest to the Harney Hills and the pines of the Ochocos. Prior to 1900, the nearest railroad point was The Dalles, nearly 150 miles to the north, over a rugged road whose course was dictated by cliffs, two river crossings, and many steep grades.

In the winter months, the dual community of Farewell Bend

and the Staats place, as well as the Sidney Stearns ranch a short distance downstream, was virtually isolated from the outside world. Heavy snows generally blocked roads to the south. Frequently the road to Prineville was covered by drifts. A winter drive to The Dalles was practically impossible, and the roads over the McKenzie and Santiam divides were used only in the summer months.

The old Staats place has a history that dates back to the late sixties. In 1868, Edwin W. Follett, later of Michigan, came to the Deschutes region to hunt and trap. He was accompanied by several companions. Their headquarters during part of the time was in a cabin near the Staats' home of later years. At that cabin and in nearby lean-tos the trappers stockpiled their deer hides. Furs and hides were floated down the Deschutes at least part of the way by boats. Many years later, Follett told of losing most of a winter's take of deer hides when a boat overturned in the river.

Through the years, other stockmen settled along the east bank of the Deschutes just north of Farewell Bend and the Staats home. One of these was D. C. Hubbard, the rangeman who located on the river near the spot where the Pilot Butte Inn was later built. Another of the early-day settlers on the Bend site was James Montgomery. His place was near the Hubbard cabin. On the Montgomery place was a large brush corral, into which stock were herded seasonally following roundups. Reaching up a bench east of that corral was a sweeping wing. Stock rushed into that wing, with the enticing water of the Deschutes just ahead, only to find themselves in a corral. In the Oregon centennial year, a gatepost of that old corral, dating to 1888, still stood, the oldest remaining man-made landmark within the city limits of Bend.

Even before Jim Montgomery built a home for his big family close to the Deschutes water edge and erected a corral, the spot had been used by rangemen. First use was possibly made by "Yank" Sullivan, who as a boy in 1873 took part in a cattle drive north from California to the Silver Lake area. There, Sullivan's employer, Andrew Lane, had established a home near the lush meadows of Buck Creek. Cattle released in the Silver Lake country ranged widely. Some made their way to the Deschutes, then north into the Sisters country.

Young "Yank" Sullivan rode for these cattle in 1874, finding some as far north as the Metolius River. Later he moved some cattle to the Bend area. On the east bank of the Deschutes he built a brush corral to hold the cattle and his remuda, while he rode across country some forty miles to Prineville, for a bit of relaxation. That was the first known use by a white man of the Bend site, aside from overnight stops by wagon trains.

One Bend street honors the W. H. Staats family; another bears the name of Sisemore; but none honors Sullivan or John Y. Todd, whose historic Farewell Bend Ranch gave the city of Bend its name.

CHAPTER 20

Bend, at the Edge of the Pines

HAD THE ALEXANDER M. DRAKES not been lured to Oregon by irrigation possibilities, or had they selected some other part of the west for vacation, Bend possibly would have remained Farewell Bend—a frontier village with a "ghost town" future.

Early in June 1900, a covered wagon, drawn by two weary, footsore horses, approached a wide bend on the Deschutes River east of the Three Sisters. The Cascade peaks to the west were white and beautiful above green skirts of pine, fir, and hemlock. This was the Farewell Bend area of pioneer ranchers. This was the land John Y. Todd and his riders visioned as the heart of a new stock empire.

There were no signs of life along the sweeping bend of the river as the tired horses and the wagon came to a stop under the pines, on a terrace overlooking a swift, willow-fringed river —a river that within a decade would be lost in a placid, man-made lake, today's Mirror Pond. In 1900, the river still raced north, unfettered by a power dam. Willows crowded close to the banks of the clear, cold stream, which, because it was swift, occupied a comparatively narrow channel. For several days, the horses grazed beside the river, and eastward into the pines.

Upstream a short distance, the early-day W. H. Staats ranch was hidden in timber around a curve in the river. Still farther upstream, on the same side, was the historic Farewell Bend Ranch. To the north, within sight of the stream, were other small ranch houses, little more than cabins, most of them with histories dating to the early eighties and most of them abandoned.

The small covered wagon was not an imposing outfit, but it was the temporary home of Mr. and Mrs. Alexander M. Drake, who were on a leisurely vacation trip in the West, in search of a new home and new opportunities. Long before Drake ever set foot on this soil, he knew that the Deschutes River was one of the untapped sources of irrigation and power in the West, and that this was one of the few places on the upper Deschutes where water could be diverted and spread over thousands of acres. Also, the United States had just approved a new reclamation bill, the Carey Act, under which irrigation segregations could be established.

Before coming to Oregon, Drake, a Midwestern capitalist, met by chance a man who had been in the Farewell Bend country and was familiar with the Deschutes region. This was Charles Cottor, guide, cook, and general handy man for the Drakes on the long drive to the Bend site. The possibility of new irrigation development was likely the major lure that attracted Drake to Central Oregon, but there was another strong lure: he was an ardent angler. Cottor had already scouted the choice pools in the river, some of which were close to the place where the Drake wagon stopped.

Bend's History Shaped

Regardless of the major attraction, irrigation or fishing, that June day in 1900, when the Drakes and Cottor set up camp on the Deschutes, marked the turning point in the history of Farewell Bend and much of the upper Deschutes country of Oregon. Soon word spread through the scattered ranches of that country, and even into the Ochoco Valley, that a capitalist from the East was interested in this region, with its irrigation possibilities, its power potential and its untapped timber. There was even a rumor that Drake had already purchased several ranches.

This rumor reached upriver, where Mr. and Mrs. W. P. Vandevert made their home on a picturesque spot overlooking broad meadows on the edge of the river. Soon the Vandeverts had a visitor from the covered wagon. Cottor made the twenty-five mile trip upriver to purchase a horse from Bill Vandevert. The horse bought was "Tuf," named for the brand it bore. The fact that Drake had sent Cottor that distance to get a fresh horse was taken as an indication that the man in the covered wagon for some reason planned to move on.

Vandevert later rode downriver to Farewell Bend to visit the new arrivals. For Vandevert, the Farewell Bend community held many memories. He was the son of Grace Clark Vandevert, who was shot and partly scalped in the massacre on the Snake River in 1851, when her mother was killed. Survivors of that massacre made their way to the Deschutes to camp and rest for a few days, while the girl regained strength before heading northwest to cross the Barlow Trail to the Cottage Grove area. Forty years afterward her son returned to the upper Deschutes country to establish the "Old Homestead" and raise a pioneer family.

Vandevert and Drake met at the covered wagon and soon discovered they were old acquaintances. Many years before, Drake had visited the Fossil Forest of Arizona and engaged a guide. That guide had been Bill Vandevert. The pair now had a long visit and, from Vandevert, Drake learned of the vast possibilities of the Deschutes region. This chance meeting was one of the factors that made Drake decide to settle here.

Soon the Drakes obtained land and, in the early fall of 1900, started construction of a mountain lodge, back a short distance from the high, east bank of the river. This became a model for lodges. Its outer walls were of unbarked pine. Inner walls were covered with paneled burlap, painted maroon, with beamed ceilings of peeled pine providing a striking contrast. Illumination was from lanterns which Mrs. Drake had purchased in China. The rugs were oriental and the furniture was rustic. There was even a bath—something new in Central Oregon at the turn of the century. It was a restful lodge in a beautiful setting.

After erecting his lodge on the river, Drake constructed three pumping plants: one at Staats', upstream; one below the present

Tumalo Avenue Bridge, and a third close to the Drake lodge. It was Drake's Pilot Butte Development Company that first delivered water to the lands immediately adjacent to Bend. Early in the summer of 1904, water started flowing through the new Pilot Butte Canal.

Furrows Mark Bend Streets

On a spring day in 1903, passing stockmen noted an unusual activity in the vicinity of Drake's lodge, about a mile downstream from the Farewell Bend Ranch. A man with a team and plow was turning black furrows here and there in the junipers and pines east of the river. The stockmen were amazed. They still considered the river at this spot as their own watering place for cattle, horses, and occasionally a band of sheep. Even before white men came, deer and antelope grazed in from the desert to quench their thirst at this easily accessible bend of the river.

Though the riders were interested, the few local residents paid little attention to the man with the plow, as the black furrows appeared in the dry needles of the old pines on that spring morning. Yet those furrows were important: they marked the streets of the new Oregon town, Bend on the upper Deschutes River. This town, still without a name, had been surveyed and platted by Drake in 1901 and 1902, but the plat had not been filed, and so far as residents of the range area were concerned, the town of Bend was "merely a rumor." In Prineville, easterly across some forty miles of sage and juniper, people did not believe the rumor. Most of them thought the marking of the streets of a town still in the blueprint stage was the dream of a promoter, but the emerging town that pioneers knew as Farewell Bend was much more than a dream to Alexander Drake.

As a result of that careful study that preceded the founding of Bend, the city had an ideal mill site when mills were ready to come, and it was at a place that could easily be reached by rail. Within a stone's throw of the Drake lodge was a power development site, on the edge of a great pine forest.

Drake even selected names for the streets. He planned for one set of streets to be named for old-timers of the community, another for trees native to the region, and still another for native flowers, with the streets to run in alphabetical order—Awbrey, Brock, Cottor; Ash, Beach, Cottonwood; Aster, Buttercup, Crocus. This happy combination unfortunately never materialized. Greenwood, Bond, Wall, Oregon, and Lava Road are the only streets now retaining their names received in 1903.

After the first plan for naming streets was discarded, it was announced on June 12, 1903, that a new plat of Bend had been prepared. On this plat, the dusty street that ran along the rocky wall enclosing the Drake lodge appeared as Wall Street, the name passing teamsters had given it earlier. Though for many years an occasional pine and gnarled juniper remained on the street, this did not handicap races held there as late as 1909. Bucking contests also took place on that street as features of Fourth of July celebrations. Over Wall Street—in the years when it was muddy in winter and dusty in summer—rolled much of the north-south traffic through Central Oregon. This street later became the route of the arterial highway, U. S. 97.

Bend Gains Village Status

By the fall of 1903, Bend—having lost the "Farewell" part of its pioneer name—was large enough to be recognized as a village, but its boundaries were still nebulous and its future was uncertain. It was considered an upstart by its neighbors—Prineville, Silver Lake, Antelope, Mitchell, and the new town of Shaniko at the end of the rails, ninety miles to the north. However, the little hamlet was growing; it now had a population of 258, according to a special 1903 census.

Redmond had not yet appeared, and Sisters was a mere group of houses, a village attempting to detach itself from pioneer Camp Polk on Squaw Creek. Prineville was a bustling range town, the trading center for Bend and the source of mail from Shaniko and points north. Shaniko, on the great windy flats of Wasco County, was the rail metropolis of the interior country. Several other communities along the Deschutes River were also striving to become the nucleus of the new area. At Deschutes, also known as Staats, were a post office and store, and general accommodations for travel in a horse-and-wagon era. Lytle, a mile or so north of the Drake lodge, had high hopes of becoming a booming town, with ideal sites for power development on the river. People of the village of Laidlaw, six miles downstream—later to be known as Tumalo—could not see a need for a new town in the high country.

Bend was strung along the east bank of the Deschutes, a distance of several miles. It extended from the old Farewell Bend stopping place at the Sisemore Ranch, north past Staats, and along the river to Lytle. In October 1903, there were three general stores in operation in the new town. Other businesses included two meat markets, a drugstore, a millinery and dressmaking establishment, three hotels, a blacksmith and wagon shop, a busy livery stable, two little sawmills, and two saloons—inevitable in pioneer times.

Bend gained the status of an organized city and was incorporated by virtue of an election held on Monday, December 19, 1904. This election possibly was the most stirring occasion in Bend's pioneer history. The sparse population of the sprawling community entered enthusiastically into the town's first political campaign. Two well-defined tickets were in the field, providing voters a choice of leaders. There were rallies and posters. Caricatures of opposing candidates were displayed around town, and even in the building where votes were cast. Feeling ran high. When ballots were counted, the Bend Coronet Band marched to the home of the newly-elected mayor and serenaded him as conqueror. Despite predictions of a close vote, the outcome of the incorporation election was one-sided. A total of 104 persons favored incorporation; only three preferred to have Bend retain its hamlet status.

A. L. Goodwillie, a former Chicago banker, was the new

city's choice for its first mayor. He defeated Gerald Grosebeck, a remittance man. Before coming to the Deschutes country, Grosebeck sold gaspipe rifles to South Americans for current rebellions. After the election, the defeated candidate shouldered a shotgun and stalked through the streets, his pockets laden with pistols. Later he passed from the Bend scene. When elected, Goodwillie was serving as vice-president of the Central Oregon Banking and Trust Company.

Councilmen named were C. W. Merrill, C. H. Erickson, J. I. West, D. McMillan, C. M. Redfield, and F. A. Shonquest. Shonquest ran for the council post as the result of the toss of dice. He and Hugh O'Kane, a colorful figure of early-day Bend, were prospective candidates. They shook dice to determine which should enter the political field. Unlike the defeated candidate for mayor, O'Kane remained to become one of the city's most substantial citizens; in 1916-1917, he erected on Oregon Avenue a two-story office building that still bears his name.

A jockey and skilled prize fighter in his youth, O'Kane was a lover of horses and a teller of stories about early-day Bend and its people. It was his practice, in the final years of his colorful life, to place his chair in front of the main door of his building, as afternoon shadows crept across Oregon Avenue, and chat with passersby. He frequently enjoyed siestas there in the shade, and none who passed disturbed his slumber or his dreams. One of those dreams was that Bend would in time become a city of more then 25,000. In 1962, it reached the halfway mark of his goal.

J. M. Lawrence was the new city's first recorder and F. O. Minor its first treasurer. E. R. Lester was elected marshal, but he was without a jail.

On January 4, 1905, the Crook County court meeting in Prineville canvassed the votes cast in the Bend incorporation election and declared the result legal. On the eve of the opening of the Lewis and Clark World's Fair in Portland, Bend was now legally a city. Officers were sworn in and held their first meeting in the Pilot Butte Development Company office. Approved at the first meeting was an ordinance setting the license of saloons at $600 a year.

One of the first official acts of the common council was to order construction of a jail, a building sixteen feet square, with two cells and a six-foot corridor.

Bend had church buildings even before the town was incorporated. The first significant community religious effort had its beginning on July 12, 1902, when a union Sunday school was organized. The Reverend B. J. Harper, Baptist missionary pastor from Milton, presided at the meeting, held in the historic old range cabin in Drake Park. In July 1904, a Baptist Church was organized in Bend with twenty-two members, and a building was erected. This was the first church building in Bend. The first Catholic priest to visit Bend was the Reverend Michael J. Hickey, pastor at Kingsley, who arrived in 1904. Services later were held in a little building facing the rutted road leading south over Wall Street.

Bend Precinct

Before Bend became a village, then a city, it was a voting precinct in huge, undivided Crook County. The Bend precinct extended eighteen miles north and south and some seventy miles east and west. The summit of the Cascades, crowned by the Three Sisters, was the western boundary. From the Cascade Divide, the precinct stretched east over the High Desert. At the presidential election in 1900, only eight persons voted in the southern Crook County area that was to be known as the Bend precinct. Four of the votes were for McKinley, four for Bryan.

Although officially incorporated as a city in 1905, Bend was still an outpost on the Central Oregon frontier. The forty-five mile trip by buggy, wagon, or horseback to Prineville, over winding roads and trails, was a lonely experience. The road was dusty in summer and difficult in winter, when drifts formed barriers across ridges. Much of it was through a forest of age-old junipers. Rabbits were abundant, and there were occasional coyotes. Not a habitation broke the monotony of the trip in the first years of the century, aside from a few farms on the higher slopes of Powell Buttes, where wells or springs provided water. When Bend voted for incorporation, water for the Powell Buttes segregation was still about a year away. The trip from Bend to Prineville was waterless, except for stops at a well or two, one at a high spring on the northeast slopes of "The Buttes." Riders carried their waterbags.

Travelers from Prineville to Bend viewed spectacular scenery: ruling the western skyline was a long rosary of volcanoes, snow bearing most of the year. High mountains reached from conical Hood in the north to the Three Sisters, seemingly in Bend's backyard, and south into the Diamond Lake country, a lost landmark for the wandering immigrants of 1853.

South from the new town of Bend to Silver Lake was another region of few habitations. Freighters found that long road, up-hill from Bend to Rosland, rocky and rugged in summer. It was rough and frequently snow blocked in winter. On that route, the first stop south of Bend—except for a "breather" at Wetweather Spring—was Lava. Then came Rosland, a now-vanished village a little north of the present town of La Pine. Beyond Rosland was the old Summit Stage Station, then Silver Lake in a great basin rimmed by mountains.

Wetweather Spring was a short distance out of Bend on the long road to Silver Lake, a resting place for teamsters and their teams, about halfway between Bend and Lava Butte. In earlier years it was an important stopping place for stage drivers in the snowy winter months. There, many of the southbound drivers changed from coaches to sleds. Northbound drivers parked their sleds at the spring and hitched their horses to rigs for the drive into Bend. The Wetweather Spring site was bypassed by modern highway construction, with U. S. 97 following a new line well to the east, to gain elevation in the swing around the edge of Lava Butte.

"Hello, Prineville."

Up until the morning of August 19, 1904, the village of Bend was pretty well isolated from the outside world, aside from mail and contacts provided by riders or drivers of slow-moving teams. Then came the news that received a banner headline in the local paper: "Hello, Prineville." The headline and story referred to one of the big events of pioneer days, in the little village that had just emerged from its "Farewell Bend" cocoon of the range era. Bend had just been connected with the outside world by telephone.

Residents of the village were invited to make use of the telephone throughout the day without charge. There followed many calls with the greeting: "Hello, Prineville." Earlier in the new century, Prineville had been connected with The Dalles and with continental hookups through Portland. The new service for Bend had been provided by the Deschutes Telephone Company.

Telephone calls were few in those days, the chief revenue coming from occasional long-distance connections. H. C. Ellis, first superintendent and general manager of the Bend Telephone Company, recalled that one ardent lover contributed as much as $3 or $4 a day in calls to his fiancee in Portland. He made his calls in the evening, thereby greatly inconveniencing the operator, with her one line leading out of the Bend community. Still, the amorous calls helped bolster the company's limited funds.

In 1905, the telephone company was reorganized under the name of the Pioneer Telephone and Telegraph Company. This company constructed new lines, and installed a public telephone at the home of Charles Gist, then postmaster at Gist, a village now missing from the Oregon map.

By 1906 there were seven telephones in the Bend exchange. Incidentally, Bend residents often had plenty of trouble getting through to Prineville in those days. "Central" was a very busy man, being postmaster in Prineville, the stage agent, and a merchant. When the mail arrived from Shaniko, or when the postmaster had other urgent duties such as waiting on customers, he "cut" the Bend line. Occasionally he forgot to restore connections, leaving Bend isolated for the better part of a day.

However, Bend residents were self-sufficient when telephone service was out. In emergencies, riders hurried overland, past telephones and dead telephone lines, to carry urgent messages or get a doctor. By the end of 1917, Bend had 313 telephones in service. In 1958, the Pacific Telephone and Telegraph Company inaugurated dial service for thousands of patrons.

Lights Come to Village

Chilling breezes of approaching winter were whipping around the timbered bends of the Deschutes River on the evening of November 1, 1910, when suddenly and dramatically there were lights in the village of Bend. The swift-flowing Deschutes had been harnessed to provide lights for a small community that was still in the kerosene and gaslight age. Many who had not visited the big cities for several years marveled at electricity flowing through the metal lines and into the delicate filaments within a glass bulb. Most of the lights were open bulbs dangling from ceiling cords. At the start, power was generated only from 4:30 p.m. until midnight, and from 4 a.m. to 8 a.m., because there was little need for electricity outside those hours. There were no refrigerators, no radios or television, no electric stoves or toasters.

Business people in downtown Bend were quick to take advantage of the new type of light to illuminate their buildings. The coming of electricity to Bend had been discussed for some time. When power was turned on that November evening, many were already prepared to use the new source of light. Within the week, city officials ordered ten arc lights for downtown street corners, where board walks were high, chuck holes were many, and travel by night was hazardous.

Before the coming of electricity—made possible through construction of a power dam on the Deschutes River at the rear of the old Pilot Butte Inn—Bend generally used gaslights. Some kerosene lamps, with their wicks and their chimneys that required constant cleaning, were also in use. Gaslights for streets were ordered in October 1907, on a trial basis—"the most modern obtainable." Each street light was connected with a small gasoline tank and could be burned all night, or put out at 10 p.m., midnight, or any hour desired, through a special clock arrangement.

Villagers See First Automobile

Even before Bend had gaslights or electricity, it had automobiles. In the summer of 1904, when the village was still unincorporated, a chugging car moved noisily into town over a rutted, dusty road, and wheeled down Wall Street. It detoured junipers and bounced over sidewalks. Soon dozens of people gathered around. J. O. Johnson, general manager of the local irrigation and power company, owned that car. It was an impressive contraption, somewhat resembling a buggy, but with a rear entrance.

Most people considered the automobile a sort of plaything, a vehicle that would not be operable on roads made for high-wheeled wagons and slow-moving horses. Those roads had high centers, were badly rutted, and were often strewn with rocks.

The first Bend-owned automobile—still in good running condition when Oregon observed its centennial in 1959, and frequently seen at gatherings of the Deschutes Pioneers' Association—was brought to the Deschutes country in 1906 by H. C. Ellis, and was used in connection with telephone company work. This two-cycle Holsman, with high wheels, was just the vehicle needed on mid-Oregon roads with high centers, stumps, and rocks. The air-cooled, tiller-steered car had been purchased in Chicago, shipped to The Dalles, and brought to Bend under its own power.

In 1906, the Deschutes Telephone Company, finding it difficult to obtain horses, decided to get a "horseless carriage." Ellis accepted delivery of the vehicle at The Dalles, but could not get

Redmond had its start in a tent home set up by Mr. and Mrs. Frank Redmond, who patiently waited for the water they were sure would eventually come from irrigation ditches. This is a 1909 street scene in Redmond, one year before it was incorporated as a city.

Not a car is in sight in this picture, north along Wall Street in Bend, prior to the coming of the railroads. Frame buildings with their pioneer fronts have long since given way to modern structures, and parking has become a serious problem.

Oregon Trunk and Deschutes Railroad crews worked on opposite sides of the Deschutes Rive in the race upstream. To the left is an Oregon Trunk crew (O.T.L.). To the right is the Deschute Railroad crew (D.R.R.). They were completing a grade below Free Bridge.

The Deschutes railroad lines were the last in the United States to be built with "powder, shovel and horses." Pictured here is a cliff being blasted into the Deschutes River.

The deep Crooked River Gorge in Central Oregon was spanned with steel for a high bridge in 1910, as the Oregon Trunk Line pushed south into the upper Deschutes River region. The steep-walled canyon at this point was more than three hundred feet deep.

Left: William Hanley, Harney County stockman and close friend of James J. Hill, was in Bend Railroad Day, Oct. 5, 1911, to lay the cornerstone for the new railroad station. Right: James J. Hill, "Empire Builder," drove the golden spike at the end of the rails, marking the end of the long struggle of the Hill and Harriman railroad systems in their epochal race to Bend, via the Deschutes Gorge.

Shortly after the railroad reached Bend, the city was host to Seattle residents, who made th
trip on the first special train ever to run over the new line. Bend was considered a frontier tov
back in 1911—so a group of local businessmen greeted the visitors with a "hold up" ne
the city limits.

Dr. Earl Sm

Left: When the Great Northern extended rails south to California in 1927, equipment unkno
in the days of gorge construction was used. In center is Captain O. C. Applegate, who in pion
days guided an Army supply train through this same area, from Fort Dalles to Fort Klama
Right: Serving as a railroad doctor in the construction of the Deschutes Gorge lines, in 190
1911, was Dr. Earl Smith, later Multnomah County coroner.

fuel there. After waiting several days, he obtained a supply from Goldendale, across the Columbia in Washington. The fuel arrived in five-gallon cans, two cans to the case. Before heading for the interior country, Ellis shipped some of the fuel ahead on the Columbia Southern train, which operated from Biggs on the Columbia River, south to Shaniko. This was "spotted" along the line.

The Holsman caused considerable excitement in The Dalles when it headed east and chugged up the Columbia River to a crossing of the Deschutes at Freebridge. At the time there was only one other car in The Dalles, a Reo owned by Dr. J. A. Reuter—a one-cylinder vehicle.

From Freebridge, Ellis headed the Holsman south, moving up Rattlesnake Canyon to Moro, at the pace of a lively buggy team. There was a delay at Moro while more canned fuel was taken aboard. Finally, as darkness came to the Shaniko plateau, the little car reached the head of Cow Canyon. With its steep rocky grade and its sharp curves, Cow Canyon Road was feared even by veteran freighters.

In the gathering darkness, with junipers draped like ghosts over rocky embankments, the Holsman moved slowly down the rugged canyon. Ellis picked the "trail" by the dim illumination of the car's bobbing kerosene lights. As the grade narrowed near Haight Toll Station, fenders on one side of the car were ripped and dented by sharp, protruding rocks on the narrow grade. By the time Ellis reached the bottom of the grade, where Trout Creek emerges from its dark canyon, the fenders were mere scraps of torn metal. He had the fenders removed at the Heisler Stage Station on Trout Creek, where they remained for years, relics of the start of the motor age in the land of cow trails.

The historic Holsman was used by Ellis and members of his telephone line crew for seven years. Since there were no gas pumps or service stations, gas for the car was freighted in from Shaniko and retailed by E. A. Sather, operator of one of Bend's first stores. Price of the "imported" gas was a bit high—seventy-five cents a gallon in Bend and one dollar at Rosland.

Even though they moved only twenty or twenty-five miles an hour, the first cars to use Central Oregon roads and Bend streets kicked up great clouds of dust. At times when a tail wind was blowing, goggled motorists, appropriately wrapped in "dusters," had to stop to get their bearings. Occasionally roads branched and there was no way of telling, in 1906, which branch was the main road. Moving at speeds which at times climbed to a risky thirty miles an hour, or up to the state speed limit of thirty-five, motorists occasionally wandered away from the main "highway," ending up at some ranch house or in pine timber. Something was needed to direct the hurried motorists.

Finally, a color scheme was adopted to guide them over roads of their choice. All "arterial routes" were designated by different colors. The main route through Central Oregon, ancestral to The Dalles-California Highway, was the "White and Blue" road. Commercial clubs of the area splashed these colors on telephone poles, posts, and trees. These white and blue bands were still visible many years later.

Dusty Streets Bother Autoists

Motorists complained of the dust on Bend streets in the decade starting in 1910. Wagon traffic through the village was still heavy, and the volcanic soil was being churned into drifting clouds. Irate housewives pointed to Bend's civic motto of the day: "Bend, the Beautiful." At last the city was persuaded to purchase a sprinkler, an improvised outfit mounted on a wagon. It was proudly announced that the sprinkler would stop "once and for all time the disagreeable dust clouds" and that the City of Bend would again become a place of beauty. Barney Lewis, in charge of the dust-settling project, used his big dray team to haul the six-hundred-gallon tank daily through town. The tank represented an investment of $160.60, donated by thirty-one persons. The scheme was noble but worthless. In warm weather, the spray from the sprinkler evaporated about as fast as it touched the hot dust. When the water did penetrate the dust, it was quickly lost in the volcanic soil. In some places, water for a time remained on top of a hardpan, then chuck holes rapidly developed.

Later, waste oil from garages was used to lay the dust, but oil mud was then tracked into homes and business houses, creating a new problem. Finally came the start of paving, controversial at first because asphalt cracked, broke, and bent. As street surfacing methods improved, Bend and its sister towns of Central Oregon eventually emerged from the dust.

Pistol Shots Sound Alarm

Up until 1905, Bend had little protection from fire. The town's first fire alarm was sounded by pistol shots.

Billy Robinson, sleeping on a billiard table in the Hugh O'Kane saloon at the corner of Oregon and Bond, was awakened at 3 a.m. on April 27, 1905, by hot embers falling from the saloon ceiling. He jumped from the billiard table, raced to the door, emptied a revolver into the sky, and lustily yelled for help. But few heard Robinson's cries and pistol-shot alarm. Before help arrived, the saloon was in flames. Efforts then turned to saving the adjacent buildings—O'Kane's bowling alley and cigar stand, the Estebenet Saloon, and Ole Erickson's lodging house.

Two boys who lived several blocks from the saloon rushed down the steep grade with a tank of water from the river. Fire fighters soaked blankets to pack around the smoking sides of the cigar stand and other buildings. A small outdoor building that might have served as a link for the spread of the fire was tumbled over, in Halloween fashion, by the volunteers. Eventually the nearby buildings were saved, but the O'Kane Saloon was a total loss. The only articles salvaged were the cash register, some bottles of liquor, a wall telephone, and a painting of the Three Sisters. This was Bend's first fire. Late in July 1905, the town's first fire department was formed, with S. C. Caldwell as chief. The department was composed of two companies, totaling thirty-one volunteer firemen.

The area's worst early-day blaze destroyed the Henry Linster sawmill near the north edge of town on July 18, 1908. By the war year of 1918, it became evident that the hose-cart method of fighting fires was no longer efficient; a year later a new fire department was organized, with Chief Tom Carlon in charge. By mid-century the Bend Fire Department was a smooth-working organization, with an expanded staff and modern equipment.

Bend's early-day water problems were not entirely concerned with fire control; there was also a need for domestic water—a need that was met by the ranchers of a previous era by dipping their buckets in the cold Deschutes. In later years, some of the riverside residents used water wheels for filling buckets. Bend's first water system was a horse-drawn wagon carrying a high, square, home-made tank. A team of bay horses slowly drew the wagon through Bend's streets, with Lucky Baldwin handling the reins. Baldwin daily filled the tank at a low place in the river, near the present Portland Avenue Bridge.

In that year, 1904, when Lucky Baldwin decided he could make some easy money delivering water with his "two-horse power plant" to Bend's three hundred homes at twenty-five cents a barrel, the town's only source of water was the Deschutes. Baldwin filled the rear-porch barrels each morning. Generally a barrel lasted a family through an entire day.

Lucky Baldwin's venture into the water business was short-lived. In January 1905, the newly-incorporated City of Bend granted a franchise to the Bend Water, Light & Power Company, with A. M. Drake as manager. A thirty-thousand-gallon wooden storage tank was constructed on the lava bluff known as Hospital Hill—the location later of St. Charles Memorial Hospital. Service through the Drake water system, with its 8,700 feet of main, began on July 28, 1905.

Early Irrigation

The first irrigation developments in the Bend area, on a district-wide basis, were those of the Swalley and the Three Sisters Irrigation Districts, and later Drake's Pilot Butte Development Company. All three operated under the new Carey Act. Also in the field, competing for Deschutes water, was the Oregon Reclamation Company. West of the Deschutes River in Central Oregon, the first diversion of water was through the Wimer Canal, named for the George W. Wimer family. That canal diverted part of the flow of Tumalo Creek into a canal. Faint traces of the old canal are still visible west of Tumalo Creek near Bend.

Succeeding the Three Sisters Irrigation Company, the Columbia Southern came into existence under terms of the Carey Act in 1902, with a 27,000-acre segregation set aside. Eventually the Columbia Southern Irrigation Company was to become the Tumalo Project. The Pilot Butte Canal was in use by May 1904. Water flowed east past Bend, then out into the sagebrush and juniper country toward Powell Buttes. In a few days, Deschutes water had covered the entire fifteen miles of the new canal and tumbled into the old bed of Dry River.

The Pilot Butte Company won a legal victory over another group, the Oregon Irrigation Company, and obtained rights to take some water from the Deschutes south of Bend. First work on that canal was started in 1904, when canals were blasted across the lava terrain. Men with teams did most of the work. Soon a canal system was reaching into the desert, over a sage plateau and through a forest of old junipers.

With water on its way in 1904, teams were used in plowing lands about as fast as brush and trees could be removed. News of the development spread fast. That same year Drake announced inquiries from some three hundred different families seeking irrigated land. When success of the irrigation experiment was assured, as was Bend's future, the Pilot Butte Development Company, the Bend Townsite Company, and various other holdings of Mr. and Mrs. A. M. Drake were sold to a syndicate composed of F. S. Stanley, E. A. Baldwin, John Steidl, and J. E. Sawhill. The new owners comprised the Deschutes Irrigation and Power Company, generally referred to as the "D.I.P. Company."

Shortly after purchasing the Drake company, the D.I.P. Company announced plans for another large main canal, to take water from the Deschutes north of Bend to irrigate 85,000 acres. The canal was to be twenty-eight miles long, with its terminus at Dry River to the east. Not all the acreage included in the original plans received water, but soon the Deschutes flow spread over the sage desert.

Meanwhile, to the north, the new town of Redmond was taking shape.

CHAPTER 21

Watering the Wilderness

WATER DIVERTED FROM THE DESCHUTES River at Bend, and trailed through the old range country in canals, played a big role in the growth of two towns, Madras and Redmond, founded near the center of irrigation tracts. Madras waited long for water, some forty-five years. Redmond was still a hamlet of tents and temporary buildings when water flowed out of the south and reached the rim of the Crooked River gorge in 1906.

The Redmond Story

The upper Deschutes country of Oregon was mostly unclaimed stock range in 1905 when Mr. and Mrs. Frank T. Redmond—both former North Dakota school teachers—pitched their tent on a sage flat about midway between the O'Neil Post Office on Crooked River and Tetherow Bridge on the Deschutes. To the south, Bend had just been founded. Twenty miles to the west was the village of Sisters. On the western skyline, as viewed from the opening of the Redmonds' tent, were the Three Sisters, pilot peaks for wagon trains.

The Redmonds had no intention of starting a town. They came west because they had heard of the opening in the Deschutes country of Carey Act segregations—lands set aside for reclamation through use of water. Terms of the Carey Act were accepted by the State of Oregon in 1901. In the following year came passage of the United States Reclamation Act. Word spread over the nation that water would soon transform Central Oregon sagelands into green fields.

The Redmonds' tent home in the sage was some four miles from water, but before coming west, the couple had taken a good look into the future. That look was largely directed by blueprints of a big irrigation project proposed for the segregation. The Redmonds selected land on a ditch already surveyed, but not constructed. They were also interested in reports that a railroad was to be extended south from Shaniko, believing that the line would pass close to their homestead.

The railroad extension talk proved to be without foundation, and the irrigation company's promise to start construction of a canal did not immediately materialize. The Redmonds, first purchasers of Carey Act land in the area, for more than a year were forced to haul water from the deep canyon of the Deschutes in the Cline Falls area. But they were patient. They cleared land while waiting for a ditch and water. Soon their little ranch in the junipers and sage became a popular stopping place for travelers and stockmen.

In establishing their home in the sage, the Redmonds guessed well. Water eventually spread through laterals to bring life to thousands of acres in the immediate area, and land seekers came in increasing numbers from all parts of the United States.

The Central Oregon Irrigation Company, which undertook reclamation of the area, in the fall of 1905 conceived the plan of establishing a "desert town" in the dusty sage and juniper land east of the Deschutes. That town was situated on the line of the main irrigation ditch leading north from Bend The spot selected was to become one of the largest single bodies of irrigable land in the Northwest. In locating their ranch, Mr. and Mrs. Redmond had the heart of the big project as their target.

Near the center of the segregation was a vacant section of school land. By chance, the section adjoined the Frank Redmond ranch. There, on the vacant section, the irrigation company decided that the new town should be founded. In tribute to the faith and pioneer spirit of the first settlers in the area, the irrigation people named the town Redmond. Redmond officially dates its start to 1905, when the first influx of settlers occurred. Not until 1910, however, was Redmond incorporated as a city.

Population of Redmond at the time of its incorporation was 216.

One of the first needs of the "desert town" of Redmond was water. A well was drilled through layered lavas in 1907, and a few lines were laid to serve the little village, but most people came to the deep well with their buckets to get their domestic water. By August 1910, a big tank of ten thousand gallons was set up. A few years later, the new town bought a water system that had been privately installed. This was developed into a modern system in later years, with storage on an old volcano, Forked Horn Butte.

In 1911 the first trains came out of the north, over a high steel span across the Crooked River gorge. The first Oregon Trunk train moved into town amid great rejoicing, over Mr. and Mrs. Frank Redmond's "dream line" of earlier years.

Redmond's growth in its early years was not spectacular, but it was steady. In later years, as Redmond developed into a dairy center in a land known for its varied crops and fine clover, population gains were large. Soon Redmond, which in pioneer days called itself "The Hub" of the region, became the intersection point of two arterial highways, U. S. Highway 97 and U. S. Highway 126.

In a few years Redmond became a school center as well as the agricultural heart of the area. First classes were held in 1907-08 and the year 1910 marked the beginning of the Redmond High School. Later, a union high school was established, consisting of Redmond and eleven surrounding districts. With the consolidation of the schools, Redmond faced the problem of providing living accommodations for out-of-town students. To solve this, a high school dormitory costing $10,000 was constructed. The minimum rent for students staying at the dormitory was $6.25 per month.

By 1930, Redmond had developed into a busy city at the crossroads of Central Oregon. Its roots are not deep in the pioneer past; most of its history covers the reclamation—through irrigation—of thousands of acres of fine agricultural lands, the establishment of an important dairy economy, and the construction of highways that lure tourists to a region noted for its scenery. But in the Redmond area there are many old-timers who recall the pioneer range era of not so many years ago. That rangeland past was recalled when Redmond, in 1955, observed its fiftieth anniversary.

The Madras Story

Unlike Redmond, Madras was not founded as an "irrigation town." There was some irrigation along Willow Creek, which seasonally carries water west from the high Ochoco slopes, but the acreage was small. Madras waited until 1946 before making a bid for recognition as the "green spot" of interior Oregon.

Near the start of the present century, population of the area rapidly increased and farming operations expanded; but ranchers were forced to make long drives to Prineville or Antelope to transact business or do their buying. Realizing the need for a trade center, John A. Palmehn decided that a town should be founded, to serve that part of western Crook County. On July 18, 1902, he filed a plat in Prineville for the new town, the name of which appeared on the legal papers as "Palmain." The difference in spelling appears to have been a mistake in recording.

When an application for a post office was made, it was found that there already existed in Oregon a post office named Palmer, so "Palmain" was rejected because of the possibility of a confusion in names. "Madras" was then suggested. The origin of the suggestion remained controversial for years. Some contended that the name was taken from a bolt of Madras cloth in a store where a new name for a post office was being discussed. Mrs. Max Wilson said the town was named for Madras, India, not a piece of cloth, explaining that her husband had proposed the name when he applied for the position of postmaster. The late Howard W. Turner, historian of the Madras country, noted in *Jefferson County Reminiscences* that he was convinced that Mrs. Wilson's version of the name was correct.

Town lots were sold in Madras as early as 1902, and some buildings were started that year. One of the first was erected by Dr. W. H. Snook, who had homesteaded near Old Culver before Madras was platted. He was the area's pioneer doctor. The Madras Townsite Company was incorporated on November 14, 1904, by John A. Palmehn, A. E. Hammond, and Don P. Rea. The City of Madras was incorporated on March 2, 1910, with Howard Turner as the first mayor and John H. Jackson as the first city recorder.

Transportation Changes

Madras was some ten miles west of the main-traveled road as the hamlet took shape. Mail from Shaniko, which was reached by railroads in 1900, was routed down Cow Canyon to Heisler Station, on Hay Creek. A carrier took mail from Heisler to Sagebrush Springs, some twelve miles north of Madras. The mail stage, however, continued on to Prineville, across the high country east of Madras, through Lamonta.

Heavy traffic moved to and from the interior country as Madras slowly grew in its sheltered valley near a low western rim breached by Willow Creek. Most travel followed the main stage route, south from Shaniko, up the McPherson Hill grade, then into the high country near Hay Creek Ranch, and south to Grizzly Gap. Traffic using the Madras route came south over Crooked River at Trail Crossing.

As Madras grew, it found itself the "big town" in a cluster of communities—Metolius, Culver, Ashwood, Lamonta, Opal City, Gateway, and others. Off to the southeast was Grizzly, where Postmaster Robert Warren served the public as early as 1879—long before Madras was platted. High on the eastern horizon was the range community of Blizzard Ridge, near the edge of the Hay Creek Ranch empire. On the brink of the Deschutes gorge, facing spectacular Cove Canyon, was Grandview, a town that was to fade to ghost status. Near the wild gorge of Trout Creek was the Pony Butte settlement, in an area that was to gain national attention for its fine agates and thundereggs. Southwest of Madras was Opal City, which served as the end of the rails for a time in early 1911 as construction of the Oregon Trunk Railroad was temporarily stopped while a steel bridge was being built over Crooked River.

The Water Problem

The first ranchers to file on lands north of Crooked River and west of the pine-covered Ochocos possibly never dreamed of water flowing through canals to irrigate fifty thousand acres in the Madras area. With a few exceptions, the early years of homesteading were damp. Because crops were good and fine grass covered the range country, there appeared little need to spend millions of dollars to impound water in an upper Deschutes River basin and move the stored flow in a fifty-mile-long ditch to dampen the "basin" near Madras and adjacent areas.

In World War I, there was a great demand for wheat, and thousands of acres of it were plowed and planted in the Madras country. Nature generally had been kind; moisture from clouds was sufficient to bring crops to maturity. However, there was no water for domestic use. Some farmers were hopeful that water could be reached by drilling deep wells. One farmer on the Agency Plains drilled a well and tapped water at four hundred feet. Another contracted for a well that was to be drilled two thousand feet, at a cost of two dollars a foot, but he did not get enough water to meet the needs of his farm.

A few settlers faced the water problem even before reaching their lands: at some stopping places they paid as high as twenty-five cents a bucket to water their horses. The greatest worry of the farmers was the high winds that swept top soil from their cultivated fields. Dust plagued housewives. Some of this dust was from fields and some from roads that had been rutted by the wheels of wagons.

As the Madras country became thickly settled, the need for irrigation became apparent. In 1913, an application was made for a permit to use 400,000 acre feet of Deschutes water yearly for the irrigation of 100,000 acres. This was the start of an effort that was to last more than thirty years. On July 21, 1938, work started on a multimillion-dollar U. S. Bureau of Reclamation project that was completed in 1946, to make Madras the "green spot" of the old range country.

Opal Prairie's "City"

Early settlers knew Culver as Opal Prairie, named from nearby Opal Springs in the deep canyon of Crooked River. The little community was founded on February 22, 1911, but it has a history that dates to 1887. Like Antelope, it is a town that pulled stakes and moved, following its pioneer start. At first Culver had been known as Haystack, because of a landmark of that name thirty miles northwest of Prineville. Later it was moved to a point near the present Haystack Reservoir of the North Unit Project. Deciding that the "town" in its new location should have a new name, residents of the area called it Culver. That was the ancestral spelling of the name of the first postmaster, O. G. Collver. When the Oregon Trunk Railroad made its survey across Opal Prairie, Culver was again moved, this time five miles west to its present location.

Culver suffered a loss of business when the route of U. S. Highway 97 was changed from the town's center to a line several miles east, not far from the original location of the town; but when water flowed through North Unit district canals in 1945, Culver found itself near the heart of a thriving agricultural community, and it prospered.

The Metolius Story

About halfway between Madras and Culver, on the old route of U. S. 97, is Metolius, named for the river whose rims can be seen in the west, across the Crooked and Deschutes River gorges. It is a town that started with a church colony, became an important railroad point in 1911, then a farm center when water ran through canals to southwestern Jefferson County. In 1902, the community became a dry-farming area when a colony of German Methodists settled there. Some fine homes were built, and a church took shape on a hill, with a cemetery nearby. For a time the elevation overlooking the interior country was known as "Methodist Hill." Metolius became important when it was designated by the Oregon Trunk as a division point, and a roundhouse was constructed there. The town eventually lost most of its railroad division business and dropped in population, but the arrival of irrigation has given new life to the community.

Warm Springs Reservation

Through the years, Madras had had a friendly and important neighbor to the northwest—the Warm Springs Reservation, the allocated domain of a small group of Indians. Its history dates back to 1855. Completion in 1949 of U. S. Highway 26 through the tribal lands to the Mt. Hood area brought Madras and the reservation people even closer. Madras is the trading point for the reservation. In 1963 the Warm Springs people voted to proceed with the development of a fine, modern resort at Kah-nee-ta Hot Springs in the spectacular Warm Springs Canyon. The first phase of the resort was placed in use in 1964.

Like Madras, Warm Springs also felt the stimulus of the construction of two huge hydroelectric plants in the Deschutes Gorge. One of the plants is at the Pelton site, the other upstream near Round Butte. Some of the revenue from these Portland General Electric Company dams is being used by the Warm Springs tribal council for the betterment of the Agency.

Gateway to Central Oregon

Gateway, some twelve miles north of Madras, is a community center, not a town—but in early days it was a well-known locality because of natural features that made it a control point for travel.

Here, Trout Creek, during long centuries, deeply eroded the region, providing a natural gateway for railroad and vehicular travel north and south through Central Oregon. At this point, Union Pacific trains came out of the Deschutes Gorge, up Willow Creek, in the race with the Oregon Trunk to Bend in 1909-1911. A post office was established in the gap in 1913, and it was named Gateway. The location was about three miles west of the Youngs post office of earlier years.

In pioneer days, the north-south road through Central Oregon, that was to become U. S. Highway 97, passed near the Gateway location, before swinging north through Lyle Gap, or south up a steep grade to Weber Wells, later known as Paxton. Modernized U. S. Highway 97 bypasses Gateway. Like other Jefferson County communities, this hamlet under the lava rims, facing the wild grandeur of the Trout Creek Canyon to the north, took a new lease on life with the arrival of Deschutes water.

CHAPTER 22

News on the Frontier

NEWS ON THE CENTRAL OREGON FRONTIER was sketchy prior to 1900, primarily because of the lack of established lines of communication. Trails to the west crossed mountains blocked by snow six months each year. Roads to the north and east were poor. The route to the south, into the Klamath basin, was virtually impassable, but a branching road into the Silver Lake region was usable, in season. There were no telephones, nor was there telegraph service. Not until the beginning of the Twentieth Century was communication speeded by the establishment of telephone lines radiating out of Prineville.

Following the days of early explorers, communication between Central Oregon outposts and forts depended on thin lines. Mail for a short time, in the early 1860s, was carried in Pony Express mail bags between The Dalles and Canyon City, in competition with Henry Wheeler's stages. There was limited communication between the gold country and Boise to the east.

First mail from The Dalles, over an established route, was taken to Prineville under a pony express contract, about 1879. The route was from The Dalles to Dufur, then overland past Wapinitia to Simnasho, Wasco County, and Warm Springs. The mounted carrier crossed the Deschutes on a ferry near the Ed Campbell place, not far from the spot where Peter Skene Ogden and his fur seekers forded the river in 1825.

Years after ruts made by immigrant wagons had faded and wheel tracks of army supply wagons had been overgrown by sage, a definite north-south pattern of travel through the area was established. This reached down Cow Canyon from the Bakeoven highlands. Over that rugged road and past a station where

Lige Haight collected toll, moved traffic from The Dalles. The old Cow Canyon Road was mostly along the bottom of a rocky creek. This was the section where ranchers of the region made a "major improvement" in 1869, after collecting $750 from merchants in The Dalles. Down that same canyon, many years later, the Oregon State Highway Department constructed a million-dollar road.

After the Oregon highway system was mapped in 1917, and The Dalles-California Highway became a major route, interior Oregon slowly emerged from its frontier epoch of poor roads and bad trails. The road system bypassed historic Antelope, but that village got a surfaced road, in 1958, from Shaniko. Two years later, the surfacing reached down Antelope Creek to join U. S. 97 at Willowdale.

News "Passed Along"

Although communication was poor prior to the turn of the century and for a decade later, residents of the sparsely-settled Central Oregon frontier got news from the "outside"—generally first hand, but possibly weeks old. Freighters driving inland from The Dalles, and also from Shaniko after the arrival of the railroad in 1900, were always a good source of news, as was the occasional "peddler," such as Jack Tunney, who drove from home to home in the ranch country, to display his stock of goods carried in a small, covered wagon drawn by two horses. Tunney not only brought news of happenings in the Oregon country, but he frequently had old papers with accounts of world events, such as the Boer War and the Russian-Japanese conflict.

Itinerant dentists were also a source of news, which was related as they extracted aching teeth. Some of the news was badly garbled and became more so after being relayed through the range country.

Prior to the extension of the railroad from Biggs up through Sherman County to Shaniko, the Farewell Bend community got its mail from Prineville, with delivery made by horseback in the

1880s. Mail was brought to the Collins Ranch on the Deschutes River at the "Old Orchard," near the north city limits of modern Bend. Later, mail was brought from Prineville to Bend by buck-board; at first, three times a week.

Not until 1911, when the railroads came, did Bend look to the east. Earlier, communication between the Bend community and Burns was by way of Prineville and over the high country at the head of Crooked River. In 1911, Bend businessmen contributed about $600 for the survey and improvement of a road to Burns. That was the start of the Central Oregon Highway—fast, straight U. S. 20 of the present.

Prior to 1917, the route of the major north-south road that was to serve Central Oregon, and eventually become U. S. 97, was uncertain. Would it be through Prineville and south up Bear Creek to Silver Lake and beyond? Or would it be surveyed south through Bend? The line through Bend was approved, with travel using the Trail Crossing span deep in the Crooked River Gorge near Smith Rock. Years later, on July 16, 1927, the high steel bridge at the Ogden Park crossing of Crooked River was placed in use when Governor Ike Patterson cut a ribbon symbolizing completion of the project that finally "firmed" lines of travel through the interior region.

The Printed Word Comes

News in Oregon's isolated interior country took a long step forward in the fall of 1880, date of the publication of the region's first newspaper, the *Ochoco Pioneer*, in Prineville. John E. Jeff-rey, possibly confident that a new county would be created and that there would be some good county-seat printing business, established a weekly, but it lasted only a few months. In 1881, H. A. Dillard—who pioneered journalism in Harney County with his *Harney Valley Items* six years later—launched the Prineville *News*. D. W. Aldridge was partner in the Prineville enterprise and became editor and publisher.

Through the years various other papers appeared on the

Prineville scene, to record the story of the range country that called itself America's "last frontier," but they made little mention of two other towns that were appearing in Central Oregon—Bend and Redmond. One of the strongest of early-day Prineville papers was the *Crook County Journal*, which was in competition with the *Ochoco Review*.

As a result of the merger of the Prineville *Call* and *Western Stock Grower* in 1922, the *Central Oregonian* was established. The Prineville paper continues to date under this title, with Mrs. E. A. Donnelly as publisher. The Prineville papers hold the most valuable record of early-day events in Central Oregon.

Years after the gold trail from The Dalles to Canyon City grew dim, the weekly *Herald* was established in Antelope. It was started on July 22, 1892 by E. M. Shutt. This newspaper operated sporadically through the years, finally disappearing in 1925. However, it managed to win national attention as the paper on which the young H. L. Davis served his apprenticeship. Davis attended school in Antelope, where his father was high school principal; he spent his spare time gathering news for the paper and setting type. His *Honey in the Horn* (1935) became a Harper's and Pulitzer prize winner.

Publisher Wins Spurs

Antelope was not only the scene of the writing apprenticeship of H. L. Davis, but it was there that Max Lueddemann, a native of Alabama, assumed the role of publisher of a string of newspapers—one of the first mass ownerships of newspapers in Oregon. Following the great fire in Antelope in the summer of 1898, Lueddemann took over the Antelope *Herald*. This was the start of a decade that was to bring much business to weekly newspapers, in the publication of "legals"—mostly homestead and timber claim notices required by law. Lueddemann conceived the plan of establishing weeklies in various Central Oregon towns. One of these papers was the Bend *Bulletin*, and another was the Ashwood *Prospector*. Lueddemann also acquired the year-old Madras *Pioneer,* established by Timothy Brownhill in 1904. The *Pioneer,* which had various owners, continued into the 1960s under the ownership of Elmo Smith, ex-governor of Oregon; and W. C. Robinson. Possibly the biggest news story ever carried by the *Pioneer* was the virtual destruction of Madras by fire in September 1924.

When Wheeler County was organized in 1899, the new county found a newspaper already in business and ready to handle county publications. This was the Fossil *Journal.* The founder was H. H. Hendricks, attorney. Population of the range town was only three hundred, but legal-minded Hendricks saw an opportunity to get some revenue from land-settlement notices. Sloan P. Shutt, connected with other early publishing projects in Oregon, was the first editor. Down through the years and into the 1960s, the *Journal* continued to serve the area, under different owners, one of whom was James S. Stewart. On Stewart's shoulders fell the leadership in the successful fight to create Wheeler County.

Even the little town of Mitchell, deep in the gorge of Bridge Creek, had its weekly newspapers. First was the Mitchell *Monitor,* launched in 1894 by "Rocky Mountain" Smith, a peripatetic printer-editor, and W. F. Magee, a school teacher. The Condon *Globe* greeted its new journalistic neighbor in a manner that was just short of libelous even in those days:

> The first issue of Mitchell's new paper, the *Monitor,* reached our table last week. "Rocky Mountain" Smith, the notorious temperance reformer (who tries to drink all the liquor himself in order to discourage others from drinking) and W. F. Magee, a school teacher, were partners until the first issue came out and in it their dissolution notice appears.

The *Monitor* was followed by the Mitchell *Sentinel* and the *Wheeler County Chronicle.* Finally Mitchell shifted its newspaper allegiance over the Ochocos to Prineville, with the *Central Oregonian* presently taking care of the town's journalistic needs.

A newspaper that was to get attention in Oregon's land fraud cases early in the century, the *Deschutes Echo,* was printed on a small press set up in Bend's rival community, Deschutes. The *Echo* was founded by A. C. Palmer, and the Grass Valley *Journal* commented: "Mr. Palmer has started his paper a little early in order to catch some of those always-welcome-to-the-printer timber notices." It was charged that Stephen A. Douglas Puter, who turned state's evidence in the historic land fraud trials in 1905, had lined up 108 "dummies" as entrymen to obtain timber land in Crook County. Since the claims had to be advertised for nine weeks in a newspaper nearest the land, Puter needed the services of a newspaper. This was the *Echo,* printed with a $50 press and distributed from a pine stump. Puter paid the *Echo* editor $10 per claim. The total of $1080 was not bad for eight weeks' work in 1905.

Advertisements in the little paper included mention of the "Hotel Staats," the pioneer stopping place on the Deschutes near the Bend site. G. M. Cornett, operator of the Shaniko-Prineville-Bend Stage Line, advertised that stages left Shaniko every evening, following arrival of the Columbia Southern train, and reached Bend twenty-four hours later, via Prineville. That brief advertisement did not note the changes of horses on the long drive, the winding road down Cow Canyon, or the long haul up McPherson Hill out of Hay Creek.

Bend Bulletin *Established*

In mid-March of 1903, a freight wagon wheeled in from Shaniko over a muddy road and backed up to the lone door of a log cabin in the village of Bend. Unloaded from the wagon were a hand press and a couple of cases of type. Editor Don P. Rea took an inventory of his equipment, found he had enough type to get out a paper despite loss of a case in transit, and went to work. A. H. Kennedy was the printer. By March 27, the men had completed the cleanup of the rat-infested cabin and the "shakedown" of the little press. That evening the little weekly was printed. It was destined to become Central Oregon's first daily newspaper, on December 6, 1916, one week before Deschutes County was created.

One of the first stories in the young paper—printed within a stone's throw of the rippling Deschutes—was a prophetic news item. That story, in April 1903, predicted that before long, two giants of the railroad world, E. H. Harriman and James J. Hill, would compete in a race to the rapidly developing Bend country. It was forecast that the race would start from Shaniko and that lines of steel would reach down from the brushy plateau into Trout and Hay creeks, then south to the pine forests of the Deschutes. Shaniko at the time was the end of the rails.

The railroad race between the giants did start a few years later, but its locale was the rocky Deschutes Gorge, not the Shaniko plateau. When the big railroad news "broke" some six years later, it made headlines for the *Bulletin* from 1909 through 1911.

In its first issues the *Bulletin* had about as much advertising from Prineville and Shaniko as from Bend. The ad of the Reception Saloon in Shaniko, ninety miles to the north, suggested that timber locators should stock up on gin and whiskey before going into the remote Deschutes and Fremont woods. Hotel Prineville proudly advertised it had "electric lights throughout the house."

The weekly paper remained in its cabin home—in Bend's Drake Park of the present—for about a year and a half, with members of the staff frequently taking a "break" by going to the nearby Deschutes and returning with fine catches of trout. In the late summer of 1904, it moved uptown to the J. M. Lawrence building. Lawrence followed Lueddemann as publisher. Six years later, the paper passed into the hands of George Palmer Putnam, a dynamic young writer from the East.

Under the editorship of Putnam, the *Bulletin* rapidly gained status as one of Oregon's top weeklies. Serving as special correspondent for the *Oregonian*, Putnam "covered" the battle of the railroad giants in the Deschutes Gorge, in the race to reach Bend. For a time, Putnam was secretary to Governor James

Withycombe, and there was also time out for service on the Mexican border, when the young publisher, already widely known in the east as a writer, sought new adventures. In later years, he married Amelia Earhart, the first woman to cross the Atlantic in an airplane.

In 1917, Putnam sold the *Bulletin* to a young Harvard law graduate, Robert W. Sawyer, who, while working for The Bend Company, served as "mill correspondent" and attracted Putnam's attention with his prose and poetry. Sawyer and his associate, Henry N. Fowler, sold the *Bulletin* to Robert W. Chandler in 1953, the year the paper observed its golden anniversary.

Through the years, headlines in the *Bulletin* became the history of the Deschutes country: "Gold rush takes place on Cline Butte," "Homestead of L. D. Wiest receives first water diverted from Deschutes," "Telephone line arrives," "John E. Ryan purchases 40,000 acres of timber," "Bend without mail for ten days," "E. H. Harriman and sons invited to Bend." Through the decades, the paper has had periodic competition, with dailies, weeklies, and bi-weeklies temporarily in the field.

Laidlaw Also Has Paper

Another paper published in the Bend area was the *Chronicle,* with Laidlaw (Tumalo) as its home. A. P. Donahue was the publisher, and the first issue appeared in 1905. Two years later, the *Chronicle,* which heralded the possibilities of Laidlaw as the Central Oregon metropolis, was still in the field. Laidlaw based its metropolitan hopes largely on the coming of the Corvallis and Eastern Railway over the Santiam Divide. In 1911, it suspended publication.

Redmond's first newspaper was launched in 1909 when that town was still in Crook County. The paper was the *Oregon Hub,* with W. D. Walker as publisher. In 1910, the Redmond *Spokesman* was started, and it has been the only paper in its field since 1915. In nearby Culver, the *Deschutes Valley Tribune* was in existence for several years. The weekly paper that Lueddemann set up in Ashwood was the *Prospector*. It faithfully recorded the news of the community when men were digging into aged hills in search of gold and silver. The major news recorded concerned the "Oregon King" mine. A paper that achieved a circulation of 627, while published in a town with a population of only 40, was the *Intermountain* of La Pine, established in 1911.

Silver Lake, a town not much larger than La Pine, had two papers—the *Leader* and the *Central Oregonian*. Eventually the *Central Oregonian* disappeared from the field, to leave the name free for the Prineville paper of later years. The *Leader* continued publication until 1928. Even some of the virtually unknown communities of the semi-desert region in northern Lake County had their weekly papers. One of these was Fleetwood, where strips of newspaper "boiler plate" were found in 1962 in an area once occupied by a hamlet, but now covered with dunes.

CHAPTER 23

Round Trip to Shaniko

DESPAIRING OF EVER GETTING A RAILROAD, Central Oregonians in 1905 turned their attention to the possibilities of a "road train" to serve the region. Such a "train," actually a bus, temporarily materialized and made transportation history: it was the first intercity bus in the United States.

Bend at the time was a slow-growing hamlet on the upper Deschutes River, its progress hampered by inadequate transportation. Shaniko, ninety miles distant, was the nearest railroad. Operating between Shaniko and Bend, via Prineville, were stage coaches of the Concord type and freight wagons pulled by four-, six-, eight-, or ten-horse teams. Shaniko and Bend were days apart—and in muddy weather, or during winter when roads occasionally were blocked by deep drifts, they were weeks apart.

Settlers were surging into Central Oregon from all parts of the country, attracted by national publicity about the "new Bend country of Oregon" and by the thousands of acres that were to be irrigated from the Deschutes. Some were lured by timber claims or the prospect of reclaiming ranches from the sage country to the east of Bend. Many of the prospective settlers turned back at Shaniko, discouraged by long waits at the end of the rails and by the rutted roads and deep gorges ahead; the trip to the interior was too much of a challenge to many easterners who had never been outside of big cities. In Shaniko, the land seekers heard about the terrible road down Cow Canyon, and about the deep-rutted roads across the sage plateau. Freighters, back from muddy trips inland, told of doubling teams to get out of the Trail Crossing gorge of Crooked River. Some land seekers endured the long trip to the inland region, but on arrival they were in no mood to continue another hundred miles or so into the southeast to look at lands. Before reaching Bend, most of the land hunters had been bounced in horse-drawn stages for twenty-four hours or more.

The situation was serious and a solution to the transportation problem was sought. Deschutes Irrigation and Power Company officials in Bend came up with a plan: why not build a big automobile to meet the train at Shaniko? This was to be an auto stage. Some would call it a "road train." William A. Gill of Portland was engaged by the Deschutes Irrigation and Power Company to build the rig, and he completed it in March, 1905. The bus had four seats, solid rubber tires, four six-inch bore cylinders, and a top speed of forty miles an hour, but a full load slowed it to twenty-five. It weighed 6,800 pounds and was equipped with air brakes and an air whistle. Not another vehicle boasted air brakes in that year—or for many years later.

A clause in Gill's contract with the new Shaniko-Bend Stage Company called for a round-trip test run between Shaniko and Bend. Gill made the run with Dewey Tyler as driver. The "train," which included the big gasoline auto with a trailer attached, was assembled in Shaniko. It failed in its first attempt to get down Cow Canyon, despite earlier efforts to build an automobile road from Shaniko to Bend down the rocky gorge. That road was constructed to a point about five miles from Madras, where it ended in the old range country because a sheep rancher refused to grant a right-of-way across his lands.

Finally, though, the big "road train" started moving. The *Madras Pioneer* of April 20, 1905, described its grand entry into Madras:

Coming with a rush down the hill north of town and giving a series of warning toots which aroused a general exclamation from dogs and chickens, the big gasoline automobile belonging to the Central Oregon Transportation Company arrived in Madras Friday. It was commanded by M. W. (Dewey) Tyler, accompanied by W. A. Gill, Don P. Rea, and Frank Lucas. The monster was immediately the center of attention.

The big engine, while traveling from Shaniko, averaged a little more than eight miles an hour over difficult roads, very much unsuited to this type of vehicle. The auto is the largest ever constructed in the United States, and is truly a monster machine. It has four engines. Should one of the engines break, the machine can still be propelled, providing gearing is intact.

The machine eventually reached Bend, where it was the center of much attention. Schools were dismissed and pupils were given free rides. Bend residents were driven to points of interest, including the Lava Butte area, ten miles to the south.

The big "auto train" made only a few trips from Shaniko, Madras, and Bend. Cost of operation was heavy and roads were rough, rutted and rocky. The trailer, intended to transport freight and baggage, bounced wildly on its solid tires. There were many breakdowns and long delays in obtaining repairs.

Actually, the auto train had been designed to operate over a sixteen-foot roadbed, a short section of which was built. That section of the route was first plowed, then scraped and leveled, and finally packed with a ten-foot roller. This packed surface was treated with a coat of petroleum, to become the first "oiled" road in Central Oregon. The roadbed started at Cross Keys, twenty-three miles south of Shaniko. Before reaching the surfaced road, the "road train" had to move over the Shaniko flats with its many mounds, then down narrow, fender-scraping Cow Canyon.

Bend was the southern terminus of the road built for the "auto train," but the prepared route never reached Bend. Construction was limited to a fifteen-mile section. Over most of the ninety miles, the "auto train" made its own way through the sage. Soon, though, it became badly damaged by the uncushioned jolts from the hard tires. The venture made headlines for a time, but within a few weeks the project was forgotten—a failure in the history of Central Oregon transportation.

Bus via Mt. Hood

Where the Central Oregon Transportation Company failed in pioneer days, a Bend man, Myrl P. Hoover, succeeded in later years. He founded a transportation firm, now Pacific Trailways, that serves three states. Four persons who missed a bus on a June day in 1929 indirectly received credit for the start of the Bend-based transportation system, which had its origin as Mt. Hood Stages, Inc.

Hoover had been a Bend city fireman, a for-hire automobile operator, and a service station owner. On a pleasant June day, he started to drive to Portland but stopped in Redmond to get a new gas line for his car. At the station he found four men who had missed their bus to The Dalles and faced a day's delay in a trip they had planned to Portland. Hoover asked them if they were willing to take a chance and travel with him over the old Barlow Trail, an unimproved, rutted road across the southern shoulder of Mt. Hood. The four decided to take the chance. To the surprise of all, the Hoover car reached Portland ahead of the bus the men had missed.

That was a fateful ride for Myrl Hoover: on that trip an idea was born. He decided to establish a bus line to Portland from Bend over the Barlow Route, known generally as the Mt. Hood Route. He traded his new model "A" Ford for a 1926 Cadillac sedan, filed for a PUC license to operate a stage service on alternate days between Bend and Portland, and, on June 24, 1929, made the first run of Mt. Hood Stages, predecessor of Pacific Trailways. It was from that beginning, that an American success story evolved.

Using the modernized Mt. Hood Route now are big buses that operate in Oregon, Idaho, and Utah.

CHAPTER 24

Law in the Sage Country

LAWMEN FACED DIFFICULT TASKS IN CARRYING ON THEIR WORK in the Central Oregon range country. Distances were great, roads were rugged, and trails were winding. Communications were poor, or did not exist. Up until about 1910, officers traveled mountain and plateau trails on horseback. A sheriff frequently rode alone, and occasionally he was required to enter, without armed "cover," the isolated ranch home or cabin of a suspect. Despite these problems, the officers who rode the trails muddied by showers or covered by snow usually got their men.

On sheriffs or their deputies rested the task of law enforcement in the Central Oregon counties prior to the establishment of the Oregon State Police in 1931. Sometimes a sheriff was joined by a posse, especially in a search for a killer. Before the creation of Crook County, in 1882, it was common for groups of men serving as sworn deputies to take over law enforcement. This occurred in the Antelope country in the early 1890s when a man, identified only as Harvey, shot and killed a well-known stockman, Rod Grant. The posse traced Harvey into the Shaniko Flats, found him at dawn beside a campfire, and shot him down.

Earlier in the last century, the long "gold trail" from The Dalles to Canyon City was the scene of a number of murders— not all of them attributed to raids by Indians on miners moving to and from the upper John Day country. There were numerous robberies by whites who attacked the men carrying the gold nuggets. That was an era when there was little law in the region, and few of the killers were caught. But attacks by whites and Indians gave place names that remain a century later. A famous one of these is Murderers Creek in Grant County, where a party of eight prospectors died in an Indian attack.

Prohibition Posed New Problems

The Prohibition Era, from 1919 until 1933, posed new and difficult tasks for county, state, and Federal officers, and few parts of the Pacific Northwest had more moonshine stills in operation during the "great experiment" than Central Oregon. Much of this activity was on the sparsely settled High Desert, the no-man's-land of the interior plateau.

Both the isolation and the topography of the region aided the makers of illegal liquor. It was easy to detect the approach of officers, and there were many secluded places where stills could be set up. Some of the choice spots were in the openings of lava caves; others were in the sheltered coves of the High Desert's waterless river; still others were in abandoned cabins of the earlier land-rush era.

The Central Oregon moonshining industry began shortly before the end of World War I, when men with little or no knowledge of liquor-making fashioned crude stills from copper boilers and coils, then launched their great experiment with sugar, corn meal, barley, and wheat. At first the potent product from the desert stills was sold in nearby towns to a select trade. Later, as competition increased, the market expanded, and moonshine runners took their liquor into Portland and Seattle. Some of this liquor produced in caves of the High Desert bore Canadian labels.

Sheriff's officers attempted to check the growth of the moonshine industry, but they found it was difficult to carry out scouting work: the local officers were too well known. Even their absence from town, or a drive east on the High Desert, might serve as a signal that would leave stills quickly vacant. Stills were easily located, but not their owners. Another reason that moonshiners were rarely found with their stills was their manufacturing procedure. The distillers would mix their "batch" for fermentation, then take to the hills and watch from a distance. Sometimes investigators traced them down through large purchases of ingredients in Bend, Prineville, Redmond, Madras, or other towns.

Occasionally, though, persons operating stills were "at home" when officers arrived. Consider the case of the "Ventriloquist of the Woods."

In 1924, Deputy Sheriff Henry A. Dussault of Madras and federal men received a tip that a moonshine still was in full operation high in the lake country of the timbered Cascades in western Jefferson County. The deputy, his aides, and federal officers headed for the hills. At dawn, six officers, all armed, surrounded the mountain cabin that was suspected of being the center of a moonshine operation. As full light came to the woods, a tall man emerged from the plant and started cutting slabs of wood. The officers prepared to move in.

While waiting for a bit more dawn light in the timber, they heard voices. Some were high, some low, and some seemed to be argumentative. The concealed officers went into a huddle. One expressed a fear held by all, "Our posse is too small to charge that gang. There must be a dozen or more men around that cabin."

But finally, with guns ready, the officers moved in. They found only one man, the woodchopper. He had been talking to himself, "in many languages and in many moods." At times his voice was high, and it echoed from the cliffs and trees.

The "Ventriloquist of the Woods" was taken prisoner without difficulty, and his plant was confiscated. Later, it was found that the "ventriloquist" was only the employee of a big-time operator.

Death in a Dugout

State prohibition officers took over when it became evident that local officers could not curb moonshining, but they worked under no such handicaps as those that faced the well-known local peace officers. State men came into the area as strangers, at times to make liquor purchases, but generally to trace the illegal liquor to its source.

In mid-February of 1926, three prohibition officers who were stationed in Bend got a "fix" on a moonshine plant in the Bear Butte Hills, over the county line in Crook, near the edge of the High Desert. The plant was in a small gully screened by junipers, on a high slope of the butte. The officers found a small dugout, in which a big batch of mash was brewing. There they awaited the return of the operator, concealing themselves inside. After they had waited for eighteen hours, a young man, leading a packhorse, rode up to the dugout, apparently noticed the tracks, and placed a blocking plank against the door. Then he lighted a match, placed his hand through an opening and attempted to look inside. Immediately an officer grabbed his hand. Two of the men broke the door open. As they did so, a shot was fired and the youth was killed. At an inquest that followed in Prineville, the officers were exonerated of any blame in connection with the shooting, but feeling ran high in the range country. It was felt by some that the youth who was killed was not the actual operator of the still.

Two weeks later, a terrific blast rocked part of Bend and demolished an apartment in which the state officers lived. One of the investigators and his wife were asleep in the apartment at the time, yet escaped injury, despite the fact that the explosion ripped the building apart. Officers strongly suspected that the attempted dynamiting of the state men was an aftermath of the Bear Butte shooting.

Three Trappers Murdered

Not all of Central Oregon's crimes of the 1919-1933 epoch could be traced to moonshining operations. Fox furs, not liquor, apparently were responsible for one of the most gruesome of all crimes of the area. That was the brutal murder of three trappers as they stepped from their mountain cabin near the shore of Little Lava Lake in the winter of 1923-24. The exact date of the

This was the Fast Freight and Express between Bend and Burns, about the time the railroads arrived. Here the freight is ready to start out over the High Desert, with detours around junipers and lava mounds.

An auto-stage, the first real intercity bus in the United States, began operating in 1905 between Shaniko and Bend, in Central Oregon. It had solid rubber tires, four six-inch bore cylinders, a top speed of forty miles an hour, and was equipped with air brakes. Not another motor vehicle boasted such brakes until 1941. At the wheel here is Dewey Tyler.

A common admonition heard on Central Oregon highways, in the days when automobiles frequently stalled, was "get a horse." This car is being towed by a covered wagon drawn by four horses.

Seven Mile Hill on the old Santiam Road challenged motorists in early days. This planked section was built over sand and lava.

Teams and "big wheels" like these were used in the early days of logging in the Deschutes country.

, six-horse team hauls a load of logs through Bend in a 1908 celebration. This was the era of horse-logging in the Deschutes woods.

At the turn of the century, the summer supply of ice came from Arnold Ice Cave. Great chunk of ice such as these were cut from the cavern and lifted to the surface with block and tackle.

When George Millican, Central Oregon pioneer, found the Prineville stock country getting crowded in the early 1870s, he moved his stock into the High Desert country east of Farewe Bend. Shown here are the remnants of his Millican Valley ranch, with the village of Millic on the distant skyline.

triple murder will never be known, for the bodies were not discovered for months after the tragedy.

The three men, Roy Wilson, Dewey Morris, and Ed Nichols, had gone into the high country at the head of the Deschutes River to spend the winter at a fox farm at Little Lava Lake. When they did not return to their homes in Bend, relatives grew fearful they had met with some mishap. On April 13, 1924, H. D. Innes and Owen Morris hiked over deep snow to Lava Lake. They found the mountain cabin vacant. On the table was an unfinished breakfast. Evidently the men had left the cabin hurriedly in the midst of their breakfast.

Tracks of a sled led from the cabin door to the nearby lake, which in April was still covered with ice and snow. Out a short distance from the shore, a hole had been cut in the ice; nearby was the sled. Human hair was found on the ice, and blood stains on the sled. When the lake ice broke ten days later, on April 23, the three bodies came to the surface. Each had been shot in the back of the head.

All foxes in the Little Lava Lake pens had been killed and their pelts taken.

Immediately a search was launched for an escapee from the Idaho penitentiary who had been seen the previous fall in the area of the triple murder. He was identified as the man who had sold furs in Portland, apparently taken from the Lava Lake foxes. The hunt for the suspect spread over the entire Northwest. Eventually he was found and jailed, but on another charge—that of binding the hands and feet of a Bend taxicab driver with haywire and throwing him into a High Desert well. The driver was rescued several days later. Whether the suspect was the actual killer of the three trappers could not be proved.

Coyote Mountain Death Unsolved

One of the strangest unsolved murders of the mid-Oregon region was that in which a Jefferson County rancher was shot from his horse in the autumn preceding the Lava Lake murders.

The rancher left his ranch home in the Coyote Mountain country one morning, planning to ride the range for stock and return
to his family in the evening. Hours later, his horse, covered with
blood, came back to the ranch.

Officers scoured the area, but could find no trace of the missing rancher, until the man's wife told of a dream in which she
saw her husband dead on a mountain trail. Mrs. Alvin Robinson
carefully described the area where in her dream she said she
saw her husband dead. The area was high in the Coyote Mountain country on a "saddle" near the northeast base of the old
Clarno volcano. Mrs. Robinson told her story to Deputy Sheriff
H. A. Dussault of Jefferson County, who was working with Sheriff Bern Gard. Dussault recognized the place described by Mrs.
Robinson, and to please her, decided to ride back into the hills.
He was accompanied by Charles Keegan and Clarence Short,
local ranchers.

Equipped with a cutter to slash wire fences and make a direct ride into the area possible, Dussault and Keegan headed for
the "saddle" while Short swung around Coyote Mountain. As the
riders neared a deep ravine near which Mrs. Robinson had "seen"
the body of her husband in her dream, Dussault's horse became
frightened, and would not cross a ravine. Dussault dismounted,
walked a short distance, and found there on the mountain trail,
the body of the missing rancher. He had been shot twice through
the back.

The range murder occurred not far from Black Rock, where
a sheepman, Tom Reilly, died under gunfire twenty-five years
earlier, in a feud over range. The range fight was in a lonely
land that reached into the Box Spring high country from the
Muddy Ranch, on a creek just south of the John Day River.

Robbers Trapped by Storm

Five minutes past noon on May 29, 1935, two strangers
walked briskly into the Dairymen's Bank in Redmond, whipped

out pistols and declared: "This is a stickup." The holdup men quickly scooped the money into a bag and drove away, taking as hostages Cashier George Rice, his daughter Henrietta, and Ruth Roberts, members of the bank staff. They headed west over the Sisters road, toward Cline Falls. Officer Joe Miller of the Oregon State Police heard of the robbery and raced west after the speeding car. In a quick stop, the bandits released their hostages and crossed the Cline Falls bridge over the Deschutes. Miller found the getaway car abandoned on a side road. There the trail seemed to end.

Another state officer, Art Tuck, joined Miller in the search. In looking over the area, they found that a light spring shower had dampened the road leading up the Deschutes to Tumalo. In the moisture were the fresh tracks of a car. The officers followed the tracks to the home of a well-known resident of the area, near Deschutes Junction. There they traced the tracks into the ranch garage, where they found the motor still hot. Upstairs in the ranch home, the officers heard voices. With gun drawn, Officer Tuck went upstairs while Officer Miller stood guard outside.

Tuck found two men counting money in a second-floor room. The money, it developed, was part of the $1948 missing from the Redmond bank. Out in the field at the time was the owner of the ranch, who proved to be an accomplice in the robbery. All three men received penitentiary sentences, but Judge T. E. J. Duffy of Bend gave the ranch owner a longer term than the two men who actually held up the bank and abducted the cashier and the two girls.

Sheriff Killed by Bad Man

Bad men occasionally showed up in the range country, but none of the Central Oregon lawmen suffered the fate of a neighbor to the east, Sheriff W. A. Goodman of Harney County. He was shot and killed in the range country on August 27, 1924, while pursuing an exconvict, Arch O. Cody. A posse eventually overtook Cody in a running fight. He was convicted of murder and executed by the state.

Major crimes were rare in Central Oregon when stock raising was the dominant industry, but there was plenty of work for the officers who enforced livestock laws prior to the era of "gasoline cowboys." Thievery of cattle was common before the adoption of brand inspection laws. In one instance, shortly after the turn of the century, a rancher lost his entire herd of cattle, which mysteriously disappeared at night from open range close to the ranch buildings. The animals apparently were trailed east over a state line and sold.

The motor age brought cattlemen a new problem, that of thieves with portable butchering plants on wheels. They moved into stock ranges, killed and dressed animals, and sold the meat in cities.

Before the creation of Crook County, there was only one law enforcement officer in the entire region now embraced by Crook, Jefferson, and Deschutes. He was a deputy Wasco County sheriff, J. L. Luckey of Prineville, who did not even have a telephone to aid him in keeping peace in the inland plateau.

Nowadays, motorized sheriffs, their deputies, and Oregon State Police with two-way radios and office teletypes, maintain law and order in the old range country which Deputy Luckey covered on horseback.

CHAPTER 25

Giant Crook Divides

UP TO THE TURN OF THE CENTURY, CROOK COUNTY remained one big commonwealth. Then, in 1907, a "civil war" of words echoed over the stock country when a division was first suggested. The "watering of the wilderness" in the western part of the county and the talk about the coming of railroads resulted in a move, quiet at first, for the creation of a county from the western and southern part of Crook.

Prineville and its surrounding communities for many years had been a stock country. People there could not see eye-to-eye with the new settlers on the upper Deschutes, who were interested in timber, irrigation, and railroads. Actually, there was some opposition in the Prineville Valley—mostly on the part of the stockmen—to the move to obtain railroads. "West Side" residents of the Bend and Laidlaw areas felt they were not represented in the county government and were being unjustly taxed. Early in the century, there was stiff opposition among Bend residents to the construction of a new courthouse in Prineville.

On January 18, 1907, "the rupture had come." On that date, Bend launched a strong move for the creation of a new county that would include a large part of western Crook and the northern parts of Lake and Klamath. The proposed name for the county was "Deschutes." A bill calling for the creation of Deschutes County was introduced in the Oregon Legislative Assembly in Salem on February 1, but in that "panic year" of the original depression, the bill failed to get out of committee. It was killed on Valentine's Day and Oregon's birthday, February 14. Prineville rejoiced. Bend, Sisters, Redmond, and Laidlaw mourned.

County division—with Crook again the target—was once more up for consideration in 1910, when it was proposed to slash two big hunks from it, one of the new counties to be called Jefferson, and the other Deschutes. The law provided that division of a county required sixty-five per cent in the part remaining. Strategists decided that both Deschutes and Jefferson counties should be created at the same time, with each supporting the other in obtaining the required separation vote.

Jefferson Created

The proposed double slashing of Crook County was placed on the November 1914 ballot. Jefferson was approved, but Deschutes failed. The "West Siders" had to wait another two years before achieving their goal.

Oswald West was governor of Oregon when Jefferson was created, and he named William Boegli as first county judge. Appointed county commissioners were John M. King and Roscoe Gard. The court was empowered to select the county seat.

Immediately a deadlock developed and also a county-seat battle that received statewide attention when it reached its climax in a "raid" and the removal of records from one town to another. Judge Boegli favored Culver; John M. King, Metolius; and Roscoe Gard, Madras. The three towns, only a few miles apart, were all villages, but each hoped to become a metropolis in future years when Deschutes water greened lands that were seasonally dusty. Voting of the three court members on the county seat question took place at Metolius, the middle town of the trio seeking courthouse honors.

For 280 ballots, the judge and the two commissioners voted for their favorite towns. Then King switched to Culver. That was a hard blow to Metolius, and also to Madras. A temporary court building was erected at Culver, and offices of Oregon's newest county were established there.

At the election in 1916, the matter of a permanent county

seat was placed on the ballot. Madras, with the largest population, was the winner. Then the battle entered the courts. Culver
people brought suit in circuit court and were granted a temporary injunction. When the case went to court, the judge dis-
solved the injunction, clearing the way for removal of the court
from Culver to Madras on the following day, Monday, January
1, 1917. W. S. U'Ren, Portland attorney representing Madras,
heard of the dissolution of the injunction and advised Madras
people that they would be at liberty on Monday morning to appear in Culver, take possession of the records, and move the
county seat to Madras.

Culver citizens were bitter, saying they had erected a courthouse in good faith and felt they were entitled to keep the county seat. Several near-incidents occurred when the Madras group
showed up on Monday morning with sleds, wagons, and buggies
to get the records. W. P. Meyers, attorney for the Culver people,
faced the Madras people in the Culver courthouse and warned
that he would have all the "raiders" in jail within twenty-four
hours. Some of the county officials refused to give up their offices or records until audits were made. However, within a day,
all records were in Madras, which became the permanent county
seat of Jefferson.

Deschutes Vote Successful

The second and successful move to create Deschutes County
was started in the summer of 1916, following the unsuccessful
effort in 1914, when Jefferson was formed. In the intervening
years, "West Side" Crook County had greatly changed. Two of
America's largest pine-milling plants, those of the Shevlin-Hixon
Company and Brooks-Scanlon, Inc., had moved west from Minnesota and started the harvest of pine timber. By 1916, the population of western Crook County was greater than that in the
Prineville area. For a number of years, feeling ran high between
the two parts of the county. There were complaints in the Bend-
Sisters area about roads and bridges, and Bend residents objected

to long trips over dusty or snow-covered roads to transact legal business in Prineville, the county seat. Also, many of the "West Siders" were still rankling under the 1914 county division defeat.

By midsummer of 1916, plans had been carefully charted for a new attempt to create a county that would be known as Deschutes. The try was to be two pronged. One proposal provided for the transfer of the county seat from Prineville to Bend; the other for the creation of a new county from Crook. The county seat transfer bill actually was initiated but withdrawn when it became apparent that, in a second county division election, the rapidly growing population of the Bend and Redmond areas would make division a certainty.

The proposal calling for the creation of the County of Deschutes was placed on the November 1916, ballot and carried, but for a time developments threatened the validity of the election. In the little rangeland precinct of Fife, the board had certified all the votes for Deschutes County, whereas these should have been divided between the old and the new county. Opponents of the county division move entered a demurrer to the proposed correction of the votes, and the case went to circuit court—a case unique in legal records.

In December 1916, Judge T. E. J. Duffy, who also ruled on the county seat of the new county of Jefferson, overruled the demurrer.

Governor James Withycombe officially proclaimed Deschutes County created on December 13, 1916, following a canvass of votes by Ben Olcott, then Secretary of State. Oregon's newest county, named for the "River of the Falls," took its place among the big family of counties mothered by Wasco and Crook, with Bend designated the county seat.

Arrangements for county headquarters in two rooms of the new two-story O'Kane building in Bend were made, and two days later, the court approved plans for "permanent quarters" in the Deschutes County Investment Company building on Oregon Avenue. For the next eighteen years, county offices remained in the so-called Bank Building annex, but eventually it was decided that the county should have its own home. On April 9, 1935, a lease was signed with the Bend School Board for the old Central School building. But the efforts to obtain quarters immediately ran into a snag. D. W. Stone filed an injunction against reconstruction of the old school into a courthouse, attacking legality of the move. Circuit Judge Arlie G. Walker of McMinnville ruled in favor of Deschutes County, and, in mid-May 1935, county officers occupied quarters in the former school building.

On February 10, 1937, well before daylight, a glow illuminated low, frosty clouds over Bend. Soon the alarm spread: "The courthouse is on fire." Flames quickly swept through the building. When dawn came, only a shell of the building remained, and practically all county records had been destroyed in one of the worst fires in the history of Bend—which, as a growing village, had had its share of fires. Few of the records covering twenty-one years of the county's history could be replaced.

The county officers had occupied the former school building for twenty-one months when the fire occurred—the origin of which was never determined. Ironically, on the day the building was destroyed, Representative J. F. Hosch of Deschutes County was to have proposed to the Oregon Legislature a bill authorizing purchase of the old school by the county. The school district had agreed to sell the building for $33,000.

After the fire, county officials moved back downtown into leased quarters. Soon plans for a county-owned courthouse took shape, the location selected being only a stone's throw from the blackened walls of the building lost in the fire. A special levy for a new courthouse was passed late in 1937 by a vote of 2,369 to 2,308. From its rocky, landscaped knoll, this "new" courthouse still faces the imposing Three Sisters skyline on the western horizon.

Part Five

RAILROADS INTO THE PINES

CHAPTER 26

Battle of the Gorge

A SPECTACULAR AND COSTLY CHAPTER in the history of American railroads was completed on the sunny afternoon of October 5, 1911. On that day "Empire Builder" James J. Hill drove a golden spike at the end of the rails in Bend. Not one, but two railroads had been completed up the deep, narrow, and rocky gorge from the Columbia River to the Deschutes Plateau.

There was an urgent reason for the competitive construction by the two railroads up the Deschutes Gorge to Bend: billions of board feet of yellow pine timber along the eastern front of the Cascades and in the Paulinas and Ochocos was ready for harvest. Also, the coveted gorge route formed a natural gateway for both systems in their plans for the extension of rails—the Hill system south from Bend to California and the Harriman system over the plateau from Bend to the eastern part of the state. The Hill dream eventually materialized, the Harriman plan remained on paper.

Pioneer Engineers Guessed Wrong

The slow pounding of Hill's hammer against the gold-gilded spike at the Bend railroad station—before a crowd of some two thousand persons—proved that the U. S. Army Topographic Engineers in their pioneer horseback survey had been wrong. More

234

than half a century earlier they had studied the Deschutes canyon to determine whether trains could be brought up the narrow, rock-walled gorge. They reported it could not be done.

The driving of the spike also marked the end of one of the bitterest and costliest struggles in railroad history. Two of America's mightiest railroad systems—those of James J. Hill and Edward H. Harriman—had battled two years for right-of-way in a rugged canyon where a saddle horse could hardly get a footing.

The contest between the railroad giants in the race from the Columbia River to Bend cost just short of $25 million, with the Hill line bearing the lion's share, about $16 million. With the exception of a short section in the upper gorge, the two lines built separate tracks to Metolius. The Hill people built the steel span across Crooked River. At the time, this was one of the highest bridges in the world—350 feet long and 320 feet above the water level.

Long before that railroad battle in the Deschutes Gorge, surveys for various lines had been made through inland Oregon, and many railroads had been "built on paper"; but aside from the Columbia Southern, which reached the Shaniko flats in 1900 in a southerly extension from Biggs, no railroad construction was undertaken until 1909.

The first serious study of a railroad route through this country dates back to 1855. For more than a dozen years previous to this there had been agitation for railroad construction in the West. Then in the fall of 1854, young Henry Larcom Abbot, a West Point graduate, was assigned to the Pacific Railroad Survey. Jefferson Davis, then secretary of war, instructed him to make explorations for a railroad in the Deschutes country as a part of a general study under Lieutenant Robert S. Williamson, who was under orders to find the most practical and economic route for a railroad from the Mississippi to the Pacific Ocean. However, Lieutenant Abbot kept most of the records and did most of the work.

The survey party arrived in San Francisco by boat on May

30, 1855. Pack animals and supplies were assembled, and other members of the party reported, including Dr. John Strong Newberry, who was the geologist and botanist for whom Newberry Crater was named; and George Crook, for whom Crook County was named. Philip H. Sheridan joined the party later. The explorers with their military escort entered Oregon south of Klamath Falls, moved north along the Williamson River to Klamath Marsh, then followed a trail to Crescent and on to the Rosland area. From their camp in the upper Deschutes country, Sheridan and Williamson sought a railroad pass toward the "snow mountains" to the west, while Abbott moved north along the Deschutes. Williamson scouted the eastern slopes of the Three Sisters to Trout Creek and emerged from the timber near the Sisters site. From there, the Williamson party rode south to Tumalo Creek, where Abbot joined the group, on the night of September 3. The next day, Abbot headed north to The Dalles for supplies, while Sheridan and Williamson explored the high country westward from Trout Creek.

On his way to The Dalles, Abbot scouted the wild Deschutes and adjacent areas, and continued his exploration on his way back to Sisters, to rejoin the Williamson contingent. On leaving the Sisters country, Williamson and Sheridan rode south and crossed the present Willamette Highway route to western Oregon, in the Eugene area. Abbot explored the Cascades west of the Metolius and the Deschutes and crossed over the Warm Springs Reservation and the Cascades, coming out on the west side near Estacada. The Williamson and Abbot parties met at Fort Vancouver.

In his report on the region, Abbot wrote:

It will be seen that the Deschutes Valley is mostly a barren region, furrowed by immense canyons, and offering very few inducements to settlers. Its few fertile spots, excepting those in the immediate vicinity of The Dalles, are separated from the rest of the world by almost impassable barriers, and nature seems to have guaranteed it forever to the wandering savage and the lonely seeker after the wild and sublime in natural scenery.

Geographic names serve as reminders of the quest for a railroad route in the Deschutes country—a quest which was unsuccessful because of the rugged nature of the country and because of the seemingly insurmountable barrier presented by the Deschutes River Gorge. A mountain in the Cascades near the Deschutes source honors Williamson, as does a river in the Klamath Basin. A timbered butte in the Sisters area bears Abbot's name, and a volcanic peak near the base of Bachelor Butte bears Sheridan's.

Colonel Hogg's Railroad

Railroad builders of later years did not take such a dim view of the country. One, however, attempted to build a railroad over the Santiam Pass—and failed. He was Colonel T. Egenton Hogg. In 1871, Colonel Hogg conceived a plan to make Yaquina Bay and vicinity the big seaport of Oregon. The railroad was to go over the low Santiam Pass of the Oregon Cascades from Yaquina Bay to the eastern part of the state. Hogg got control of the Cascade Valley and Cascade Mountain Wagon Road, plus the adjacent sections of land grants assigned to the road company for its construction efforts. He used the grants to float bond issues in the East, for funds to carry out his road construction. A section of the railroad actually was constructed on the Santiam Divide, mostly by Chinese laborers. There still can be seen on the high Cascade Divide part of the railroad grade on which Hogg's car moved back and forth to preserve his rights. These rights called for operation of a railroad "over" the Santiam. Out of this venture, with its thousands of acres of grant lands, came the Oregon and Western Colonization Company, with ownership of farm and range lands in its hands, and timberlands in the ownership of the Hill family.

Hogg Rock, now skirted by the Santiam Highway, was named for this early railroad builder.

Another railroad that was built on paper through Central Oregon was the Oregon Short Line & Utah Northern Railway, which sought a line from Vale to the Bend site in 1889. It followed closely the line of the Willamette Valley & Coast Railroad survey of 1885. From Farewell Bend on the Deschutes, the Oregon Short Line was to turn south, following up the river to where the town of Crescent now stands. No work was ever done on that proposed line. The Willamette Valley and Coast Railroad would have connected with the Corvallis and Eastern.

Prineville Builds Own Line

One of Central Oregon's railroads is unique in America. It was city built in the war year of 1918, when a federal order was required to obtain steel; and it is city owned. This is the Prineville Railroad, which extends down Crooked River and over the O'Neil hump nineteen miles to Prineville Junction. There it links with the north-south track over which operate Oregon Trunk, Union Pacific, and Great Northern trains. Through this connection, Prineville moves its produce to continental lines.

The story of the Prineville City Railroad dates back to February 16, 1916, when the city council decided that something should be done to obtain rail transportation. Behind this decision was the need of a carrier to move the wealth of Ochoco timber to markets. Over in the Deschutes country, Bend had had rail service since 1911, and two of America's largest pine mills were preparing to start operations there. Bend was growing. Prineville councilmen decided that since a railroad would not come to Prineville, the city would build a line to the railroad. At its February 16 meeting the council asked for a vote of the people on a bond issue to build a railroad. The $100,000 issue was approved on March 28. Another $100,000 was added in a later vote that year. Eventually the bonded indebtedness for construction of the railroad was to reach $385,000.

In midsummer, 1918, the new railroad was completed, but it did not bring new life to Prineville overnight. For years the railroad did not pay and the city defaulted on interest and bonds. The debt was around $175,000, and the future of the line was dark. A small engine, the "Galloping Goose," moved daily up and down the track, sometimes with empty cars. Then came the big sawmills of 1937 and 1938; and the railroad, whose construction had attracted national attention, quickly became an asset as the wealth of the Ochoco pine country moved down Crooked River to the main line. By 1960, two modern diesel engines were operating over the trackage that was once the trail of the "Galloping Goose."

Oregon Trunk Line

As the nineteenth century ended, the challenge to build a railroad into the vast country immediately east of the Oregon Cascades was being widely accepted. In 1899, the Oregon Railroad & Navigation Company made a survey from The Dalles through Dufur to Tygh Valley, down White River to the Deschutes, and up the Deschutes to Bend. That survey called for a line through the Deschutes Canyon past the Cove, where Crooked River pours in from the east, but maps were never filed, the route being considered impracticable. Three years later, in 1902, the Columbia Southern made a location survey to extend the line from Shaniko through Antelope and Madras to the Bend site. However, no work was done south of Shaniko because of engineering problems.

In 1906, attention centered on the Deschutes Canyon as the most feasible route for a railroad into the inland plateau, despite the warnings of engineers of the Williamson survey party in 1855 that this region was one of "almost impassable barriers."

On February 24, 1906, the Oregon Trunk Line—a name that was to echo through the rugged Deschutes region—was organized in Nevada. A survey was made into Central Oregon from Dufur, end of the Great Southern. The survey was via Kingsley, Tygh Valley, White River, and the Deschutes, practically following the route abandoned by the O. R. & N. seven years earlier. The portion from Dufur to the mouth of White River was subsequently abandoned, and the line adopted followed up the Columbia River from The Dalles to the mouth of the Deschutes, then up the Deschutes and Willow Creek to Madras. Maps covering the line were filed in 1906 and 1907. No one realized it at the time, but this was the beginning of a project that was to mushroom into a multimillion-dollar undertaking and a grim struggle between barons of the railroad world, James Jerome Hill of the Great Northern and Edward Henry Harriman of the Union Pacific.

Gorge Battle Lines Drawn

The Oregon Trunk, it developed, was to become a Hill subsidiary. Soon the Harriman competition took shape, in the form of the DesChutes Railroad, with the firm adopting a spelling of the name of the river in common use at the time. The DesChutes firm soon made and filed maps of a line following up the Deschutes and Trout Creek to the plateau near Madras, but changes were made when construction started. At first there was little interest in the moves of the two railroad giants; Western America had not yet sensed the significance of this project at the mouth of the Deschutes, where the Columbia flows westward to the Pacific.

No work was done on either line in 1908, but that year the Central Oregon Railroad filed maps for a line from Madras to Bend over Crooked River. The new railroad, ownership of which apparently was known to few, was incorporated on June 18, 1908. In the following year it was taken over by the Oregon Trunk Line, Inc., through purchase of stock. Thus James J. Hill made a giant leap into Central Oregon, and, by acquiring the Central Oregon Railroad Company's rights, obtained a vital site for a railroad crossing of Crooked River—a move that was to be of great importance in the final phase of the Battle of the Gorge. By acquiring the crossing site, the Hill people had virtually blocked the Harriman move to build a parallel line to Bend.

Porter Brothers, a firm of contractors, suddenly appeared on the gorge battle lines when they bought stock in the Oregon

Trunk Line, in the amount of $170,352.50. Then they sold the stock for the identical price "in the interest of the Great Northern Railway." At the same time, John F. Stevens, world-famous engineer who had quietly scouted for a line through the Deschutes country a year before, became president of the Oregon Trunk Line.

The Battle of the Gorge had begun. In construction work, Porter Brothers represented the Hill interests and Twohy Brothers, the Harriman system. Through Twohy Brothers, the Des-Chutes Railroad moved crews to the east bank of the Deschutes while the Porter Brothers kept their crews on the west bank. As early as the summer of 1909, one of the surveyors recorded in his diary that crews from the opposite sides of the river were lobbing bullets at each other. "Fortunately," he added, "no one seems to be much of a shot."

Even before surveys were completed, contractors were busy in various parts of the long gorge that Peter Skene Ogden had crossed in 1825. Within a few days after the news broke that the Hill and Harriman people were engaged in a multimillion-dollar race into Central Oregon via the Deschutes route, contractors established camps up and down the river. More than one thousand men, working under twenty different contractors, were on the job for Porter Brothers within days after the battle was joined. At the same time, the O. R. & N. Co. moved twenty-six cars of laborers to various camps in the gorge. In July 1909, The Dalles *Chronicle* reported:

Harriman has begun work on the disputed route through the canyon and is prepared to seize the strategic points without waiting for the courts to settle the condemnation suits now pending with the Oregon Trunk. Camps established at various points between Deschutes (at the mouth of the Deschutes River) and Sherars Bridge are reported determined to repeat tactics which have proved effectual in the past, in an effort to secure any desired route against a possible rival.

First dirt was moved by Porter Brothers shortly before 12 o'clock, Monday night, July 26, 1909. When the Harriman forces awakened the next morning, crews found that not only were they cut off from a wagon road they had built, but that the line of construction they had mapped was covered with Porter Brothers men. Most of the camps were in the central gorge area, west of Grass Valley and Shaniko. Equipment, teams, and wagons were assembled in The Dalles area and moved to the construction scene. Within a few weeks, ranchers as far away as Axehandle and Ashwood could hear the rumble of blasting in the rocky gorge.

By September, preliminary skirmishing was over and all concerned were ready to settle down to the business of building railroads. The normal sources of labor supply were Portland and Spokane. Labor was in good demand and men were hard to hold. Common laborers received twenty to thirty cents an hour; carpenters and concrete men from thirty-five to forty cents; and well drillers were paid seven dollars a day. Teamsters received around six dollars. Camp lodging was furnished and meals were twenty-five and thirty cents.

Shaniko Branch Used

The nearest railways on which men, supplies, and equipment could be shipped in were the Shaniko branch of the Oregon-Washington Railroad & Navigation Company line, running from Biggs to Shaniko east of the Deschutes; and the Great Southern, running from The Dalles to Dufur west of the Deschutes. From these two railroads there was an average haul of twenty-five miles over mountainous wagon roads to reach points along the first seventy miles of grade, upstream from the Columbia.

Work in the narrow canyon of the Deschutes was not only costly and spectacular—it marked the end of an era. This was one of the last big jobs virtually "done by hand." Performing that work were thousands of laborers, mostly from southern Europe. Black powder, placed in "coyote holes" drilled into lava cliffs, tore away sheer walls of the gorge. Equipment mostly consisted of picks, shovels, wheelbarrows, hand-drilling tools, hand cars, and twenty-pound rail. Crews in the late summer of 1909 worked in the sweltering heat of the rocky canyon in areas occasionally infested by rattlesnakes. In winter, blasting crews often found these snakes rolled into balls.

Heat and reptiles were not all that bothered the men. Opposing crews had little tricks to make life miserable. Each side often placed spotters on cliffs overlooking the gorge. These spotters watched for places where their opponents stored powder. On dark nights, a crew of five or six men would slip across the river and detonate the caches. The result was that both sides faced delays because powder was not always available when needed.

The adopted lines of the two companies conflicted at several places, but all differences were settled when the Union Pacific (the Harriman system) agreed to hold to the east side of the Deschutes, and the Oregon Trunk pledged to stay on the west side. However, conflict continued in the area of the Warm Springs Indian Reservation. The Oregon Trunk built a grade across the DesChutes Railroad's survey line at Mile 75, blocking the Harriman crews. The upshot was that the Government enforced what was known as the Canyon Act, resulting in a joint track usage agreement covering eleven miles, between what became North Junction and South Junction. On May 17, 1910, the opposing contractors reached a "cease fire" agreement which was to last for "a period of 999 years." That action by the government foreshadowed the Interstate Commerce Commission jurisdiction over railroad construction.

One of the last fights for right-of-way between the two lines occurred on the homestead of Frank Smith in the North Junction area. The Oregon Trunk maps had been approved in Washington, D. C., before Smith secured title to his homestead. Johnson Porter of the Porter Brothers offered $2,500 for the place. The next day, the DesChutes Railroad offered $3,500 and posted armed guards. For a time, Porter Brothers carried construction material around the ranch, in a narrow section of the canyon. It appeared that the Harriman people had effectively blocked Oregon Trunk work in the canyon area. Finally the Oregon Trunk asked that the Canyon Act be enforced, and a compromise was effected. On May 17, 1910, a contract was signed whereby both roads agreed to use the Oregon Trunk tract for eleven miles in the canyon.

James J. Hill Looked to South

The plans of James J. Hill included a railroad not only to Bend but beyond. His ultimate goal was to penetrate California by way of Klamath Falls, with Bend his immediate objective. Early in the gorge struggle, the Oregon Trunk let a contract for construction from Madras to Bend, keeping men at work on approaches to the Crooked River bridge to hold the right-of-way. The DesChutes line had done nothing beyond Culver, where the lines of the two systems ran parallel, and only a hundred feet apart. First draft of the agreement for joint usage of the line from Metolius south provided only for entrance by Harriman to Redmond. Later, on September 6, 1911, this contract was amended to give Harriman the joint use of the Oregon Trunk Line from Metolius to Bend, with joint terminal facilities.

By this time the work of clearing a right-of-way for Hill's planned line to California was well under way, but the Hill railroad did not go south that year. Work was suspended because there seemed little prospect of immediate timber development. Old stumps of the clearings are still visible in the jackpines of the La Pine area and southward.

Sixteen years passed before the Oregon Trunk renewed its plan to push into the south. In that year, 1927, the Oregon Trunk applied to the Interstate Commerce Commission for a permit to construct a line from Bend to Klamath Falls—as originally intended. Finally it was the Great Northern, not its subsidiary the Oregon Trunk, that was granted I.C.C. permission to extend the line from Bend, thereby fulfilling the dream of James J. Hill and his great engineer and line president of a later day, Ralph Budd. The Great Northern pushed farther south than Klamath Falls though: it extended to Bieber, California, for a junction with the Western Pacific and a clear track to the Bay area of California. The first train over the extension south from Bend made its run on May 1, 1928.

Gradually through the years the Oregon Trunk and the Union Pacific consolidated trackage in the Deschutes Gorge. On July 10, 1923, an agreement was reached for the Oregon Trunk to use the DesChutes Company line between South Junction and Metolius, but not until July 1935 did the DesChutes Company abandon its line from Ainsworth to North Junction. By mid-century both lines operated over a single track between the Columbia River and Bend; the grim Battle of the Gorge had been fought in vain.

On October 5, 1911, when Bend celebrated Railroad Day, the Oregon Trunk was represented by its "top men." Watching James J. Hill drive the golden spike was William McMurray, general passenger agent of the Union Pacific. A colorful figure from the Harney ranges was William Hanley, who laid the cornerstone for the new Bend station.

What happened to the golden spike that was driven at the end of the rails in Bend in 1911? It was immediately withdrawn, then passed around for inspection, and was last seen in the hands of Jim Hill. One version is that after the ceremony and the break-up of the crowd of two thousand, Hill gave it to Bill Hanley, sage of the Harney rangelands, saying as he handed the spike to his long-time friend: "I was building the railroad to come and see you."

CHAPTER 27

Pines in the Spotlight

THE FIRST TRAINS that came out of the Deschutes Gorge to roll south over a new trackage to Bend in 1911 stopped at the edge of a forest that held some sixteen billion board feet of pine— great, tall trees, their bark yellow in the Central Oregon sun, trees that spread from the Cascades to the edge of a desert where conifers gave way to sage and juniper.

There were no large sawmills in Bend when the golden spike was driven at the end of the rails, but railroad men were willing to wait; they knew that back in the hills and around the flanks of the Paulinas was a vast stand of pine that would eventually be harvested, and hauled by train to the lumber-hungry East.

The railroad builders, James J. Hill and Edward H. Harriman, had estimates on the timber potential long before their railroad builders battled in the Deschutes canyon—but their figures were only guesses. The full wealth of the Deschutes timber, and that which mantled the Ochocos, was not known until cruises were completed in later years. Those cruises indicated that six and a half billion feet of pine timber on the Deschutes plateau was in national forests, with about nine and a half billion board feet privately owned. Ten billion or more board feet covered the Ochocos. Forests of pine reached to the Fremont rims.

The wealth of timber was scarcely touched when the railroads arrived, except in some marginal areas where pines had been felled and converted into lumber for local use, mostly in building frontier towns, ranch dwellings, and homesteaders' cabins.

Region's Mill History Traced

The settlers in the Prineville country obtained their building material the hard way; they cut small trees at the edge of the Ochoco timber, converted them into logs and built their first homes. Some preferred "lumber," and this they roughly trimmed from log slabs. C. C. Mailing of Grizzly noted the need for boards and, by 1877, had a mill on Willow Creek in initial operation. It was Central Oregon's first sawmill, the source of lumber for many pioneer homes, cabins, barns, and bridges.

Another of the early-day sawmills was on upper Trout Creek, where Charles Durham set up a plant close to the edge of the Ochoco timber to provide lumber for many of the first homes built in the communities north of Crooked River. Constructed in May 1901, the Pilot Butte Development Company plant was the first commercial sawmill in Bend. Its original location was at the rear of the Pilot Butte Inn of the present. Steidl & Reed also set up a sawmill in Bend in 1903. Its machinery was moved in with difficulty; a runaway of a four-horse team scattered the mill equipment over the Grizzly Mountain terrain, injuring the driver, John Tweet. Various other small mills were established in the region, to serve their immediate communities. Their annual cut was small—it scarcely dented the edges of the great pine forests.

Farm horses, all accustomed to hauling heavy loads, were used for dragging the big pine logs out of the woods to little mills operated by steam. The hauls were not great, for the mills were set up near the stands to be logged. There, little communities were founded, one at the Charles Durham mill up close to the edge of the Ochoco pines on Trout Creek. That mill, operated by a small crew, supplied lumber for hundreds of ranches and homesteads. Another of the pioneer mills, set up in 1906, was at the old Cowles Orchard area on the Deschutes west of Madras, where anglers now whip the river for trout. Virtually every range community—some half as large as present-day counties—had its own mill.

Early-day residents of Prineville and Bend, where big mills were later to take shape, were not greatly interested in the potential wealth of pines covering three mountain ranges, the Cascades, Ochocos, and Paulinas. There was no market for timber, aside from the few wagonloads of boards sawed daily by the small mills. Prineville was content to be recognized as a livestock center; Bend as an irrigation town. Stockmen seasonally grazed sheep and cattle in the high pine country, where range was lush and water was abundant, but they made no use of the wood. Occasionally when sheep came out of the mountains in the fall, fires blazed back in the timber, set by herders who believed that fire in the forest would provide more accessible grass in future years. Instead, manzanita spread over the old burns, to create impenetrable buckthorn thickets.

Actually, timber was available for the established ranchers of the region and the homesteaders. Under the Timber and Stone Act of 1878, ranchers could purchase 160 acres of non-mineral land at $2.50 an acre. This act was intended as a help to settlers who needed timber and stone for construction. However, in early years few homesteaders took advantage of the act, because they were usually able to pick up plenty of stones on their claims for building purposes, and they required only a few wagonloads of lumber for their homes and barns.

Rush for Timber Recalled

Near the turn of the century, settlers discovered that timber claims were gaining in value. Eastern lumbermen became increasingly aware of the great forest of untapped pine in the region. Around 1904, there was a renewed interest in the Timber and Stone Act, mostly by persons who did not even have homesteads to improve. Applicants for the timberlands were required to pledge that they would not transfer title to the 160 acres they could get at $2.50 an acre, but this "small print" was overlooked. "Entrymen" came from the East by the trainload, their way paid by persons seeking huge stands of timber. These entrymen filed on the claims and then transferred the title to others.

Out of this procedure grew the Oregon land fraud cases that attracted nation-wide attention. The timber rush ended in 1905 when forest reserves were placed in the U. S. Department of Agriculture and timber was withdrawn from entry. But this was after hundreds of thousands of timbered acres had been acquired by individuals from all parts of America. In later years, this privately owned timber was segregated into contiguous blocks, and huge stands were purchased by Midwestern lumber operators seeking new timber frontiers.

The original land now included in the Deschutes National Forest was withdrawn from the public domain by President Grover Cleveland on September 28, 1893, and was named the Cascade Range Forest Reserve. It embraced the area west of the Deschutes between Jefferson Creek on the north and Cottonwood Creek of the Diamond Lake country on the south. Much of the original forest land now in the Deschutes National Forest, east of the Deschutes, and in the Fort Rock country was withdrawn by President Theodore Roosevelt on July 31, 1903.

On September 17, 1906, the first national forests were created on the Deschutes plateau. They consisted of the Cascade National Forest on the west side of the Deschutes, and the Fremont on the east side. The Deschutes National Forest was created on July 1, 1908, and it included the present Ochoco National Forest. From time to time through the years, the boundaries have been changed.

When preserves were created and various timber withdrawals made, the federal government undertook the protection of the pine that covered the mountains of the interior country. This protection was inadequate, yet it was a beginning. Early in the century, a guard station, the first in the Deschutes woods, was established on the Metolius River at the pioneer D. W. Allingham homestead.

Two Men Guard Entire Forest

Cy G. Bingham was a forester who left his mark in the eastern Cascades. The first official ranger in the Deschutes timber, he received his appointment around 1900, when all the public domain was still administered by the General Land Office. W. P. Vandevert, an upper Deschutes rancher, had been on the job earlier, though his duties were more those of a fireguard than a ranger.

The boundaries of Bingham's district are not known, but they must have included practically all of the Cascade portion of the Deschutes forest and some of the Willamette west of the Cascade crest. His name can be seen inscribed on many trees throughout the area. Bingham and a companion—whose name of "Connolly" also appears on letters cut into trees—had cabins in the high country southwest of Bend. In 1908, Bingham was transferred from the Cascades to become supervisor of the Malheur National Forest at John Day.

Through the years, Central Oregon pinelands suffered from many large fires; and old scars on blackened, rotting stumps indicate that even before white men came, devastating fires swept through the woods. Pioneers said it was the practice of Indians to start "hunting fires," to get game out of the thickets. Lightning undoubtedly caused many of the early fires; scars on trees show that bolts frequently slashed into pines.

One of the largest fires in the Deschutes woods occurred in the Paulina Mountain country, in the arid August of 1908. That fire raged on an unbroken fifteen-mile front and became so serious that E. P. Petit, head ranger at the old Rosland station near La Pine, issued a call for 150 men. Coming from Shaniko, Moro, and other points along the Columbia Southern Railroad, they fought the wind-whipped fire for $2.50 a day and board. A providential rain finally checked the conflagration.

On June 6, 1910, the weather was hot and arid in the upper Deschutes country, some thirty miles southwest of Bend, when smoke curled up from the Edison Ice Cave area. Flames spread rapidly through the intermixed pine and lodgepole as erratic breezes whirled through the dusty timberlands. Before it was controlled, nearly a week later, the Edison Ice Cave fire had burned through seven thousand acres, to leave a wilderness of blackened snags.

A few years later, residents of Bend watched with fear as a great cloud of smoke billowed up from the Arnold Ice Cave area, twelve miles to the south. That fire destroyed ten thousand acres of timber in the country near the northern Paulina foothills. In 1926, another great fire occurred in the Fox Butte area east of the Paulinas. Bend residents drove to the top of nearby Pilot Butte to watch the clouds of smoke roll northeast into the High Desert.

The high Pine Mountain country on the skyline south of Bend was the scene of a twelve-thousand-acre fire in August 1926.

Greatest of all the fires in the Deschutes region was the Aspen Flat conflagration of July 23, 1959. It blackened some twenty-one thousand acres of marginal timber northeast of Fort Rock. Equipment brought into use to control that fire was unknown to early-day foresters—big tank-bearing planes that flew low over the fire front to drop borate slurry on the advancing flames. Smoke jumpers from the Redmond Air Base joined in the attack.

What a contrast with pioneer days when Cy Bingham and Bill Vandevert watched smoke curl into the sky from some distant mountain fire, kept an eye on it for a few days to determine whether it might prove dangerous, then—if conditions warranted —"took action." That action generally consisted of a one-man attack on the flames with shovel and axe.

CHAPTER 28

Sawmills on the Deschutes

THE PEOPLE OF BEND had changed their opinion about the value of the vast stand of pine in their immediate backyard, and had become restless there at the end of the rails when the big news came: two of America's largest pine-manufacturing plants planned to erect mills at the edge of town. One was to be on the east side of the Deschutes River, the other on the west side, and they were to face each other across the big curve in the river, known to pioneers as Farewell Bend.

The year was 1915. A great war was being fought in Europe, with the United States still on the sidelines. The demand for lumber was heavy, and an even greater demand was expected when the war ended. Midwestern lumber firms, whose pine stands in the Great Lakes region were running short, looked to the Pacific Northwest. Already several Minnesota lumber firms had blocked off huge stands of pine on the Deschutes plateau.

The Shevlin-Hixon Company of Minnesota, on May 10, announced plans for the construction of a plant on the west bank, that would be one of America's finest pine mills. Downtown in Bend an impromptu parade was held. Later there was a public meeting with many speeches. The weekly Bend *Bulletin,* which recorded the start of World War I in 1914 with small type, "bannered" the mill news. Then, on August 18, Brooks-Scanlon, Inc., revealed its plans for a mill which would virtually duplicate that of the Shevlin-Hixon firm, both in construction and in capacity. These companies were to manufacture billions of board feet of lumber from Deschutes pines and other species.

252

Selection of Bend as the location for the plants was not something that happened overnight. There had been much long-range planning. Huge stands of timber had been acquired and consolidated into logging units; lands for the mills had been purchased; and surveys had been made for the mill pond. The pond planning started as early as 1907, when the Central Oregon Development Company made its surveys. To protect the area for mill pond use, this company obtained property from John Sisemore, the pioneer who lived on the Farewell Bend Ranch. The pond was to cover 265 acres and would hold five million board feet of timber.

After the mill pond was first surveyed, John Steidl, who had a part in the shaping of Bend, prophesied, "Very few of our people realize what such a pond will some day mean to Bend. If the railroad ever comes to Bend, the area is assured of several mills."

Some of the holdings from which Brooks-Scanlon was to cut timber had been selected by M. J. Scanlon, when he visited the pinelands in 1898. At that time he drove by team over the rugged Santiam Divide, the route of pioneers, examined forest areas in which he would like to have holdings, and later issued orders for the acquisition and consolidation of the selected lands. It was Dr. D. F. Brooks, senior member of the firm, who eighteen years later, announced the decision to build a plant at Bend.

Tom Shevlin of Yale

The Shevlin-Hixon plant on the Deschutes was rapidly taking shape when Bend had a distinguished visitor—Thomas L. Shevlin of LaCrosse, Wisconsin, president of the Shevlin-Hixon firm and its affiliated interests. At the time, the Shevlin-Hixon people owned more than two hundred thousand acres of timberlands on the Deschutes plateau and in the eastern Cascades. Tom Shevlin was highly pleased with work underway on the plant and predicted that Bend would soon become one of the big cities of the region. It was known that Shevlin's special interest in Bend, snuggled close to the Cascade timber, dictated the decision to build on the Deschutes.

Shevlin was a nationally famous figure—not as the head of one of the country's big lumber concerns, but as a football player. He was known as "Tom Shevlin of Yale," early in the century. While at Yale, he played an end position and served one year as team captain. It was said that no opposing player ever got around the end guarded by Tom Shevlin. In 1906, he was graduated from Yale, but was called back several times in later years to assist as coach.

Following his graduation, Shevlin spent six months in the Deschutes country, working with Mike Kelley, a cruiser. Together they blocked out Shevlin timber for the harvest of the future. In 1912, Shevlin became head of the big Minnesota lumber firm that was preparing to move into the Deschutes woods. Always he kept in close touch with developments in the Deschutes region, and he was on hand to view preliminary construction work on the plant buildings. After visiting Bend, he returned to Minnesota, where, on December 29, 1915, three months before the big plant he established on the Deschutes started production, he died, a victim of pneumonia. Gloom spread through the town of Bend, that had "adopted" the lumberman; but the death of the ex-Yale football star did not slow his Deschutes lumber production timetable: the first logs moved into the ripping edges of saws in mid-March 1916.

Bend was no longer an agricultural town at the edge of the pines; it was now a mill town and growing rapidly. Its growth became phenomenal in the history of Oregon. The coming of the lumbering industry resulted in an increase of 910 per cent in population from 1910 to 1920. Population again soared in 1923, when both Brooks-Scanlon and Shevlin-Hixon added modern units.

Railroads Reach into Forest

Both Shevlin-Hixon and Brooks-Scanlon started their preliminary logging operations close to Bend, where for a short time,
the sound of saws and falling timber could be heard in town.
Gradually the logging operations reached into the deep woods;
there the companies set up camps and designated them by numbers. Occasionally the temporary location of camps gave names
to areas, such as Shevlin south of La Pine.

Construction of logging railroads was started about the same
time that the first crews moved into the woods and it increased
through the years. Over these tracks rolled big steam locomotives and long strings of flatcars. The trains moved daily out into
the woods from Bend. Laden with pines, they returned in the
evening to dump their loads in the new millpond. Eventually
Shevlin-Hixon track reached south into Lake County and the
southern Paulinas. Brooks-Scanlon steel skirted the northern foothills of Newberry Crater and extended into the Fort Rock area, a
distance of some eighty miles.

Later, Brooks-Scanlon built its railroad line northwest into
Jefferson County past Sisters, with Black Butte looming as a
pine-clad landmark on the skyline. After forty years, logging
railroads in the Deschutes country were to be replaced by wide,
fast roads over which rolled fleets of big trucks from distant
woods. By the 1950s, the last of the mill trains and their giant
locomotives had disappeared from the Deschutes scene, to join,
in memory, the era of "big wheels" when logs were hauled to
loading docks by teams of horses that were kept in large barns
at the south city limits. In mid-century Bend placed a set of
these "big wheels" on display in picturesque Drake Park. The
wheels continue to attract the attention of thousands of tourists.

In their first thirty-five years of logging in the Deschutes
country, the two mills cut approximately ten billion board feet
of timber. This, it would appear, left only some six billion board
feet remaining; but the original estimate of some sixteen billion

feet on the Deschutes plateau did not include the new growth, and changes in logging methods made it possible for lumber firms to harvest timber that had been bypassed in lava fields and on steep slopes during earlier years. Also, at first, only pine was considered desirable merchantable timber. Several other forest types have been added to the timber crop since then—Douglas fir in the High Cascades west of the Deschutes, Western White Fir, and lodgepole pine, an excellent pulpwood.

Even in their first years of "shakedown" operation, the two mills in Bend were nationally high in the production of pine, and when the plants got on normal schedule they were milling around 200 million board feet annually. As more head rigs were added and the demand for lumber increased, the Bend mills, operating on triple shifts in the late 1920s, were cutting around 500 million board feet each year. Eventually the Deschutes National Forest, looking toward continuous lumber production under the sustained yield program, set the allowable cut from the forest at 138 million board feet.

In 1950, thirty-four years after the first logs moved under ripping saws, the directors of the two mills reached a decision that directly affected the city: they decided that timber of the area, now virtually all on federal land, could be most advantageously harvested under one operation. The result was that Brooks-Scanlon purchased the plant and the timber holdings of the Shevlin-Hixon firm. After Shevlin-Hixon cut its last log— December 23, 1950—there was deep gloom in the city that recalled the time when more than two thousand men were employed by the local pine plants in the woods and the mills. Bend felt the loss of the Shevlin-Hixon payroll for several years—then continued its slow growth into a city of 11,748 in 1960.

Road System Modernized

As the Bend mills cut their company-owned timber, purchases from the U. S. Forest Service rapidly increased. This

miniscent of pioneer days, but actually a scene of the present, are these horses racing through the sage, headed for new pastures as a season changes. On the skyline is Fort Rock.

Ever since pioneer days, cattle have been moved seasonally from Central Oregon ranches
summer pastures in the high country. This herd is grazing on Sparks Meadow, close to
western base of Bachelor Butte.

Oregon State Highway De
Sheep raising is an important agricultural pursuit in Oregon, and is scattered over the sta
This band of sheep is crossing a bridge in the Redmond area of Central Oregon.

Joe Van Wormer

A telescopic lens brought into sharp focus this typical creature of the High Desert, the proud pronghorn antelope of the rim country. Dim in the distance are groves of junipers at desert edge.

Oregon Game Commission

Mule deer are found throughout Oregon east of the Cascade summit. They summer in the Cascades, but as fall storms appear, they generally migrate to lower elevations on the eastern slopes. They are the largest of all mammals common to the High Desert fringes. Note the large ears that give them a mule-like appearance.

Huge crowds gathered to see the first North Unit water flow into laterals such as this, to feed thirsty lands. By 1946, harnessed Deschutes water had made Madras the "green spot" of the old range country.

In 1958, Pelton Dam was completed on the main stem of the Deschutes River, with an installed power capacity of 124,000 kilowatts—putting the river to work in a major way producing electric power.

stumpage was purchased through competitive bidding, and the successful bidder agreed to develop the roads under federal specifications. By 1960, a fine, modern road system, opening up many new recreation areas, was taking shape, leaving only as memories the roads of pioneer days. Work was extended to include the improvement of forest highways into resort areas, such as Newberry Crater, into which the first "auto road" was constructed in 1913 from La Pine—steep, dusty, often rocky and winding. By 1960, a fine, surfaced road ascended into Newberry Crater from U. S. Highway 97 north of La Pine. A surfaced road was also constructed into the Elk Lake country, and into the south as a unit of the new Cascades Lakes Highway.

Brooks-Scanlon, now Bend's one big plant, modernized its entire operations in 1958, at a cost of more than three million dollars. Automation was primarily the goal of the modernization, with a new plant constructed and new machinery installed. Across the river, in the meantime, the old Shevlin-Hixon mill had been razed, yet many of its buildings remained to provide locations for lumber remanufacturing plants.

East of the river, Lelco, Inc., was founded, to provide Bend with a new payroll. That plant developed its own millpond in an area once covered by sage. Oregon Trail Box Co. added another payroll, as did other lumber firms new to the Bend scene. Bend definitely continued as a mill city—but it was making a strong bid for a new source of income as a recreation area that was gaining wide recognition.

City Retains Scenic Beauty

Through the years, smoke has continued to billow from tall mill stacks, but Bend, astride the Deschutes River, has retained much of its primitive beauty. From the mill area, the river spilled its clear water into the upper reaches of Mirror Pond, where it was becalmed into a mile-long lake reflecting pines and homes, lawns of which reach to the river edge. Parks have also been developed along the river bank; and from the millpond north through the power plant—about a mile and a half—not a single manufacturing plant has been established along the river. Forests that provided the city's great lumber industry became even more important when the area made a bid for tourists and other recreation seekers.

Recreation possibilities of the Deschutes country were known to the early-day settlers. After harvest each season, it was the practice of many ranch families to pack food and bedding in farm wagons and drive to favored spots in the high country, to camp, fish, hunt, and gather berries. But those early seekers of forest recreation were a mere trickle compared with the great rush to the woods that followed the second world war.

Ski Area Developed

Year-long recreation use of the Deschutes forest became a reality in 1958 when a new Pacific Northwest ski site was developed on the northern slope of Bachelor Butte, a 9,060-foot-high volcanic cone on the skyline west of Bend. In the 1961-1962 ski season, more than 98,600 persons used that ski area. Nearby, on the Santiam summit, is the Hoodoo Ski Bowl, and to the south on the Willamette Divide is another fine ski area.

Pine Harvest in the Ochocos

The story of the harvest of the Ochoco pines is largely a repetition of the Bend story, but not until the 1930s did mills come to the Prineville country, bringing an industrial boom and a great increase in population. That year, Prineville was a quiet town, still close to its rangeland past, with a population of 1,027. Twenty years later, it had a population of 3,233, an increase of more than 300 per cent. Dusty streets over which rode Vigilantes long ago were now paved, modern business houses were established, and new residential additions were founded.

By the late 1950s there were three large mills and several small mills in the immediate Prineville area, where the first settlers hewed logs for their homes. Like Bend, Prineville also became a mill town—but remained a city of great beauty, especially when viewed from the high western rims overlooking the broad green valley that sweeps north to the Smith Rock ramparts. And, as with Bend, when the big mills arrived, they found a railroad waiting to haul their lumber to the main line. That was the Prineville Municipal Railroad.

Gilchrist, on Little River

One Central Oregon town, Gilchrist, did not "back into" the lumber industry, as did Bend and Prineville. It was founded, in 1938, by the Gilchrist Timber Company as a model town built around the manufacture of timber. The small city is on the Little Deschutes River, astride U. S. Highway 97, some 47 miles south of Bend. Like other mills of the area, the Gilchrist plant competitively bids for federal timber to mill with company-owned stumpage, under a sustained yield program. Gilchrist, in northern Klamath County, is not an incorporated town.

Two Timberless Towns

Redmond and Madras are "timberless towns" with important mill payrolls. Redmond is in the sage and juniper country well east of the Cascade timber, but over highways from the west roll fleets of log-laden trucks carrying stumpage to be milled in this city of the dairy country. Mills did not come to Redmond until long after the town was founded, but in recent years they have provided an important payroll.

From downtown Madras, the only pine trees visible are those on the fringe of the Ochocos, far to the east along the head of Willow Creek, yet Madras has an important lumber industry. Logs are hauled from the nearby Warm Springs Indian Reservation, across the Deschutes to the west. There is also a big sawmill on the Agency, near the Deschutes.

The multiple-use concept has shaped the future of forests of both the Deschutes plateau and the Ochoco country, assuring stability for communities under the sustained-yield program. Residents of that enormous country east of the Cascades no longer look on the timbered hills in terms of sawmill payrolls—they recognize that water flowing from the forest makes possible the region's second most important industry, that of agriculture; and they know that the recreation lure of the green forests has created for the area its third most important income, its tourist trade.

By 1960, the Deschutes National Forest was third in the entire Northwest in recreation use. More vacationists camped in the Deschutes pinelands, on streams, around lakes, and in inviting meadows facing old mountains, than in any other national forest in the Oregon-Washington region.

Part Six

MILEPOSTS AND HORIZONS

CHAPTER 29

The Scene Changes

LEANING CABINS IN THE SAGE, ancient corrals on the open range, a pioneer home on the Deschutes crushed by a falling poplar, weathered piers of an old span close to a modern bridge—these are nostalgic reminders of Central Oregon's rapidly fading past. They are found in a land transformed by modern highways, crossed by tall twinpoles of power systems, scarred by gas lines, changed by huge dams in gorges followed long ago by beaver trappers.

Central Oregon for decades was considered a range country, fit only for the grazing of sheep, cattle, and horses, and the growing of hay in the well-watered country under lava rims. Pioneer Prineville, once the capital of this high plateau country on the sunrise side of the Cascades, proudly noted its rangeland past. Even in the twentieth century it considered itself the last frontier of the shrinking West. Crook County High School students adopted "Cowboys" as the name of their fine athletic teams. Seasonally, top Pacific Northwest Rodeos are held in a big arena close to high lava rims.

Bend, Central Oregon's largest town, had its start close to an old cabin and a corral on the Deschutes River, where livestock came in from the sage country, over dusty trails, to quench summer thirsts. Antelope and Mitchell in the north and Silver Lake to the south were range towns, serving stock empires spread over a thousand hills. Ashwood, even while catering to miners early in the century, continued to serve as the trading post for big ranches along Trout Creek and up into the hills that disappeared in timber beyond Blizzard Ridge.

In the broad plateau east of the Cascades, where aged, twisted junipers fringe rocky ridges, there are many reminders of the area's range days. In a long, narrow valley south of Hampton, there are corrals near a weather-bleached cabin. Between the cabin and the corral, made of long juniper posts lashed together, is a deep well. It was the watering place of some of the ten thousand horses owned by William W. Brown, the "horse king" of another era. The well is still in service, to provide water for a new "spread," that of Elton and David Jackson, who are reclaiming grasslands from the smothering sage.

Cabins with their windows broken, their doors gone, and their roofs ripped by storms, are found in other sheltered valleys on the high plateau. These were the homes of land seekers of other days.

On some of the older ranches of the region once embraced in giant Crook County are disintegrating sheep-shearing plants— low sheds facing a labyrinth of corrals. Few of the old shearing pens are intact, but on some of the ranches the high frames used in packing wool into big sacks still stand.

Bend's last reminder of its range days was a gatepost, close to the eastern bank of the Deschutes River at the rear of the Pilot Butte Inn. Horses herded from the High Desert in the early 1880s willingly moved into that wide-winged corral, enticed by the swift river just beyond. There was still a corral on the Deschutes in the hamlet of Bend when the ancestral Pilot Butte Inn was dedicated on March 17, 1917. The aged gate post remained in its original position until 1960.

Earlier, Bend lost its most important relic of its range era, when an old cabin, erected by stockmen in the Drake Park site of a later year, was torn down. On its site in 1959, Daughters of the American Revolution erected a marker to note the fact that the old cabin was the location of the first school taught within the Bend city limits.

Old Bridge Disappears

As Central Oregon's past faded, many landmarks disappeared. One was the historic Trail Crossing Bridge in the Crooked River canyon close to Smith Rock. The bridge, reached over steep, narrow approaches, was abandoned and razed in 1927 when the Oregon State Highway Department's high, steel span at Peter Skene Ogden State Park was completed, a short distance downstream.

Also changing with the times were the routes of early-day roads, originally built for teams and wagons, and later smoothed and widened for automobiles and trucks. The old roads roughly followed the paths of least resistance. They zigzagged up steep slopes, detoured rocky knolls, skirted junipers, and added miles to avoid crossing a bit of farmland.

Gradually through the years the interior Oregon arterial routes were straightened. Out of the north, across the Madras country and over Crooked River, was routed U. S. Highway 97, known in earlier years as The Dalles-California Highway. U. S. Highway 20 across the interior plateau experienced a similar modernization—to provide a fine, fast route of long tangents close to the road "constructed" in 1911 by a small party of Bend men with picks, shovels, and grubbing hoes. The original distance from Bend to Burns, over the hand-made pioneer road, was one hundred and fifty miles, some twenty miles longer than the present two-lane route. Driving time has been reduced from a full day to about three hours.

Highways played no small part in changing the Central Oregon scene, but there were other important factors. The coming of the railroads in 1910-11 ended the century of isolation that had made Central Oregon the bypassed heart of the state. When the pine mills followed the rails to the upper Deschutes, Bend changed from an irrigation town serving a stock country to an industrial city.

In the first decades of big milling operations in Central Oregon, most of the lumber was shipped east for remanufacture. Eventually, small remanufacturing plants were established in the area, to add important payrolls. Also established were plants processing farm and dairy products. Various minerals were quarried for construction use. These included pumice that came from old volcanoes, and banded and colored rhyolites widely in demand by builders.

Bonneville Power Arrives

Bonneville power, on wires carried by tall towers, reached Central Oregon in the late 1930s, to alter the way of life in rural communities where lanterns were still burning in barns and milk sheds. Radiating from Redmond, the location of the Bonneville substation serving the region, are Rural Electrification Administration lines that carry power and light to many parts of the once-isolated interior country. In May 1940, a switch was thrown into place in Redmond, to send power through the Central Electric Cooperative, Inc., lines. Farm life changed abruptly. Not only did electricity make it possible for ranchers to operate their plants with this new power, and to light their dairy sheds, their barns, and other buildings, but it opened a new freedom for farm families.

Need for power in the region south and southeast of the Deschutes country was seen following World War II. As a result, the Midstate Electric Cooperative, Inc., was formed, with headquarters in La Pine. Lines were constructed south to the Fort Rock country, to provide power for pumps that are lifting water to big ranches from underground pools. A branch was extended southeast to Silver Lake, to light the little town where an oil lamp hanging in a second-story auditorium on Christmas Eve, 1894, fell to the floor, starting a fire that claimed the lives of forty-three persons.

Across Central Oregon in 1960, construction started on another power line, one from Redmond to Burns and on south into northeast Nevada. This line passes through the plateau country where homesteaders once matched their skill with nature and lost. As the year 1965 began, crews were in the field surveying for power lines that will dwarf those of the Bonneville system that cross the High Desert. The new lines will link the Pacific Northwest and the American Southwest power systems. In the Central Oregon high country, they will directly pass across the stock empire once ruled by Bill Brown.

"Big Ditch" Constructed

South through Central Oregon in 1961 was excavated the "big ditch," a six-foot trench blasted into lava that was to hold America's largest pipeline. It was a 36-inch natural gas line which extended a distance of 1,400 miles from Alberta, Canada, to the Bay area of California. Flowing through the line is a new source of energy—a new fuel for the region.

What a change from the old days of pioneer homesteaders when coal oil in five-gallon cans, two cans to the case, was hauled in by wagon from The Dalles, or over the high Santiam from Lebanon, Albany, or Corvallis, to light lamps for homes and lanterns for barns! And what a change from the day when the only power in this frontier country was that provided by horses, or by the hands of men!

Green Years Ahead

Long ago, immigrants who were heading for the snow-covered Cascades considered Central Oregon a barren, forbidding land that took a heavy toll of themselves and their stock. People who came afterwards found the range country less forbidding. They established homes in well-watered valleys and filed on land that could be dampened from huge cold springs. They cultivated bottom lands and harvested natural meadows. Their stock ranged into the Ochocos, and into the tall pines of the Deschutes country.

The first surge of homesteaders who followed the early settlers found most of the good land and the choice streams and water holes taken. These late arrivals looked on Central Oregon as a hard land, that hoarded its water hidden in deep lavas and was stingy with its forage. As a result, conquest of the once-wild land of Central Oregon was slow. Then came the awakening of the land, as water coursed through long canals and trains rolled north and south through the long Deschutes Gorge.

Eventually water in canals spread over thousands of acres of the inland country, changed the region's economy, and gave agriculture a ranking only below the income from forests. Behind the story of the diversion of water to the thirsty acres is the history of the watering of a new Oregon frontier.

Last of the big irrigation projects completed in Central Oregon was the multimillion-dollar Prineville Dam on Crooked River in 1961. Work began on this project on October 26, 1958; and early in 1961, the dam, 184 feet high and 1,160 feet long, was finished. It serves a triple role: primarily, it is a flood control project; but is also holds water for irrigation, and its long shore lines provide a new Oregon recreation area. No longer will spring flood water surge through the narrow channel of Crooked River and spread over the Prineville area, as it did in earlier years, when settlers were clearing the fields, and even as recently as 1952, when the western fringe of Prineville was inundated. There is new promise for residents of the Prineville area of green years, and freedom from the fear of floods.

Pioneers who came over the Santiam from Linn County in the late 1860s likely never dreamed there would some day be constructed on Crooked River and tributary Ochoco Creek big dams to hold water in reserve for summer use and make green the broad valley that stretches north to the gray pinnacles of Smith Rock.

CHAPTER 30

Oregon's High Desert

SOUTH OF A SERIES OF OLD HILLS that reach east from the Mutton Mountains through the Ochocos to the Aldrich peaks of the John Day region are sagebrush plains that stretch for two hundred miles, from the Cascade foothills to the Idaho border and south to Nevada. Part of this isolated land of sage and occasional junipers, rocky rims and leaning mountains is the High Desert, spread over portions of four counties, Deschutes, Crook, Harney and Lake.

Pioneer maps of the country bear such names as Rolling Sage Plains, Great Sandy Desert, and the Artemisia Desert. Today the old names have been forgotten, and the region is universally known as the High Desert, in contrast with slightly lower lands to the south referred to in earlier years as the Low Desert.

Central Oregon's High Desert partly spreads south to merge with the greatest of all American deserts, that which lies within the Great Basin. A segment of the High Desert is in the High Lava Plains province. Part drains into the Great Basin, part toward the Pacific Ocean. It is a desert astride the faulted roof of Central Oregon.

The High Lava Plains within the High Desert can be best inspected from the air, when morning or evening shadows are long. Under the accentuating shadows, the plains unfold their ancient volcanic story—great earth faults come into view; courses of rivers and streams, dry for ages, twist across the old lava country; craters reveal their outlines, and uplifted horsts and downdropped grabens take shape. The larger faults, some with displacements of thousands of feet, trend generally a little north of east.

Dominating this ancient upland is a former huge volcano, Newberry, within the green edge of the Deschutes National Forest. Hampton Butte, 6,333 feet high and vastly older than the surrounding soil-covered lavas, shares its rule of the High Desert with volcanic Newberry and Glass Buttes. Both Hampton Butte and Glass Buttes rise some 2,000 feet above the surrounding plateau.

Ancient Past Recalled

The High Desert is an arid land, but it bears plenty of evidence that it had a damp past. During the moist climate of the Ice Age, basins between the block-faulted mountains filled to form big lakes, especially in the northern Great Basin. Waves of old lakes cut well-defined terraces along their eastern shores, against which water was whipped by prevailing westerly winds. The old terraces make it possible for geologists to trace the former extent of the lakes.

Stream beds cut their way across the now-waterless High Desert, from the Hampton highlands northwest past Millican, and across the Alfalfa and Powell Butte communities to Crooked River. The courses of the ancient streams, twisting through fault valleys and across lava barriers, can easily be traced. Dry River, largest of all the streams that drained the High Desert, was temporarily impounded in the Millican Valley, to form a lake which splashed against the south slopes of Horse Ridge.

High Desert ravines and old courses still carry a trickle of water seasonally, in years when heavy snow piles up on the interior plateau and melts under sudden "chinook" winds that whip out of the southwest. But generally the High Desert ravines are dry, even in periods of heavy rain. Along some of them are windmills, erected by ranchers who obtained their water deep in lava formations.

With the exception of springs around Wagontire Mountain, and those near the head of Crooked River, the High Desert is virtually devoid of surface water. Ranchers drilled hundreds of feet seeking water, but in many instances, the deep, costly wells were "dusters."

What Is a Desert?

There are those who say that the high interior of Oregon is not a desert, yet it does have certain desert characteristics: it is a region of low annual precipitation, around eight or ten inches. Daytime temperatures in summer are high, occasionally over a hundred degrees, and evaporation is great. Still, the region's average yearly temperature is not high, the cold of winter off-setting the heat of summer. Winter temperatures as low as -52 degrees have been recorded, and there have been annual tem-perature spreads of around 160 degrees.

High winds occasionally sweep over this desert, but they are not characteristic of the region, whose summer days are warm and nights are cool. The winds come from the southwest, and oc-casionally they bring light rain in spring, summer, and fall, and light snow in winter. Melting snows at times create temporary, or "playa," lakes, which make it possible for ranchers to move cattle or sheep in to take advantage of the plateau forage and water.

Oregon's High Desert is virtually without dunes, except for some in northeastern Lake County, close to the big Christmas Lake basin. Here great ridges of sand blown from Pleistocene lake beds are slowly moving into the northeast before prevailing winds. There has been some drifting of sand and top soil plowed from fields in the homesteading era, but most of this sand has been trapped in the sage.

Like most other desert areas of the world, especially in the Great Basin, a mountain barrier created the desert conditions that exist on the immense inland plateau. This barrier is the Cas-cades, which take moisture from Pacific clouds, chilled in pass-ing over the mountains. Most of the moisture spills as rain on the windward side of the Cascades, but some drifts over the summit to dampen foothills. West of the divide, Eugene measures on an average 37.88 inches of moisture annually; Bend, east of the mountains, records 12.15 inches. Fremont, much farther east, gets only 8.78 inches of rainfall annually.

The Living Desert

The High Desert is far from a lifeless terrain, devoid of vegetation and animal life. Belying its "desert" name, it is seasonally green, when moisture conditions make plant growth possible. Desert life is far more abundant than would be indicated by the lonely coyote trotting through the sage, an antelope standing sentinel on a lava rim, or a jackrabbit loping across a winding road. Only the person who makes camp in the sage at night, cooks his meal over a small fire, then listens to earth noises while he watches stars wheeling into the west, is fully aware of the "little people" of the brushlands—mice, gophers, brush rats, and the tiny big-eared deer mouse.

Largest of all mammals common to the High Desert fringes are the mule deer. Antelope are seen in the rim country; often they race across highways, or pace automobiles. That desert bighorns once ranged over the area is indicated by the occasional sight of bleached and twisted horns, but now only their transplanted kin are found, on Hart Mountain overlooking the Great Basin.

Jackrabbits, or desert hares, are still found on the desert, but not in such great numbers as in the homesteading era, when they nightly invaded fields by the thousands, to destroy crops. Cottontails also play in the sage, as do squirrels and chipmunks; but kangaroo rats, mice, and various other kinds of rodents greatly outnumber all other creatures of the plateau desert.

Bobcats live in the rim country, and when trailed, seek refuge in junipers. One of the smaller carnivores is the skunk, not abundant, but obnoxious around ranch homes. Ground squirrels are plentiful, and badgers are common in areas where squirrels live. There are even some cougars in the region.

Flowers of the High Desert

Following seasons of abundant moisture and mild temperatures, parts of the High Desert become great gardens of wild flowers that spread over the old lava prairies and cover the weathered slopes of fault-block mountains. The number of flowering plants contributing to the beauty of late spring in the High Desert can be numbered in the hundreds, and possibly in the thousands, in such areas as the high Steens Mountain and its desert slopes. Central Oregon's high country blooms in late May or early June, but in sheltered valleys of the Deschutes and Crooked Rivers, the flowering season is a month earlier.

Some sturdy plants flower seasonally in the region, yet they are few compared with the outburst of blooms that follows damp winters and mild springs. Among the High Desert plants are some of the type called xerophytes—the "dry plants" which have adapted themselves to desert conditions. They are able to weather intense heat and prolonged droughts. The plants survive the hot summers and cold nights by remaining in the seed stage. In rainy seasons, they sprout, grow quickly, and produce seeds that can be stored through the dry seasons. During dry spells that parch the desert, several types of plants become dormant, but when the rains arrive, they quickly come to life.

Most High Desert plants conserve water through special adaptations. Mingled with the plants that must make the best of the short moisture are perennial, flowering herbs; shrubs, and deep-rooted trees, including the twisted junipers which appear to have a root system that nearly equals the amount of growth above ground.

Each of the provinces of the Great Basin has certain types of plants not found in other areas, but generally the Great Basin plants—from the Nevada deserts to the Oregon high country—are common to the entire province. However, it is not unusual to find different species respresented.

Most characteristic shrub of the Great Basin and Columbia

Plateau deserts is the sagebrush, known to botanists as *Artemisia tridentata*. This is a gray-green shrub occurring widespread over high deserts throughout the Western United States. It is common on the High Desert, with low growth in some places and growth as high as a saddle pony in other areas. Known as the three-tooth sage, this is the shrub that gave its name to the Oregon Artemisia Desert of early-day explorers.

Popularized in western fiction, this sage has an aromatic fragrance, especially after desert rains. When used for campfire fuel, the brush has an aroma that filters down valleys in low-lying smoke layers, to spread out over sandy basins once occupied by pluvial lakes.

Carpeting the High Desert floor in favorable seasons are such plants as the mountain lupine, various penstemons, many rock-loving plants that grow in crevices of lava rims, mariposa lilies, scarlet gilia, columbine, yellow lamb's-tongue, purple and white iris, blue dicks, and camas. Also common to the region are the apricot mallow, sand verbena, moss rose, and pink phlox. Some of the smaller lake depressions are carpeted with blooms.

War Games in the Desert

On Central Oregon's brushy High Desert, more than one hundred thousand troops engaged in extensive war games in the days of World War II in 1943. In dust, in storms, in brilliant sunshine and the chill of an early winter, the soldier trainees engaged in a maneuver that virtually engulfed perimeter towns and spread over parts of four counties.

Taking part in these war games, officially known as the "Oregon Maueuver," were soldiers of the IV Army Corps, commanded by Major General Alexander M. Patch. Principal forces in the corps were the 91st, the 96th, and the 104th Infantry Divisions. These troops were only part of the buildup that then made Central Oregon one of the country's most important military areas. Yet the old range country—in the vast area bounded by Bend, Redmond, Prineville, Burns, and Silver Lake—"swallowed" the thousands of armed men and their vehicles. When darkness came to the region, with campfires doused in the make-believe conflict, the High Desert appeared vacant. It seemed as lonely and lifeless as in the days that followed the departure of homesteaders after their ill-advised attempt to reclaim the sage wilderness.

Even before General Patch's young soldiers spread over the High Desert in opposing armies and bivouacked under the clear plateau stars, an important airbase had been constructed near Redmond, and another large base had been established on the gently sloping plains west of Madras. To the south of Bend, on the east side of the Deschutes River, an Engineer Replacement Center was constructed, with accommodations for ten thousand men. The engineers' camp, on the river fifteen miles up the Deschutes from Bend, was named in honor of an army engineer of another era, Henry Larcom Abbot.

Participating in these war games were thousands of young men who never before had been out of large cities. After a preliminary series of division tests in their home cantonments, they were sent into the Oregon high country for the corps tests. Most of them had never slept on the ground. Many had never seen a snow-capped peak, a juniper forest with twisted trees; a desolate sagebrush plateau, or cattle on the open range—not to mention jackrabbits, which in some areas were as common as the sage. Almost every one of these men was to play some role in theaters of war in Europe or the South Pacific. In its summary of the maneuver, the War Department noted:

The area was found to be ideal for maneuvers as prescribed . . . . The generally clear, cold weather facilitated long foot marches and permitted almost continuous operation of aircraft. Often a range of fifty degrees in temperature in twenty-four hours was encountered; and the last two corps problems, conducted when the temperature was six degrees above zero, caused no great discomfort when river-crossing phases found all personnel thoroughly wet. The health of entire command was excellent.

Since sleep is a rarity in war, or in preparation for battle, maneuver problems ran continuously for two or three days. Aside from the sounds and deaths in actual battle, there were no attempts to change conditions of the maneuver from actual war conditions. Even the "wounded" were gathered from make-believe battlefields, tagged as to nature of their injuries, and sent back along the chain of medical commands.

The training armies surged back and forth over the plateau. When forces found their way blocked by fences of ranchers, the fences were cut—and later repaired by the Engineers. Over the opposing armies swept planes, most of them operating out of the Redmond airbase. Central Oregon's streams and rivers also played their part in the war games, claiming a number of lives. Bridges, some of which were in use over the Deschutes twenty years later, were constructed by the Engineers. Rivers were crossed on pontoons.

Across the Deschutes near Camp Abbot was built a fine bridge that was given the name of the IV Corps commander, General Patch. Another bridge honored the Camp Abbot commander, Colonel Frank S. Besson.

Completed in the spring of 1943 and occupied in early May, Camp Abbot was constructed at a cost of more than four million dollars and was used for a little more than a year. When it became evident that World War II was in its final phase, the camp was deactivated and the razing of concrete and wooden structures soon followed. Eventually, the Hudspeth Land and Livestock Company of Prineville acquired the broad meadows where the Engineers trained.

War games on the High Desert in 1943 ended within artillery shot of a place long before touched by actual war between white troops and Indians. The place was Silver Creek, some forty-five miles west of old Fort Harney. There at dawn on a Sunday morning, June 23, 1878, Lieutenant R. F. Bernard, a Civil War veteran, led his men in a fierce charge against a large war party of

Bannocks and Paiutes who had trailed across the Harney country from Idaho, killing settlers and burning farm homes.

In the Silver Creek area, Bernard, a veteran of an earlier scrimmage with Indians in the same region, faced an imposing war party. It was estimated that some fifteen hundred warriors and their families were in the camp that the cavalrymen elected to surprise in the June dawn. More than six hundred of the Indians were well equipped for fighting. The dawn battle was brief, but it was bloody, with considerable hand-to-hand fighting. Though the whites were under heavy fire from Indians hidden behind rocks, only three of the soldiers were killed. Bannocks and Paiutes suffered a considerable loss before withdrawing and bringing to an end the uprising known as the Bannock War.

This is the only recorded "war" within the boundaries of the broad land known as Central Oregon. Soldiers in the High Desert war games eddied around the Silver Creek battle site on a number of occasions—but it is doubtful whether a single soldier engaged in the make-believe battles ever heard of the dawn scrimmage on Silver Creek, sixty-five years earlier.

Few Changes Seen

Through the years, the High Desert has changed little. A century ago, its grassy basins and slopes, that were green in the spring, enticed George Millican from the Crooked River Valley, but he found conditions stern: deep wells had to be drilled to tap water for cattle and horses, and seasonally the livestock had to be moved to sheltered valleys away from the plateau with its generally severe winters. William W. Brown followed with his "horse empire," but found only temporary wealth in the hills. Homesteaders, hopeful of transforming the high country into wheat fields, established homes and tore up bunch grass with plows—but they also failed.

The only major change in the High Desert scene today is a fine highway, U. S. 20, which reaches from Bend to Burns, crossing river beds, skirting slanting mountains, and detouring the rims of old earth faults. It is a highway that makes accessible one of the most interesting of all western lands called deserts.

In the high country east of Bend, only three of the many towns established in the era of homesteads have survived. They are Millican, named for the rancher of another century who ranged his stock over the basin; Brothers, location of an Oregon State Highway Department maintenance unit, a store, service station, and picnic area; and Hampton, the old "halfway" point between Bend and Burns.

What of the Desert's Future?

Through the years, the High Desert has challenged attempts at conquest, as it did in 1845, 1851, and 1853, when it quickly erased the wagon tracks of immigrants. There is still hope, though, that the high country may yet yield to man's attempts to make use of the brushy plateau. Already thousands of acres are being cleared through chemical spraying and draglines. As early as 1937, an experimental program in the investigation of semi-arid range for livestock use was started at a cooperative government station, Squaw Butte, near the eastern edge of the High Desert. This is now a part of the Squaw Butte-Harney Range and Livestock Experiment Station. Mission of that station is to "determine the best methods of grazing desert range lands to permit the highest sustained production of livestock, and methods of management of range cattle, both on the winter feed ground and on summer range."

High Desert soils are rich, but they lack water, which lies deep in the earth under lava folds. Recently, high twin poles appeared in the sage, from Redmond southeast into the Alvord Valley and Nevada. Through lines on the high poles flows a new source of pumping power for the region—electricity.

The High Desert of Central Oregon, in a region of old volcanic rims, will probably never be a land of green, well-watered meadows; but stockmen are confident that eradication of the sage and availability of water pumped from deep wells will bolster the economy of inland Oregon. Regardless of its future, the High Desert will remain a challenging land of varied interests to those who read stories from ancient hills and picture the area's remote past when strong streams flowed through ravines now choked with sand.

CHAPTER 31

Scenic Geology

THE HILLS OF CENTRAL OREGON hold many lures for those who would probe into the region's ancient past, read the record of the rocks, study the quite-recent volcanic story, and gather rare minerals from folded mountains.

Riders of the open ranges and the homesteaders who followed them paid little attention to volcanic skylines, ancient beaches warped into mountain tops, or varicolored rocks at the base of weathered cliffs. The stockmen gave names to some of the geographic features, such as the Ochocos, Maupin Butte, Paulina Peak, Mutton Mountain, and Haystack. But they were little interested in stony skulls protruding from colored John Day clays, impressions of leaves on rock slabs torn from creek bottoms by floods, or the gem-like stones. It remained for a new generation to show interest in the mid-Oregon wonderland of old fire-domes and peaks, plume agates, petrified woods, and artifacts found at Indian camps of long ago.

Our Fence of Mountains

Directly west of Oregon's high and picturesque inland country is a grand "rosary of mountains" reaching from the Columbia River to the Klamath country. These peaks, all old volcanoes, are the Cascades of Oregon, which divide the state into separate geographic and climatic areas. George Vancouver, the English explorer, referred to the Cascades as a "ridge of snowy mountains." He described them well, for snow clings to the higher peaks the year around. Five of the aged volcanoes are all more than 10,000 feet high. They are Hood, Jefferson, and the Three Sisters.

Motorists driving across the High Desert over U. S. Highway 20 from Burns first spot the cone-like mountains from a ridge near Brothers. On drawing closer to the mountain barrier, they soon become aware that the Cascades are not like the Rockies, or the high, eroded rims that loom over desert basins to the east. The Cascades are not folded mountains, fault-block masses, or glaciated overthrusts; they were once fire mountains—thundering volcanoes that left their mark on the Oregon country.

Highways over the Oregon Cascades provide easy approaches to the cloud-tipped or snow-blanketed Cascades. Each mountain pass has its own unique scenery. U. S. Highway 26 from Central Oregon virtually brushes the base of majestic Hood. U. S. Highway 20 brings into perspective two ancient mountains—Three Fingered Jack and Washington, both of which have been denuded by great glaciers. Oregon Highway 242 takes the motorist into the heart of a region of spectacular volcanism—the McKenzie Divide between the Three Sisters volcanoes and Mt. Washington.

Geology Crowds to Roadside

On the mile-high McKenzie Divide, now largely bypassed as the result of the construction of a fast, modern highway along the McKenzie River via Clear Lake, geology crowds to the roadside. At the summit, jagged flows of lava from Yapoah Crater, on the southern skyline, and little Belknap Crater, to the north, merge and interfinger near the Dee Wright Memorial, a rocky platform which honors a pioneer of the region. The volcanic region visible from the memorial is unsurpassed in America for its wealth of recent lavas, its ice-dissected volcanoes, and its wild scenery. Youthful cinder cones and rivers of blocky obsidian add variety to the mountain landscape, in this summit region of lava compressed between two forests.

There is abundant evidence, in this land of frozen streams of rock, that glacial ice as well as volcanic fires played major roles in shaping the scenery. Where the highway dips from the lava at the west edge of the McKenzie lava flows, the grooved trails of glaciers are visible under the mantling black rock.

Motorists driving west over the lava fields, who leave their cars at the Huckleberry Camp, and hike into a nearly timberless "island," will discover high in a mountain bowl one of the unique scenic features of the region—a cataract of frozen lava formed hundreds of years ago when a tongue of liquid rock from a crater chilled on the steep slope of a mountain.

North of the McKenzie Highway at the Cascade Divide are lava features that include a "hornito"—a low, oven-shaped mound that once sheltered a volcanic vent. Glazed sides of this big vent, which leads into the darkness of the lavas, indicate that in the final volcanic action at Little Belknap, hot gases escaped from deep in the mountain. The "hornito" is reached over a trail that winds several miles over lava fields.

Paulinas Rule Skyline

Visible on the skyline some forty miles south of Bend is an isolated mountain range, the Paulinas, dominated by the remnants of a volcano, Mt. Newberry, that was a giant in its time. The Paulinas, directly east of the Three Sisters Cascades, hump up from the High Desert. Highest point of the range is Paulina Peak, 7,985 feet above sea level.

The Paulinas consist of the rimmed mountain, Newberry, and scores of flanking parasitic volcanoes, many of them still unnamed. The Paulinas are entirely within the Deschutes National Forest, and are best known for their two trout lakes, East and Paulina. These lakes occupy separate parts of a once-large caldera, formed when the broad dome of ancient Mt. Newberry broke away in concentric faulting.

Newberry Crater seasonally is visited by thousands of tourists, attracted by the strange story of a volcano that "lost its head." Interesting caldera features are a big obsidian flow, volcanic cones, hot springs at East Lake, and the fine view obtained from Paulina Peak. From that peak, easily reached over a mountain road, are visible parts of four states—California, Washington, Nevada, and Oregon.

A surfaced mountain reaches into Newberry Crater from U. S. Highway 97 near La Pine, a distance of approximately twenty miles. This is part of the Central Oregon area in which astronauts—preparing for lunar landings—trained in 1964.

Ochocos Part of Circle

Forming part of the great rim of mountains encircling the heart of Central Oregon are the Ochocos, an outlier of the Blue Mountains, one of Central Oregon's largest uplifts, with spurs reaching into several counties. The "Blues" are one of a series of mountain ranges composed largely of high ridges much older than the far-reaching Columbia River basalts. These ranges extend from the Mutton Mountains, overlooking the Warm Springs Indian Reservation on the west, to the Wallowas of Eastern Oregon and the Seven Devils Mountains in Idaho.

West of the rugged Picture Gorge country of the John Day River—and near Paulina east of Prineville—rocks folded into mountains hold many fossils, some of them ferns older than the Age of Mammals; others the bones of creatures that lived in the land long before the Columbia lava spread widely over the region. The Ochocos entomb many of these older fossils—yet this part of the Blue Mountain uplift is not geologically old. Geologists frequently refer to the interior Oregon ranges as the "Central Mountains."

The buff-colored Smith Rock formation fronting on Crooked River near Terrebonne is a westerly snout of the Ochocos, which dip under the Deschutes lavas in a sharp downwarp, apparently to bend under the comparatively recent Cascades and reappear in the Goshen area south of Eugene.

Within the grand fence of mountains encircling much of Central Oregon are prominent landmarks—Powell Buttes, Glass Buttes, Hampton and Cline Buttes, Pine Mountain, and Grizzly.

Some are weathered fault blocks; others are remnants of ancient volcanoes.

Escarpments Reach to Clouds

South of the Central Mountains of Oregon are some of the American West's most spectacular features—great escarpments which in winter storms reach into the clouds, and in the summer add color to distant skylines. Majestic Steens Mountain rules much of this isolated range country of the Northern Great Basin. The nine-thousand-foot fault escarpment of the Steens is made up of volcanic rocks which are often interbedded with ancient lake beds.

Fault-block mountains, steep on one face and gently sloping on the other, are abundant in the northern lands of the Great Basin of Oregon. They are an attraction known to few Oregonians—yet they are accessible over surfaced highways. One of the most striking fault mountains is the high Abert Rim, skirted by fine highways, Oregon 31 and U. S. 395. To the southeast, Oregon 78 crosses a spur of the towering Steens, to reveal from the east the beauty of a fault formation often mentioned in geologic literature.

Mountains of the semi-arid interior plateau and the northern Great Basin are generally timberless, tan, and barren under the summer sun—but covered with grass and flowers in spring months. Closer to the Cascades and in the John Day region, mountains are timber covered. Southeast of Canyon City is the Strawberry Range, highest peak of which is 9,038 feet. Close to the center of the state are the timbered Maury Mountains, which slope east to Camp Creek.

Caverns Lure Tourists

Ranchers of the upper Deschutes country were the first to discover long tunnels in sloping lands, and they made some use of them as natural refrigerators for meat in hot summers, and as shelters for stock in winter storms. One of the first-discovered lava tunnels was Dillman Cave, twelve miles south of Bend. This is now the location of Oregon's unique Lava River Caves State Park. Ranchers of the area in pioneer days chilled their venison in the long tube, from which cold air flows on hot days. Not far from Bend, Horse Caves provided shelter for livestock in many hard winters. Smaller caves near ranches to the southeast of Bend served as natural barns for range stock.

The tourist era brought renewed interest to the lava caverns, and now they attract thousands of visitors, especially at the Lava River Caves Park. There a caretaker is on duty and lanterns are available. Originally tourists could walk a mile back into the cave, but the present area of the tube available for inspection covers only about half of the original distance.

The Lava River Cave of the Bend area is an immense, mile-long, rock-walled tube that reaches west toward the Deschutes River. Like other caves in the Mt. Newberry foothills, it was formed thousands of years ago when lava from cones and fissures filled old channels. The thick flows cooled on the top, the sides, and base, but the interior remained fluid. At points downhill near the snouts of flows, the molten rock broke out, forming drainage channels generally conforming with the old valleys. Some of the lava drainage tunnels were long, some short; but all had the same pattern: domed ceilings, nearly vertical sides, and slag-covered bottoms. In some of the caves, the arched ceilings are fifty feet above the floor. Widths range from ten to thirty feet.

Visible on the walls of the tunnels are the marks of lava recession, left when the lava slowly drained. Only with ample light can visitors grasp the immensity of the lava tunnels. Charts near the caretaker's quarters at the entrance to Lava River Cave provide information as to the length of the cavern, the direction of the conduits, and the thickness of the rocky ceiling.

All of the long tunnels of the upper Deschutes country are of the lava type, but the presence of ice has resulted in some of the conduits being called "ice caves." Best known of these is the

Arnold Ice Cave, twelve miles south of Bend, from which the village obtained ice in early days. Ice forms only in caves whose entrances are sheltered from the hot summer sun. Also necessary is a supply of water, generally from melting snow; and a free circulation of air. At Arnold Ice Cave, a miniature glacier near the entrance has "flowed" back into the cavern darkness.

Other well-known caverns of this type in the area are the South and East Ice caves of the northern Fort Rock country, and the Edison Ice Caves, southwest of Bend.

Lavacicle Cave Attracts Scientists

One of the most fascinating of the many caverns of the Deschutes region is the Lavacicle Cave of the Fort Rock area, discovered by chance in 1959 when a fire crew was "mopping up" following the twenty-one-thousand-acre Aspen Flat fire. This tube, about a half mile long, apparently remained sealed after lava drained. Intense heat within the cavern resulted in a remelting of ceiling lava, which formed stalactites and stalagmites, and some rocky rosettes. To protect the delicate formations, the Deschutes National Forest set aside the cave as a place of scientific interest, with only guided parties permitted to enter. The entrance is locked, but arrangements to visit the unique tunnel can be made through the U. S. Forest Service.

Second in scientific interest to the Lavacicle Cave is Charcoal Cave, twelve miles south of Bend in the northern Paulinas. In this cave, Dr. L. S. Cressman, University of Oregon anthropologist, discovered a mass of charred wood. The wood apparently was thrown into the cavern, then carried back under an overhang. It has been determined that this wood was cut with a stone axe, but anthropologists cannot account for the great pile of partly burnt timber in the cavern; possibly, they say, it was used in ceremonial fires; or perhaps it was burned to melt ice. In earlier years, many artifacts were found in the area.

A long lava tunnel in the Devils Garden country of the Fort Rock basin was surveyed in 1963 by a team of scientists, as a phase of the lunar landing studies. If caves exist on the moon, they may have shelter value for the first astronauts to land there. For this reason, the Derrick Cave was extensively studied and tests were made to determine whether its underground course could be detected from the surface, through use of gravimeters and other equipment.

Indians Used Caves

Not all caves of the region are of the lava tunnel type. Under cliffs in the Fort Rock country and in the Deschutes and Crooked River canyons are low caves, eroded from river walls by water and wind, that provided shelter for early Indians. The far-famed Fort Rock Cave, near the town of Fort Rock in northern Lake County, is the best known of these. There are many others in the northern Great Basin region, facing the flat country once covered by lakes. These caves were primarily shelters for nomadic hunters of long ago, and the old cavern homes of the first residents of the area held many artifacts, most famous of these being the material obtained from the Fort Rock cave.

A cave at Cougar Mountain, a short distance east of the Fort Rock Cave, also yielded a fine collection of artifacts, as well as a skeleton. Pictographs are found in some of the caves, but most of the "Indian writings" are on the smooth walls of gorges.

Twenty miles east of Bend in Dry River Gorge, close to U. S. Highway 20, an old Indian encampment was discovered some forty years ago. Considerable material was unearthed at the site, under rocky cliffs covered with pictographs, but vandals have destroyed almost all of these fine writings, inscribed on rocks by the ancient campers.

One of the most recent discoveries of an old Indian encampment was made when a trench for a gas line was excavated in lavas about a half mile east of Lava Butte, ten miles south of Bend. Hundreds of artifacts were found by Washington State University anthropologists in a small area. Apparently the site was used by ancient hunters as a camp near a deer trail.

Tourists find Central Oregon's noted Wind Cave one of the most interesting lava caverns of the region. Located in the Arnold Cave group south of Bend, this cave is noted as a "breather" —on cold winter days it "inhales," and in hot weather it "exhales." At times the force of the outpouring wind is so intense that it can be heard at a considerable distance, and will lift objects into the air. The opening of the cave is narrow, of the skylight type, and it is through this restricted passage that the cavern air flows.

Volcanoes Tell Own Stories

Scattered over the interior plateau, mostly around the flanks of Mt. Newberry, are hundreds of volcanic cones, some of them mere "chocolate drops," others several hundred feet high. Each of these tells its own story, through lava layers, rocky flows, breached sides, craters, fissures, or cinder lips. Best known of the Deschutes cinder cones is Lava Butte, ten miles south of Bend on U. S. Highway 97. It is the location of a U. S. Forest Service scenic viewpoint and observatory.

The Lava Butte story is typical of many of the cones of the area—a small volcano came into existence in a zone of weakness, on a fissure. About the time the cone reached a height of around five hundred feet, lava welled up through a central crater, but did not reach the top. The massive pool of molten rock within the crater breached the south wall of the cone, to form one of the grandest and most recent lava flows in the region.

Mokst Butte Imposing

High on the north slope of Mt. Newberry is spectacular Mokst Butte—a fine crater known to few, but now accessible over an improved road. Lava welling up in Mokst Butte carried away the entire south half of the cone and spread over several sections of land. One of the rocky flows in this area engulfed a grove of pines to form the so-called Lava Cast Forest—in reality a "forest" of rocky tree molds.

Geologists estimate that around the base of Mt. Newberry are more than two hundred parasitic cones. They skirt the entire foothills of Newberry. Many of these cones not only tell their own stories, but reveal the direction from which the wind was blowing at the time of eruptions: prevailing winds from the southwest dropped cinders and ash on the northeast rims.

On the south slope of the South Sister volcano is LeConte Crater, of interest because its recent surface was peppered with debris from a buried vent. The vent was buried under the Great Mesa flow. There are a number of small cones in this area. Northwest, on the trail to Broken Top from Green Lakes, is Cayuse Butte, remarkable because of the variety of volcanic bombs it scattered over the area. These bombs, common in the Deschutes country, were great gobs of lava which cooled while whirling in the air.

Land of a Thousand Lakes

Of interest to vacationists as well as anglers are the many lakes of the Three Sisters Cascades, in upper Deschutes country, and the mountains that reach north to Jefferson and beyond. Many of these lakes are known only to foresters and the Oregon State Game Commission field men, who seasonally visit the high country to plant fingerlings—and, on some occasions, to give names to the lakes in which the tiny fish are planted. Many of these names appear only on detailed maps.

Flows of lava tumbling from mountain vents, and glaciers moving down steep slopes were factors in forming lakes of the Central Cascades of Oregon. Tongues of lava created lakes by damming streams, as at Elk Lake near the South Sister, and the nearby Lava Lakes. Glaciers created many lakes by gouging out basins or by dumping terminal moraines into valleys. Suttle Lake, on U. S. Highway 20 west of Sisters, formed behind a glacier moraine.

A summit glacier on the South Sister created a tiny lake, at the very top of that mountain, by scooping a basin. Three of the region's best known lakes—Crater, East, and Paulina—were formed by volcanic action in mountain summits.

Fossils Tell Stories in Stones

Scattered over Central Oregon are scores of fossil localities, some world famous for their record of ancient plant life, others widely known for the stony remains of Oregon's ancient mammals, from the "Dawn Age" of Clarno times to the Ice Age. The rich record of the eons was first brought to the attention of the scientific world just a century ago when soldiers scouting through upper Crooked River and the John Day country found marine shells on mountain tops, fine leaves in shales, and animal bones in colored clays.

Best-known mammal beds are those found in the John Day Valley, mostly near Spray, or in the Clarno country, where the late A. W. "Lon" Hancock of Portland discovered bones of the "thunderbeast" and its kin in rocks close to the high, flat rims of Iron Mountain.

There are few areas of Oregon that have not yielded some fossils, to make it possible for paleontologists to trace the story of ancient lands—but most of these finds have been made in the interior country.

Leaves of ancient plants and needles from old forests have added to Oregon's prehistoric picture. Leaf beds in Central Oregon are even more abundant than the mammal beds. There are · many fine leaf localities near Mitchell, on Taylor and Bear creeks. Others appear along upper Crooked River, and in Jefferson County near Gateway, and at Vanora Grade. The Clarno area is world famous for its leaf fossils, and the nut beds on Pine Creek have attracted national attention from paleobotanists—the scientists who study ancient plant life. Traces of one of Oregon's oldest forests have been found in a late Paleozoic formation of the Suplee country, east of Prineville.

The interior country has also added to the story of ancient

Portland General Electric Company's Round Butte Dam, completed in 1964, forms beautiful Lake Billy Chinook, a 3600-acre reservoir reaching into three river canyons.

Picturesque Lake Simtustus, the reservoir behind Pelton Dam, offers scenic cruising through awesome geologic formations—and consistently good fishing.

Standing guard on Central Oregon's High Desert is this gnarled and long-dead juniper. Carpeting the desert floor are several types of sagebrush, including the famous three-tooth sage with low growth in some places and growth as high as a saddle pony in others. When used for campfire fuel, the brush has an aromatic fragrance that filters down valleys in low-lying smoke layers, to spread out over sandy basins once occupied by pluvial lakes.

marine life, with discoveries made in old ocean beds near Mitchell and in the Izee highlands to the east.

The multimillion-year story of the horse has been read from the rocks of Central Oregon, from the epoch of the tiny four-toed creature of Clarno days to the big animals that raced over lake shores in now-arid northern Lake County, during the Ice Age. Fossil Lake, east of Silver Lake, has given up many bones of the Pleistocene horse, represented by several species.

Gorges Slash Ancient Lands

Interior Oregon is a semi-arid land—yet it is a country that has been deeply cut by rivers, some of which still flow through deep canyons. Many others have vanished; one of these is Dry River, a stream that slashed its way across the High Desert, east of Bend, to leave the trace of its main course and of many branches in the brushy plateau. This is the river that created a deep gorge through Horse Ridge, as it cut through lavas on a northward course to Crooked River.

Recently the spectacular Horse Ridge Gorge was brought within view of passing motorists. This was done when the Oregon State Highway Department re-aligned its old, winding section of U. S. Highway 20 over Horse Ridge. The new section of highway reaches upgrade close to the "fossil canyon," around three hundred feet deep in places.

Some of Oregon's most awesome gorges occur in the interior country. One of these is the deep Deschutes Gorge, the full spread of which can be seen from the Portland General Electric observatory, high above Lake Billy Chinook. That lake inundated the Cove Orchard camp area, which has since been replaced by a new park.

Oregon's Highway Department recognized the tourist value of the gorge country when it constructed a rim road as part of its Cove Palisades Park development in Jefferson County. This road provides four viewpoints, each facing a different geologic story in the Crooked River-Deschutes canyons. The Highway

Department also took advantage of a lofty rim overlooking Prineville from the west, to develop a wayside park and provide a grand view of the upper Crooked River Canyon.

Upstream from Prineville about twenty miles are the impressive palisades of Crooked River—towering cliffs seemingly held up by giant pillars formed by columnar basalt. This is a spot for picture taking—and a bit of probing into the old story of the Crooked River Canyon.

Land of Captured Rainbows

The John Day country east of Antelope near Clarno, at Twickenham not far from Mitchell, and in the Spray region, is a land of rainbows imprisoned in lava-capped hills. The color is provided by the John Day beds, formed from the ash of volcanoes millions of years ago. Under varying climatic conditions and in different zones of moisture, minerals within the volcanic ash took on different colors; the result is truly a land of rainbows.

A short drive down Bridge Creek from Mitchell will bring into view the gaudily colored John Day beds. There, the Oregon State Highway Commission has set aside the Painted Hills Park. Banded, colored domes vie for attention, but cannot detract from the sloping, green hills in the distance, where the John Day beds come into full and glorious view. However, the John Day Canyon is not entirely a region of soft, varicolored hills. The river also has its narrow, rocky gorges, especially downstream from the Burnt Ranch community and in the range lands north of Clarno. In those areas, the muddy John Day is a stream that challenges the skill of river runners.

"Lost Rivers" Leave Record

Central Oregon has its share of lost rivers. One of these, ages ago, flowed past the present city limits of Redmond, to leave a deep, wide gorge, the bottom of which is now farmed. This gorge loses its identity near Tetherow Butte. Possibly the old gorge was a temporary channel of the Deschutes, when that stream was battling lava blockades.

East of the little town of Terrebonne near Crooked River is the broad mouth of a canyon that is only about five miles long. That gorge, more than a mile wide at its mouth near Crooked River, but narrow near Prineville Junction, was possibly created by the gushing waters of a "thousand springs." Those springs apparently flowed under lava, and possibly had their origin in the Deschutes near Bend, during an epoch of lava dams.

Ghost Towns of the High Country

Part of the region's recent story can be traced from "ghost towns" of the inland country. One of these is Antelope, the story of which has already been told. Another is Shaniko—the end of the rails in Central Oregon from 1900 until 1911. A third is the hamlet of Ashwood, deep in the canyon of Trout Creek close to tawny, nearly treeless Ash Butte. Each of these towns has its own interesting story.

Shaniko, Antelope, and Ashwood can easily be visited in a single day. Shaniko is on U. S. Highway 97, in southern Wasco County. From Shaniko, a surfaced road reaches across brushy flats to Antelope, in a broad valley under high western rims. The venturesome can reach Ashwood over seventeen miles of country road; but those who are in a hurry should use the surfaced route down Antelope Creek to Willowdale, then take the new rural road up past the world-famous Pony Butte agate localities.

In the old range country of Central Oregon, there are sites of many other ghost towns, but not even a cabin stands to mark their location.

END

Chronology

1825 – Peter Skene Ogden made first recorded exploration of Central Oregon.
1834 – Nathaniel Wyeth passed near Bend site in first recorded trip into upper Deschutes basin.
1843 – John C. Fremont crossed through Central Oregon; discovered Summer Lake and Abert Rim en route to California.
1845 – Meek's Lost Wagon Train crossed westward over High Desert; camped at Prineville site.
1851 – Survivors of Clark massacre on Snake River reached Bend site; camped on Deschutes.
1853 – Elliott cutoff party segment reached Bend area after wandering over High Desert.
1854 – Wasco County created, January 11. Included all Oregon east of Cascades.
1855 – Williamson railroad survey party passed through Deschutes country, seeking rail route.
       – Warm Springs Indian Reservation established.
1859 – Andrew Wiley discovered Santiam Pass, over which wagon road was constructed in 1866-67.
1860 – First bridge built over Deschutes at Sherar site, opening important gateway to Central Oregon.
1862 – Marion and Felix Scott made first crossing of McKenzie Pass with wagons; spent winter on Trout Creek.
       – Howard Maupin established stopping place on Antelope Creek, near present site of Antelope.
1864 – Camp Watson established on Fort Creek, five miles west of Antone.
1865 – Army volunteers crossed Santiam to occupy Camp Polk, on Squaw Creek near present town of Sisters.
1867 – Chief Paulina, frontier raider, killed near Trout Creek by ranchers whose stock he had stolen.
       – First settlers reach Ochoco, to build log cabins in Prineville area.
1868 – School, first in Central Oregon, opened on Mill Creek, in Ochoco country.
       – Barney Prine started store in his home on edge of Crooked River. This stopping place gave Prineville its name.
       – General George Crook brought Indian unrest in Central Oregon to successful end.
1871 – Antelope Post Office established on August 7, at stage station started by Howard Maupin.
1872 – Name of Prine Post Office changed to Prineville, December 23, dating Prineville's start as town.
1874 – Lake County created, October 24, from parts of Wasco and Jackson.
1877 – John Y. Todd rode into upper Deschutes country to establish Farewell Bend Ranch.
       – John Templeton Craig died in winter storm on McKenzie Pass while carrying mail.
1878 – Bannock War touched fringe of Central Oregon when battle was fought on Silver Creek.
1880 – Prineville, county seat of Crook County, incorporated.
1882 – Vigilantes founded in Prineville, following slaying of two ranchers.
       – Crook County created from southern part of Wasco, October 24, with Prineville named county seat.

1888 — Sisters Post Office established at present location after being moved from nearby Camp Polk.

1889 — Lakeview, county seat of Lake County, incorporated.

1891 — Fossil, county seat of Wheeler County, incorporated.

1894 — Christmas Eve fire at Silver Lake took lives of forty-three persons.

1899 — Wheeler County created February 17, named for pioneer stage operator, Henry H. Wheeler.

1900 — Railroad constructed from Biggs to Shaniko, making Shaniko one of the largest wool-shipping centers in the world.

1901 — Antelope and Shaniko in Wasco County, incorporated.

1904 — Bend platted by its founder, A. M. Drake, June 7. Incorporated January 4, 1905.

1906 — Redmond platted near center of large irrigation segregation; incorporated in 1910.

1909 — Hill and Harriman started historic railroad construction struggle in Deschutes Gorge.

1910 — Madras, county seat of Jefferson County, incorporated.

1911 — Golden spike driven at end of rails in Bend, October 5.

1913 — Metolius in Jefferson County, incorporated.

1914 — Jefferson County created from Crook, December 12. Madras named county seat following court struggle.

1916 — Deschutes County created from Crook, December 13, with Bend named county seat.

— Big pine mills started operating on Deschutes in Bend.

1918 — Prineville's city-owned railroad placed in operation.

1922 — Maupin in Wasco County incorporated.

1927 — Steel span over Crooked River opened to traffic.

— Great Northern extended rails south into California from Bend.

1938 — Sandals found in Fort Rock Cave given 9,000-year age.

1943 — High Desert war games held, Camp Abbot opened.

1946 — Deschutes water flowed to North Unit Project lands.

— Sisters in Deschutes County and Culver in Jefferson County, incorporated.

1958 — Spray in Wheeler County, incorporated.

— Completion of Pelton Dam on the Deschutes.

1959 — Forest fire burned 26,000 acres in Aspen Flat country.

1960 — Power line constructed across High Desert to Harney County and Nevada.

1961 — Prineville Dam on Crooked River completed by United States Bureau of Reclamation.

— Thirty-six-inch gasline through Central Oregon constructed by Pacific Gas Transmission Company.

1962 — Clear Lake Cutoff—bypassing McKenzie Pass—completed and placed in use.

— Sam Hill Bridge over Columbia River dedicated as new feeder of traffic into Central Oregon.

1964 — First phase of Kah-nee-ta Hot Springs Resort, on Warm Springs Reservation, placed in use.

— Completion of Portland General Electric Company's Pelton-Round Butte hydroelectric project on the main stem of the Deschutes River in North Central Oregon.

— During the Christmas flood of 1964, heavy rain and melting snow in the upper Deschutes country spilled into Bend the greatest head of water in history. Even the "lava sponge" at Lava Island—which normally takes care of high water—could not handle the big flow. In December 1964, Bend measured 8.62 inches of moisture; whereas the normal is about 1.62.

Bibliography

Abbot, Henry Larcom. *Explorations for a Railroad Route*, 1854-55. Pacific Railroad Reports. Volume 6. Washington, D.C., 1857

Baker, Gail C. "Deschutes Historical Record." United States Forest Service, 1949

Bancroft, Hubert Howe. *History of Oregon*. 2 vols. San Francisco, 1886, 1888

Brimlow, George Francis. *Harney County, Oregon, and Its Rangeland*. Portland, 1951

Brogan, Phil F. "Watering of the Wilderness." Bend *Bulletin*, January-June, 1931

——"Farewell Bend and Its People." Bend *Bulletin*, March-November, 1933

Brooks, James E., editor. *Oregon Almanac and Book of Facts*, Portland, 1961

Carey, Charles H. *A General History of Oregon*. 2 vols. Portland, 1936

Chaney, Ralph W. *The Ancient Forests of Oregon*. Eugene, Oregon, 1948

Condon, Thomas. *The Two Islands*. Portland, 1902

Corning, Howard M., editor. *Dictionary of Oregon History*. Portland, 1956

Cressman, Luther S. *Petroglyphs of Oregon*. Eugene, Oregon, 1937

——*The Sandal and the Cave*. Portland, 1962.

Curtis, Ralph. "Central Oregon History." Series. Bend *Bulletin*, 1923

Edwards, Mrs. Charles S. "Central Oregon History Scrapbooks," 1930-1950

Ekman, Leonard C. *Scenic Geology of the Pacific Northwest*. Portland, 1962

Farrell, Allie M., editor. *Jefferson County Reminiscences*. Portland, 1957

Frome, Michael. *Whose Woods These Are*. New York, 1962

Horner, John B. *Oregon History and Early Literature*. Portland, 1931

Lahee, Frederic H. "Lava River Caves of Oregon." Oregon State Highway Department, 1955

McArthur, Lewis A. *Oregon Geographic Names*. Portland, 1952.

McCornack, Ellen Condon. *Thomas Condon, Pioneer Geologist of Oregon.* Eugene, Oregon, 1928

McNeal, William H. *History of Wasco County.* The Dalles, Oregon, 1953

Menefee, Leah Collins. Manuscripts dealing with Lost Wagon Train of 1853.

Oliver, Herman. *Gold and Cattle Country.* Portland, 1962

Oregon Blue Book. Salem, Oregon, 1963-1964.

Oregon: End of the Trail. American Guide Series, Portland, 1951.

Packard, Earl Le Roy. "Geologic Occurrence of the Hardgrave Jurassic Fauna of Burns, Oregon." Geologic Society of America Bulletin, 1921

Pinchot, Gifford. *Breaking New Ground.* New York, 1947

Richmond, Carroll. "History of the Town of Maupin." The Dalles *Chronicle,* Historical Edition, 1948

Sawyer, Robert W. "Henry Larcom Abbot and the Pacific Railroad Survey of 1855." *Oregon Historical Quarterly,* 1932

—— "Beginnings of the McKenzie Highway, 1862." *Oregon Historical Quarterly,* 1930

Scott, Harvey W. *History of the Oregon Country.* Vol. 3. Cambridge, Mass., 1924

Shane, Ralph M. *Early Explorations through Warm Springs Reservation Area.* Portland, 1951

Shaver, F. A. *History of Central Oregon.* Spokane, 1905.

Strong, Emory. *Stone Age on the Columbia River.* Portland, 1960

Thompson, William. *Reminiscences of a Pioneer.* San Francisco, 1912

Turnbull, George S. *History of Oregon Newspapers.* Portland, 1939

Veazie, A. L. "Pioneer Monument Dedication." *Oregon Historical Quarterly,* 1938

Williams, Howel. *Crater Lake, the Story of Its Origin.* Berkeley, Calif., 1941

—— *Volcanoes of the Three Sisters Region, Oregon Cascades.* Department of Geological Sciences. Berkeley, Calif., 1944

—— *The Ancient Volcanoes of Oregon.* Eugene, Oregon, 1948

Worrington, H. M. *Ancient Man in North America.* Denver, 1957

Interviews with William P. Vandevert, Deschutes pioneer and son of a survivor of Clark massacre of 1851; John F. Stevens, Great Northern engineer; Ralph Budd, Great Northern president; John Campbell Merriam, paleontologist.

Index

DATE